AF710565

WITHDRAWN

SOCIALISM:
INSTITUTIONAL, PHILOSOPHICAL AND ECONOMIC ISSUES

INTERNATIONAL STUDIES IN ECONOMICS AND ECONOMETRICS

Volume 14

1. Harder T: Introduction to Mathematical Models in Market and Opinion Research With Practical Applications, Computing Procedures, and Estimates of Computing Requirements. Translated from the German by P.H. Friedlander and E.H. Friedlander. 1969.
2. Heesterman ARG: Forecasting Models for National Economic Planning. 1972.
3. Heesterman ARG: Allocation Models and their Use in Economic Planning. 1971.
4. Durdağ M: Some Problems of Development Financing. A Case Study of the Turkish First Five-Year Plan, 1963–1967. 1973.
5. Blin JM: Patterns and Configurations in Economic Science. A Study of Social Decision Processes. 1973.
6. Merkies AHQM: Selection of Models by Forecasting Intervals. Translated from the Dutch by M. van Holten-De Wolff. 1973.
7. Bos HC, Sanders M and Secchi C: Private Foreign Investment in Developing Countries. A Quantitative Study on the Evaluation of its Macro-Economic Impact. 1974.
8. Frisch R: Economic Planning Studies Selected and Introduced by Frank Long. Preface by Jan Tinbergen. 1976.
9. Gupta KL: Foreign Capital, Savings and Growth. An International Cross-section Study. 1983.
10. Bochove CA van: Imports and Economic Growth. 1982.
11. Bjerkholt O, Offerdal E (eds.): Macroeconomic Prospects for a Small Oil Exporting Country. 1985.
12. Weiserbs D (ed.): Industrial Investment in Europe: Economic Theory and Measurement. 1985.
13. Graf von der Schulenburg J-M, Skogh G (eds.): Law and Economics & The Economics of Legal Regulation. 1986.
14. Svetozar Pejovich (ed.): Socialism: Institutional, Philosophical and Economic Issues. 1987.

Socialism: Institutional, Philosophical and Economic Issues

edited by

Svetozar Pejovich

The Centre for Free Enterprise

Texas A & M University

1987 **KLUWER ACADEMIC PUBLISHERS**

DORDRECHT / BOSTON / LANCASTER

HX
73
.S633
1987

Distributors

for the United States and Canada: Kluwer Academic Publishers, P.O. Box 358, Accord Station, Hingham, MA 02018-0358, USA
for the UK and Ireland: Kluwer Academic Publishers, MTP Press Limited, Falcon House, Queen Square, Lancaster LA1 1RN, UK
for all other countries: Kluwer Academic Publishers Group, Distribution Center, P.O. Box 322, 3300 AH Dordrecht, The Netherlands

Library of Congress Cataloging in Publication Data

Socialism : institutional, philosophical, and economic issues.

(International studies in economics and econometrics ; v. 14)
Includes index.
1. Communism. 2. Socialism. I. Pejovich, Svetozar. II. Series.
HX73.S633 1987 335 87-1740

ISBN 90-247-3487-8 (this volume)
ISBN 90-247-2730-8 (series)

Copyright

© 1987 by Martinus Nijhoff Publishers, Dordrecht.

All rights reserved. No part of this publication may be reproduced, stored in a retrieval system, or transmitted in any form or by any means, mechanical, photocopying, recording, or otherwise, without the prior written permission of the publishers,
Martinus Nijhoff Publishers, P.O. Box 163, 3300 AD Dordrecht, The Netherlands.

PRINTED IN THE NETHERLANDS

To R. A. WARE and B. V. THOMPSON, JR.

To Whom I Owe a Great Debt

CONTENTS

Page

Preface IX

PART ONE. RIGHTS, INSTITUTIONS, AND PUBLIC POLICY

1. MAN AND THE STATE
James M. Buchanan 3

2. THE MARKET AND THE METAMARKET
Pedro Schwartz 11

3. THE LIMITS OF ECONOMIC POLICY
Karl Brunner 33

PART TWO. SOCIALISM: PHILOSOPHICAL ISSUES

4. IS SOCIALISM INEVITABLE? HISTORICAL PROPHECY AND THE POSSIBILITIES OF REASON
Hans Albert 55

5. SOCIALISM: DO THE ENDS JUSTIFY THE MEANS?
Roland Vaubel 89

6. HAYEK ON LIBERTY AND THE RULE OF LAW: THE ROAD TO SERFDOM REVISITED
Dieter Schmidtchen 115

PART THREE. SOCIALISM: ECONOMIC ISSUES

7. INFORMATION, MOTIVATION, AND THE PROBLEM OF RATIONAL ECONOMIC CALCULATION IN SOCIALISM
Peter Bernholz 147

Page

8. RATIONAL EXPECTATIONS IN CENTRALLY PLANNED ECONOMIES
Jan S. Kowalski 175

9. THE CASE OF CENTRAL PLANNING IN THE USSR
Andrzej Brzeski 209

10. THE CASE OF SELF-MANAGEMENT IN YUGOSLAVIA
Svetozar Pejovich. 239

11. ECONOMIC AND SOCIAL CONSEQUENCES OF SOCIALIST POLICIES IN FRANCE
Jacques Garello 251

12. THE CASE OF CODETERMINATION IN WEST GERMANY
Christian Watrin. 277

INDEX OF NAMES 315

PREFACE

> It was Lenin's genius to recognize the importance of embellishing the [socialist] system with all the trappings of democracy. If the people want a constitution, give them one, and even include the bill of rights. If they want a parliament, give them that too. And a system of courts. If they want a federal system create that myth as well. Above all, let them have elections, for the act of voting is what the common man most clearly associates with democracy. Give them all these, but make sure that they have no effect on how things are run.
>
> \- G. Warren Nutter

Most research by Western scholars has emphasized macroeconomics (and to a considerable extent still does) as the method of analysis and growth rates as a standard for evaluating the performance of different economies. In the early 1960s Nutter raised questions about the reported growth rates in socialist states, the importance of growth policies for human welfare, and the ability of macroeconomics to enhance our understanding of social and economic processes. In his work, Nutter used the standard price theory adjusted to incorporate the incentive effects of property rights in resources. He was castigated for defying the traditional wisdom. Not surprisingly, history has validated Nutter's theoretical framework and his conclusions. The point is that price theory has one advantage over the analysis of aggregate variables: it deepens our understanding of social and economic forces at work in alternative institutional settings.

It is clear today that the synthesis of the economics of property rights, the Alchian-Demsetz theory of the firm, and Buchanan's blend of political philosophy and public choice analysis provide research in comparative economic systems with a strong and testable analytical content. Instead of recording and interpreting economic performance in different countries ex post, we can make ex ante deductions from the effects of alternative institutional structures on the pattern of economic behavior.

Empirical evidence carries a simple but powerful message: capitalism has done much more for the common man than socialism has. The new approach to the study of comparative economic systems carries another important message: the failure of socialism should be attributed to its institutions. These institutions interfere with the right of ownership and contractual freedom, generating behaviors that are clearly inconsistent with the efficient allocation and use of resources. Thus, the problem of socialism does not stem from poor planning, poor choice of social engineers, and/or the integrity of its ruling elite.

The purpose of this book is to illustrate how and why the institutions of socialism have failed to produce efficient interactions among individuals in the community.

Chapters 1-3 emphasize this crucial interdependence between individual liberty, institutional structures, and public policy. Chapters 4-6 raise philosophical issues that have important social implications. Is socialism inevitable? Is socialism a viable social system? Are vague promises about future happiness worth current restrictions of individual liberty?

Chapters 7 and 8 deal with rather general but important economic issues: the effects of socialist institutions on rational calculations and rational expectations. The last four chapters analyze the relationship between four distinct types of socialist institutions (central planning, self-management, codetermination, and the French experiment with socialism) and economic performance.

The chapters by Albert, Bernholz, Garello, Schmidtchen, Vaubel, and Watrin were prepared for the Liberty Fund Symposium on Socialism (Interlaken 1985). Chapters by other scholars were added in order to complete the coverage of important issues.

My special thanks goes to James Buchanan for his intellectual input at the Liberty Fund Symposium on Socialism and for permission to use his presidential address given at the Mont Pelerin Society meeting in St. Vincent, September 1986. Steve Wiggins has made some very important suggestions toward the final content of this book. The financial support of the Lynde and Harry Bradley Foundation is gratefully acknowledged. Maureen Creamer and Judy Roessner have done an excellent job in editing and typing the manuscript.

Steve Pejovich
College Station, Texas

PART ONE

RIGHTS, INSTITUTIONS, AND PUBLIC POLICY

Chapter 1

MAN AND THE STATE

By

James M. Buchanan*

Among us there are some who are able to imagine a viable society without a state. These libertarian anarchists, or anarcho-capitalists, have made major contributions in demonstrating how many of the modern state's activities might be better carried out through the spontaneous processes of the market. And these arguments are exerting an effect now in the cross-national movements toward privatization. I do not want to underestimate the importance of the challenge that the libertarian anarchists have posed for all of us who defend state action.

Social order without a state is not readily imagined, or at least in any normatively preferred sense. We find it difficult to model the working properties of such a social arrangement, especially as we look at the behavior of persons in the world about us. We fall back on Thomas Hobbes to provide the description of what the genuinely stateless-lawless society might be like. The normative rejection of this model forces us to

---

*J. Buchanan is the winner of the 1986 Nobel Prize in economics. This chapter is based on his presidential address given at the Mont Pelerin Society meeting in St. Vincent, Italy, 1986.

raise a whole set of issues that the libertarian anarchist need not concern himself with at all.

Of necessity, we must look at our relations with the state from several windows, to use the familiar Nietschzean metaphor. To consider two extremes, we can, with Herbert Spencer and the libertarians, consider the state as an adversary and convert my title into "Man Versus the State." At the same time, however, we must also recognize that "man is the state" in the basic sense that it describes the set of institutions through which we organize ourselves politically and collectively for the achievement of purposes that simply cannot be otherwise secured at all efficiently.

Some understanding of the operation of the state is required before any discussion about the assignment of this or that function to the state or about policy options in the carrying out of this or that function. This very simple principle was simply overlooked by most economists until the middle of this century, and with tragic consequences.

Descriptively, we know that the state fits no single model, and that the two general models mentioned do not nearly exhaust the set of the possible. The state is not a monolithic entity empowered with a monopoly of coercion and equipped with a will of its own. It is not voluntaristic in the Wicksellian sense where all collective decisions reflect unanimous agreement among all persons in the polity. It is not the embodiment of the will of the possibly shifting median voter in majoritarian processes. It is not the instrument through which a ruling coalition, temporarily in office, enriches itself at the expense of others in the polity. It is not a freely-floating bureaucracy constrained only by its inner organizational logic. It is not the mere agent for a ruling class or establishment.

There are elements of each of these models, and possibly others, in the state as it variously exists in different nations. How we choose to model the state depends on the purpose to be served, on the questions to be asked, and answered.

Rather than concentrate attention on what the state is, however, it may be best to examine the position of the individual in relation to the state. In this context it may be helpful to think of the state as an organization that possesses the peculiar feature of <u>compulsory</u> membership, thereby contrasting it with other organizations in which membership is voluntary. As with most models, this is a limiting case. We know that states vary widely in the compulsoryness of membership, and further that the costs of exit vary widely among persons. Nonetheless, the absence of a cost effective exit option does distinguish the state from almost all other organizations. For most purposes, the individual is a member of the organization that is the state, and a member he must remain.

What does it mean to say that the individual is a member of an organization? Membership implies adherence to the rules of the organization, whatever these may be, and, in application to the state, this approach calls attention immediately to the importance of the rules, the constitution of the polity. There are two dimensions of the rules that define the organization of the state, dimensions that can vary independently. One dimension involves the extent to which the individual is subject to the state's authority, or, conversely, the extent of his private sphere protected from state intervention. The second dimension of rules concerns the structure of the decision-making process through which the state's authority is exercised. In particular, this dimension defines the participation or nonparticipation of the individual in political choice.

In a totalitarian society, there are no rule-protected spheres within which the individual is guaranteed exercise of liberty. The individual is a slave to the state-as-master, quite independently of the ways in which state decisions are made and also of the benevolence or malevolence reflected in the patterns of state choices. The answer to the question posed by Robert Nozick (Nozick 1974) is clear. Even in the final stage where the individual is subject to the will of the majority he remains a slave.

In nontotalitarian societies, however, there remain rule-protected spheres within which the individual has liberty of choice and action. But it is worth emphasizing that in all areas of action within which the state may act, the individual is necessarily subject to the state's authority. The well-being of the individual, however this may be measured, depends on the state. The individual's position in the polity is fully analogous to that of the resource owner in an economic relationship embodying rent.

The sign as well as the magnitude of the rent finally assigned to the individual are beyond his own powers of control through choice. There is no exit option. This relationship is not affected, in its fundamental aspect, by the possible participation of the individual in collective-political decision processes, save in the limiting case where the operative voting rule is unanimity.

Recognition of the necessary vulnerability of the individual to state action does not imply that "voice" is an unimportant attribute of membership in the compulsory organization that is the state. Most persons may prefer a participatory democracy to government by an elite, even if both are bound by the constitutional-legal order to the same range of authority.

My emphasis, however, is on the critical importance of the rules that limit the exercise of the state's authority, rules that are independent of the way collective choices are made within such rules. The participatory exercise of voice in an unrestricted parliamentary democracy may be valued, but limits on the range and extent of state action may be substantively of much more significance. Possible participation in the shaping of the polity's constitution, the set of rules that constrain the potential exercise of state authority, is categorically of greater import than any guarantee of voting franchise within a given constitutional structure.

In a very real sense, the set of rules that define the respective spheres for state and private action locates the individual along the freedom-slavery spectrum. Once these rules are settled, and independently of how they may have been derived, and/or how much or how little voice the individual is allowed to exercise in shaping state action, the individual remains a subject within the domain of the state's constituted authority. Within the authorized sphere of collective action, the individual remains dependent on the state. Dependence need not, of course, imply impoverishment; the individual may fare well or poorly under the dependence umbrella. But it is self-evident that recognition of dependency status invokes a behavioral pattern quite different from that which genuine independence affords.

My argument may seem fully consistent with that of the libertarian anarchists who see individuals as subjects of the state on the one hand

and as adversaries of the state along the boundary lines of state power. I part company with the libertarian anarchists, however, as noted above, when I accept, with Hobbes, that individuals would, if given genuine constitutional choice, grant some authority to the state, even in the full recognition that such a grant of authority comes as the certain sacrifice of individual autonomy.

We should never be trapped in the delusion that the enhancement of the state's authority to "do good things for us collectively," involves no cost to us as free individuals. But recognizing that this cost exists is not the same as saying that it is a cost we shall never pay. The cost in liberty will, over some ranges of state action, be lower than the expected benefit from the exercise of state authority within the defined limits. We are able to satisfy our preferences, to achieve a higher level of utility, where some of our liberties have been sacrificed and where there does exist a well-defined but limited domain for the exercise of the coercive power of the state.

But we must recognize full well that, within the limits of the authority so assigned to the state, we are necessarily subjects, or, more dramatically, slaves, to the state, as master. The slave may, indeed, enjoy a higher standard of living than the free man, but he is a fool if he neglects for a moment the elementary fact that he remains a slave. In a very real sense, the constitutional contract that sets the limits of state authority over individuals is a slave contract, and we sell ourselves into slavery with each and every extension of the state's power.

Why is a slavery contract, as such, different from any contract? Why do all of us (except possibly for a few extreme libertarians) think that the slavery contract is not normally an ethically legitimate embodiment of voluntary exchange? We reject such an "exchange" because it does not allow for a post-contract viable exit option; the person who finds himself in a slave relationship does not have effective alternatives. Membership in a state embodies this attribute of the slave contract to the extent that the state, as such, possesses the authority to direct the activities of the individual including the authority to extract a share of the resource or product that is nominally under the individual's "private" possession. We are dependents, slaves, rent-recipients (these are equivalent terms for purposes of my argument here) to the extent that we are unable to escape the extractions demanded by the state. It took me two decades to shuck off the normative trappings of orthodox economics and to write in defense of tax loopholes.

Confusion arises here because there seems to be no identifiable master in the democratic polity. As an individual, a person may well acknowledge his dependence on the state, but he may also recognize that there seems to be no single person or group that çan be identified as master. In the idealized model of majoritarian democracy, the individual's fate depends on a process, and, in the limit, no one person has more than minimal influence in determining the result. We are, in such a setting, all "slaves without masters."

We are, however, slaves-subjects only to the extent that the state is authorized to act, quite independently of the decision rules through which it operates. (Again, save in the limiting case of a unanimity rule.) We are free men within those spheres of our activity that are protected from state intrusion by effective constitutional order.

The monumental folly of the past two centuries has been the presumption that, so long as the state operates in accordance with democratic procedures (free and periodic elections, open franchise, open entry for parties, candidates, and interests, majority or plurality voting rules) the individual does, indeed, have insurance against exploitation, quite apart from any viable exit option. Modern states have been allowed to invade increasing areas of "private space" under the pretense of democratic process. (In saying this, I do not want to imply that the legal form of state expansion is unimportant. States that broadly adhere to the rule of law are, of course, more protective of individual liberty than states which discriminate among persons arbitrarily, even with the same level of total activity.)

I hope that my argument here has shifted the emphasis somewhat. Failure or success has too often been measured in terms of the standard economists' criterion of efficiency, the ability to get goods and services produced and distributed, to add to the wealth of nations. This emphasis has, I think, been mistaken, at least in part. Markets may fail against the efficiency standard, even in some relative sense. But even in failure markets allow persons to retain exit options without which liberty cannot be secured. The state may succeed against the efficiency standard, even in some relative sense. But even in success, the state necessarily closes off (or narrowly restricts) the exit option for its members, implying necessarily that while liberty may be allowed it cannot be guaranteed. In retrospect, it seems singularly unfortunate that Adam Smith chose to entitle his great work "The Wealth of Nations" rather than "The System of Natural Liberty."

Finally, let me express the main point of these remarks by reference to Hayek's notable *The Road to Serfdom* (1944). In my view, the thesis should not be that an initiation of state intrusion must lead, ultimately, to man's serfdom to the state. The thesis should be interpreted to suggest that *any intrusion* by the state insures man's serfdom, *within the limits defined by the intrusion*. Man is, and must remain, a slave to the state. But it is critically and vitally important to recognize that ten percent slavery is different from fifty percent.

REFERENCES

Nozick, Robert. 1974. *Anarchy, state, and utopia*. New York: Basic Books, pp. 290-292.

Chapter 2

THE MARKET AND THE METAMARKET

A Review of the Contributions of the Economic Theory of Property Rights

By

Pedro Schwartz*

The aim of this chapter is to summarize contributions made by economists to the economic analysis of property rights. I believe that economists have made great strides recently toward the understanding of social institutions which for many years had been ignored and that the new hypotheses formulated by economists will be of interest to sociologists, anthropologists, and students of law. In addition, the reincorporation of the study of property rights into the field of economic theory has enabled economists to solve some problems which remained unsolved in the economic theory of the market, such as, for example, what conditions are necessary for the existence of workable competition, a more accurate definition of so-called "external effects," remedies for "market failure," the formulation of a theory of economic systems, and the answers to certain questions in the theory of the firm relating to ownership and control.[1]

---

*P. Schwartz, formerly professor of economics at the University of Madrid, is a member of the Spanish parliament.

This chapter consists of four sections plus a summary. The first section will contain a brief excursus through the history of economic thought in order to give some idea of the metamorphoses in the concept of property rights.

Having explained what I mean by "property rights" and by the "metamarket," I will in the second section set out what has been called Coase's theorem, the starting point for an economic theory of property rights. In the third section I shall introduce Posner's hypothesis, which allows one to distinguish within the metamarket between those legal institutions which improve the efficient working of the market process and those which redistribute wealth obligatorily and thus reduce market efficiency. This hypothesis enables us to understand the true economic significance of private-property rights and leads us to a distinction between a positive and a normative economic theory of legal institutions. In the fourth section I shall analyze the Krueger-Posner theory of the social costs of legal monopolies.

PROPERTY RIGHTS IN THE HISTORY OF ECONOMIC THOUGHT

An interest in the evolution of civil institutions through the course of history and in the multiplicity of forms exhibited by these institutions in different geographical settings was transformed into systematic research in the works of a group of philosophers, historians, and social scientists known today as the Eighteenth-century Scottish Historical School. Montesquieu had previously put forward the hypothesis that climatic differences explained the diversity of existing institutions, a diversity which at first sight appeared to be irreconcilable with the assumption that human nature was invariable irrespective of differences of place and time. The Scottish School, among the most prominent of whom were Francis Hutcheson, David Hume, Adam Smith, John Millar, and William Robertson, preferred to choose the mode of production as the explicans. That is to say, they thought that although men were fundamentally the same at birth, they combined into societies that differed according to the mode of subsistence of each specific society. This theory was soon expanded until it became transformed into a full-blown philosophy of history. The hypothesis that the history of society should be divided into stages of development was proposed in 1762 by Adam Smith and the French economist Turgot simultaneously, yet independently of each other. It was that the evolution of humanity could be divided into successive stages, those whose activity was primarily hunting, pastoral or nomadic, agrarian, industrial, and commercial. Book III of _The Wealth of Nations_, entitled _Of the Different Progress of Opulence in Different Nations_, is a masterly reconstruction of European history from the rise of the Roman Empire in terms of the economic motive force which generates social organizations. Hegel, in his _Philosophy of Law_, took up from Adam Smith the idea that the key to the historical evolution of humanity is its economic organization, an idea further developed by Friedrich Engels and Karl Marx in _The Origins of the Family_ and _Capital_, respectively. In the course of its transmission through German philosophy, however, the Scottish idea had been recast in a determinist mold. The new determinist theory permitted one to understand by what unavoidable mechanisms humanity had passed from the feudal stage to the capitalist and would inevitably pass from capitalism to socialism.

Three further growths sprang from the economic theory of institutions: the theory of the market, the economic theory of private property, and the theory of the distinction between the laws of production and the laws of distribution.

Let me begin with the theory of the market. Then I will examine the other two theories--the economic theory of property rights and the distinction between efficiency and distribution, both of which have undergone a rebirth recently in the works of Coase, Posner, and other economists of the so-called Chivirla School (the universities of Chicago, Virginia Polytechnic, and California at Los Angeles).[2]

One of the major contributions of the Scottish School to social philosophy is the idea of the unintentional, and indeed unwanted, consequences of individual human actions. It is not accidental that the Scottish Enlightenment should show an interest in the history of languages: there are few more striking facts in sociology for those who believe in the underlying unity of human nature than the existence of a very large number of different languages spoken by mankind. Today, linguists such as Piaget or Chomsky have returned to the search for a single grammatical structure which is said to underlie this plethora of languages. My interest lies elsewhere, however. The Scots emphasized the fact that, while the language spoken in each different place is the creation of human beings, no one specifically designed it. Rather, it was the unintentional product of the interaction and evolution of individual attempts to communicate meaningfully. In similar terms, Adam Smith describes to us the institution of the market: controlled by no one, it works spontaneously, as the unintentional social result of individuals pursuing their own individual interests. Following Adam Smith, generations of economists have devoted their efforts to the analysis of those conditions necessary for the existence, uniqueness, and stability of market equilibrium.

It was David Hume who first brought together the disparate elements of what was later to be formulated as the economic theory of private property. Hume's approach to property rights, most thoroughly worked out in Section III of his _Enquiry Concerning the Principles of Morals_,[3] is dictated by his search for an overriding principle on which to base a "science of morals," a principle analogous to Newton's law of gravity, on which the modern science of physics was based.[4] This he found in "the principle of public utility."

Although Hume's definition of his theory of private property is couched in terms of social and political utilitarianism, the underlying criterion seems to be one of economic efficiency, more appropriate to the dynamic world of mid-eighteenth century commerce.

Let me go on to examine how the economic theory of the market has been enriched by one of Smith's earlier followers, the English philosopher John Stuart Mill, who also had much to say concerning the other outgrowth of the Scots economic theory of institutions.

John Stuart Mill was a child prodigy who from his earliest years was groomed to be successor to the leadership of the Utilitarian School when its founders, Jeremy Bentham and James Mill, his father, died. After a nervous breakdown at eighteen, however, J. S. Mill, influenced by the arguments of the first socialists and working class leaders in favor of a revision of classical political economy, began to subject the ideas of his mentors to a process of reorientation. One of his contributions to the humanization of the "dismal science" was his theory of market failure. In his Principles of Political Economy (1848) Mill devoted many pages to the question of whether the state should intervene in the economy. He based his discussion on two interesting distinctions. First, he made a distinction between what he referred to as "necessary functions" and "optimal interventions." "Necessary functions" were those which led to the establishment of a legal framework, which the market needed in order to function properly. Second, within the so-called "optimal interventions" he distinguished between those based on false theories and those designed to correct market failures. The risk of market failures that John Stuart Mill presents lays the groundwork for the threefold division of market failure presented by orthodox twentieth-century economists: external effects, increasing returns, and lack of information. This tripartite division of market failure is based on the three conditions necessary for the existence of perfect competition: (1) the perfect discrimination of goods, which would eliminate external effects of the consumption of some goods on the consumption of other goods; (2) perfect divisibility of factors, which would preclude the problem of increasing returns and the monopolies which arise from them; and (3) perfect information, which would preclude disequilibrium contracting.

Mill's teachings were taken up at Cambridge University by Henry Sidgwick, then by Alfred Marshall, the first holder of the chair of economics there, and then by his disciple A. C. Pigou, who succeeded Marshall in that chair. Marshall proposed the use of subsidies to stimulate firms with increasing returns, the subsidies to be financed by taxes levied on those firms with diminishing returns, thus maximizing the social product. Pigou put forward a more carefully thought-out analysis of the problem together with comprehensive conclusions. It was he who formalized the idea of "externalities" or external effects, i.e., that situation in which, due to market failure, the social costs are greater than those paid by the producer, or the social benefits are greater than those which accrue to the producer. An example would be the case of the paper manufacturer who does not pay the cost of the pollution caused by his activities or that of the scientist who obtains little or no profit from an unpatentable theory.

The economist who presented the most acute analysis of property rights prior to John Stuart Mill's attempt to separate laws of production from laws of distribution was Jeremy Bentham. Of great importance in the dissemination of Bentham's ideas about property was the selection of his manuscripts published by Etienne Dumont under the title *Traités de législation civile et pénale* in 1802. The subject of private property is first analyzed according to the general principle of security, and then, more specifically, Bentham examines the problem of how to quantify the cost in welfare derived from different kinds of limitations placed upon private property.

For Bentham, the beneficial consequences of being freely able to conserve and pass on the fruits of one's labor were spectacular; the prosperity of society was founded on this principle, the ramifications of which Bentham later worked out and explored more fully in the first part of the "Principes du Code Civil," and in the second, which concerns title deeds and the transfer of property rights.

The position from which Bentham analyzed the institution of property rights, however, tended to paralyze later research on the subject. Security and the right to own property stimulated wealth; attacks on this principle and the institution of property rights were ultimately irrational, or at least uncivic. Any research into the possible defects of a society's property rights system, or the possible inadequacy of existing rights in the light of technological progress, seemed therefore unnecessary. Thus, at the same time, any consideration of alternative social systems, other than for the purpose of condemning them, appeared to be irrelevant. John Stuart Mill's approach to the problem is scientifically much more interesting.

The last development of the Scottish theory of institutions, the distinction between laws of production and laws of distribution, was also initiated by J. S. Mill. This distinction is a serious attempt by an orthodox economist to analyze the relationship between the economic market subject to the law of efficiency, an institutional metamarket subject to the law of efficiency, and an institutional metamarket subject, as he thought, to the law of justice--between efficient production and property-rights distribution.

Mill, in order to soften the dismal science, needed to establish to what degree economic laws were unchangeable and to what extent they could be modified by institutional reforms. He needed to know this in order to ascertain, for example, whether profit sharing among a firm's employees or the establishment of cooperatives was compatible with the laws of economic science.

Mill separated society into two completely discrete areas: the world of efficient production, subject to quasi-natural laws, and the world of distribution, modifiable by institutional reforms.

Mill himself realized that distribution had repercussions in the sphere of production and vice versa. Later criticism has used primarily the theory of marginal productivity to emphasize the links between production and functional distribution. Nevertheless, Mill's distinction possesses an almost intuitive attraction. Perhaps there are conditions under which one could say that the world of economic efficiency is completely separate from the world of property rights and personal distribution.

Our interest in Coase's theorem, which we shall examine in the following section, lies precisely in that it delineates the conditions under which it is possible to separate the economic market from the institutional metamarket, thus allowing us to study those institutions which propitiate this segregation and leading us to specify mutual influences when this segregation is not possible.

One can judge the importance of Coase's contribution in this field if one compares it with the role assigned to property rights and other legal institutions in the work of a modern disciple of Mill, Lord Robbins. In his famous lectures on *The Theory of Economic Policy in English Classical Political Economy* (1952), Robbins insisted that the "system of Economic Freedom," as he called the view of society held by the classical economists, was not based on the natural harmony of self-interested individual actions. Very much to the contrary, the smooth functioning of the market depended on "the provision of a set of rules which so limited and guided individual initiative, that the residue of free action undirected from the centre could be conceived to harmonize with the general objects of public interest" [Lecture VI, section vi].

A legal framework was therefore necessary. Nothing, however, was being said about the possibility of an economic analysis of this necessity, or about the structure and organization of this framework. The work of Coase allows one to advance a step further in the economic analysis of the metamarket.

COASE'S THEOREM OR THE CONDITIONS FOR FREE CONTRACT

Before going on to explain Coase's theorem, since an important component of this theorem consists in delimiting "property rights" within the context of the "metamarket," a clarification of these two expressions is in order.

By "property rights" I mean not merely rights of ownership over tangible possessions, but also rights which extend from those over one's vote to rights of way, administrative concessions, entitlements to a contracted performance, or patents and copyrights. The essential idea is the exclusion of others from the use of a service or good and the transferability of this right, to a greater or lesser degree of attenuation, according to the institutional constraints.

I wish to introduce the term "metamarket" to describe the institutional world where property rights are defined and conferred and within the framework of which they are transferred and enforced. These rights are then the object of contracts or agreements in the market. The function of this institutional metamarket is to define the constitutional rules, laws, social customs, and ethical standards within the market. The metamarket is the locus where parliament, the law courts, arbitration tribunals, and the police carry out their activities. The metamarket is where wars are declared, strikes are organized, and thefts are perpetrated; in this metamarket, prison sentences are meted out, taxes collected, social security stamps charged, subsidies paid, and family allowances granted. In short, one might briefly define this metamarket as that institutional framework within which the actors of the economic market carry out their transactions.

By presenting case after case taken from Anglo-American legal practice, Coase was able to show that external effects could be "internalized" without any need for taxes or subsidies if the affected parties were permitted to contract freely among themselves; in other words, without any government intervention, the producers of an externality, such as, for example, that of a paper manufacturer, and the consumers of this externality, such as for instance the anglers and residents of the neighborhood, could manage to reduce this externality to an optimum level by means of a mutually satisfactory agreement, reached by compensating or "bribing" those who enjoyed property rights over the river and the atmosphere.

Professor Coase's next step was to examine the conditions necessary for the externality to disappear without public intervention. (By the "internalization of the externality" one means in this case arriving at the same level of pollution, as if anglers, neighbors and paper manufacturers all formed part of the same firm. In this case, as Stigler has pointed out, one would produce that quantity of smoke and effluent sufficient to equal the margin of utility for manufacturing paper, hooking trout, and breathing the surrounding air.)

According to Coase's theorem, whomever the cost of the externality is charged to--paper manufacturer, anglers, or neighbors--the same combination of pollution and manufactured product will be reached if three conditions obtain: (1) that property rights be clearly defined; (2) that transaction costs be zero; and (3) that payments or compensations to those who hold the rights do not affect the pattern of demand.

Of these three conditions the most important are the first two. They are the necessary conditions for the producers and consumers of an externality to be able to contract freely among themselves.

Note that the first condition excludes very little. It does not say to whom the right to do what they please with the river and with the air should correspond. It only says that the right of ownership should be defined, whether the right lies with the manufacturer or the local inhabitants. If the second condition is fulfilled (together with the third) and the transaction costs are zero, the same optimum level of pollution will be attained _no matter whom the property rights belong to_. That is to say that the property system is immaterial if it is known to whom the rights belong and if the costs of reaching an agreement are nonexistent. (Some communal property systems increase transaction costs greatly.)

The object of this chapter is not to discuss the problems of pollution and their possible solution, but rather to trace the boundary between market and metamarket and to define the relationship between both compartments of society. The first condition stipulated by Coase is the one which reduces the role of the metamarket to assigning unambiguous property rights. The second condition states that negotiations and dealings cost nothing in time or in money. Conversely, if transaction costs are positive, then the point of equilibrium reached may depend on the initial distribution of property rights. Consequently, one can only partition the laws of production and the laws of distribution as John Stuart Mill wanted, if contracting and recontracting cost nothing (and rights are clearly assigned).

Coase's theorem fruitfully reframes one of the three problems inherited from the Scottish Historical School's research program: the problem of how to express with exactitude the highly plausible situation that the ownership of property rights could be assigned under many different systems without the workings of the economy being affected in any fundamental way. The areas are discrete only if the market is perfect.

Coase's innovation consists, then, in reformulating the conditions for the existence of an economic optimum, in such a way that the attenuation of these conditions and the occurrence of externalities are linked to the malfunctioning of the metamarket. Let us examine exactly what this implies.

Coase, instead of talking about "perfect discrimination among goods" and "perfect divisibility of factors," presents us with the equivalent condition (1) that property rights should be well defined. Let us suppose that in a society it is perfectly clear who owns the property rights over all goods and services. One still has the task of ensuring that these rights are respected, and the cost of doing so could be greater than the benefits obtained if the rights were respected. Apart from this, when supply or demand changes, whether because of technological progress or changing tastes, the benefits obtainable from the enforcement of property rights would also change. Thus, for instance, the invention of television has made it profitable to redefine property rights over wavelengths, rights which previously had not seemed worthwhile even to attribute, let alone to enforce. Therefore, any modification in the conditions of supply and demand means that the existing attribution and enforcement of property rights is rendered obsolete. Despite these difficulties, condition (1) underlines the possibility of bettering discrimination of goods and discrimination of factors through the machinery of the metamarket rather than through ad hoc state intervention.

Then Coase, instead of talking about "perfect information" as a condition for perfect competition, talks about condition (2), "zero transaction costs." It is true again that this condition cannot fully obtain in the real world. Even as efficient a market as the New York Stock Exchange, for instance, needs to cover certain expenses, such as those for the use of a building, a computer, and brokers. Many markets are more expensive than this one; thus, the market made up of the paper manufacturer, the anglers, and the local inhabitants will have to spend time and resources to agree on compensation payments and who will call a halt to discussions before an optimum solution is reached, unless one had been reached by chance. Again, speaking of "zero transaction costs" rather than "perfect information," makes one think of improving markets rather than establishing a state information agency, seemingly incurring no costs.

In short, whenever the market optimum appears to be an unreachable goal, one should examine whether rights can be sufficiently defined and trading efficiency sufficiently promoted to provide for better contracting. Any felt "market failures" are not in fact failures in the market but in the metamarket, the institutional organization of which suffers from malfunctions that act to prevent optimal contracting within the market.

Coase's theorem first of all permits one to define under what conditions the distribution of rights in a society would not affect the market, that is to say, permits one to separate the laws governing production efficiency from those promoting a socially accepted distribution. Second, the theorem leads one to ascribe failures in the economic system not to the price mechanism but to the malfunctioning of the institutional metamarket. The next step is to analyze the metamarket from an economic point of view in order to discover (1) whether there exist within it de facto corrective mechanisms and (2) whether de jure it might be possible to recommend certain reforms which would bring the working of the market closer to its ideal state.[5]

POSNER'S HYPOTHESIS, OR THE SOCIAL EFFICIENCY OF THE METAMARKET

We find ourselves confronted with a dual problem: a positive or empirical problem of ascertaining how the mechanisms of the metamarket work; and a normative or social policy problem of putting forward suggestions for the improvement of the metamarket so as to reduce, as much as possible, institutional interferences in the economic mechanism.

Professor Coase is again the pioneer of the positive theory of the metamarket. In his 1937 article, "The Nature of the Firm," he explained the existence of firms by means of transaction costs in the market. This problem was to explain the nonmarket characteristics of firms and the facts of their growth and size: "Outside the firm, price movements direct production, which is co-ordinated through a series of exchange transactions on the market. Within a firm, these market transactions are eliminated and in place of the complicated market structure with exchange transactions is substituted the entrepreneur-co-ordinator, who directs production" (p. 333).

Firms appear to reduce transaction costs in the market, be they information costs, contracting costs, or costs born of uncertainty. This summarizes the economic point of view for studying the metamarket: many institutions appear as a means of circumventing high transaction costs.

Richard A. Posner, in his book Economic Analysis of Law (1973), has written an excellent synopsis of research into the metamarket. This large book covers the common law, antitrust, commercial law, procedural law, and constitutional law within the specific context of the United States, using as an analytical tool what I have chosen here to baptize "Posner's hypothesis."

According to Posner and those other American writers whose works Posner summarizes in his book, the law is susceptible to economic analysis because many legal institutions have an economic rationale. This was not the intentional outcome of any plan, nor was this the case for those institutions analyzed by the Scottish Historical School. The economic rationale of many legal institutions is the furthering of economic efficiency. There are naturally many institutions and legal decisions which, when put under the magnifying glass of economics, do not appear to increase efficiency. Posner explicitly takes into account and studies this possibility when he confronts problems of a normative nature, that is, when he proposes reforms in existing institutions in order to increase their efficiency. Posner, together with Demsetz, Pejovich, Furubotn, and other authors of this school, however, always approach the study of legal institutions on the hypothesis that these institutions function to increase the efficiency of the economic system for which they provide a framework.

Before presenting possible applications of Posner's hypothesis, I think that, in the interest of terminological precision, I should define exactly what I mean by efficiency and explain how it is to be measured. The most widely accepted definition of efficiency is that given by Wilfredo Pareto: a social state is deemed efficient when no one can better his position without harming that of someone else.

In our context, therefore, a "Paretian improvement" is that change in the market or in the metamarket which improves the situation of an individual without causing a deterioration in the position of another.[6] Efficiency is measured by willingness to pay. As Posner puts it, "efficiency means exploiting economic resources in such a way that 'value'--*human satisfaction as measured by willingness to pay* for goods and services--is maximised" (p. 10).

These abstract concepts might be better understood through the analysis of a specific case, in which the economic *rationale* of a legal institution is not immediately obvious in all its implications. Let us consider the case of a false description of a good in a sales contract. If the seller of a fake painting knowingly deceives the buyer, the latter should have the power to initiate penal or civil proceedings against the fraudulent party. The justification for this action lies not in making good the wrong done to the purchaser, since the damage has already occurred and will not influence any future allocation of resources (except to the extent to which the redistribution in income brought about by the fraud might affect this allocation). The justification lies in the fact that each successful fraud will act as an incentive to the perpetration of further fraudulent sales, and such frauds involving false description in the sales contract entail two kinds of costs for society: first, the effort involved in painting imitations of great masters; and second, the additional precautions that future buyers will have to take, such as paying for an expert's appraisal, x-ray examinations, research in archives, and so on. To be sure, if the judges in the metamarket apply the maxim of _caveat emptor_ to the buying and selling of paintings, the market will arrive at some kind of solution which will imply an equilibrium between the production of a further quantity of fakes and the increased costs in guaranteeing the authenticity of the signature. This would lead to a waste of resources in comparison with the situation in which civil and penal responsibilities fall upon the vendor and consequently contribute to deterring frauds from continuing their activities. In some cases, however, one must apply the _caveat emptor_ principle, for example, in livestock fairs and markets, in which the speed and certainty of agreements has priority over other considerations. Society has thus implicitly decided that benefits to be derived from the existence of such fairs are greater than the combined losses incurred by the costs of setting up the fraud and the adoption of preventive measures to deter such a possibility (see Posner 1973, section 4.7).

As a mechanism to increase efficiency in resource allocation the metamarket acts in two ways, which were indicated by two of the conditions in Coase's theorem: first, it betters the definition of property rights; and second, it reduces the costs of the transaction leading to the optimum.

In order to study the first case, the mechanism through which the metamarket more precisely defines property rights, I shall take as a paradigmatic example that of the _ius in rem_, that of private property in things.

Economists have chosen to emphasize two features of private property that make it peculiarly appropriate for the process of contracting. The first is that of exclusivity. In the purest forms of property rights, the proprietor enjoys the possibility of excluding all others from the usufruct of his property. The second is that of transferability. If a property right is not transferable, resources will not be moved from a less productive to a more productive application by means of voluntary exchanges. The relationship between these conditions is more complex than appears at first sight, however, since the very exclusivity of a right makes it more easily transferable and the difficulty involved in transferring the right because of high transaction costs usually makes the complete exclusivity of the owner's rights socially unacceptable, unless it bears some rights of way or other alternatives, as might occur in the context of land needed to build a railway line.

Since the coexistence of exclusivity and transferability in private property improves the functioning of the market, it would be a good thing if there were many such rights with similar features. As Posner puts it, a system of property rights ideally should extend itself until it becomes universal: "Ideally, all resources should be owned by someone, except resources so plentiful that everybody can consume as much of them as he wants without reducing consumption by anyone else . . . [as no] issue of efficient use arises in such a case" (Posner 1973, section 3.1).

The second case, the question of transaction costs, assumes even greater importance in the light of Posner's analysis, since transferability is so important. One example will perhaps help to clarify the question. Assume that there is a factory which emits smoke, thus polluting the atmosphere in the district. It is a poor area with high unemployment, and any attempt to close down the factory would be unpopular. The first question is whether the factory owner has a property right over the air, making him free to pollute it to any degree, or whether the property right is vested in the public. Coase's principle tells us that, if transaction costs are zero, it is immaterial who is vested with the property rights, as long as they clearly belong to someone. In this case, either the local residents pay for the factory owner to buy a filter to reduce the pollution to an optimum level (a combination of smoke and employment) or the factory owner compensates the local inhabitants so that they allow him to emit his optimum quantity of smoke. The costs of such a transaction, however, might be prohibitive, since the many local residents may not be able to agree on a solution, and passers-by or tourists are not always on hand and could not receive compensation for having to breathe the smoke as they passed through the neighborhood. Under these conditions, not only is it extremely difficult to arrive at the optimum, but the initial assignment of property rights is no longer immaterial. If one wishes to avoid closing the factory, so that unemployment will not increase, it would be better to confer rights to use of the air to the factory owner and then let him be "bribed" by the local inhabitants with a smoke filter so that he can reduce pollution without increasing his costs. To confer property rights on the local inhabitants might make the transaction endless.

This is how Posner's hypothesis can be used to complement Coase's principle. According to Posner, a great number of institutions of the metamarket, be they courts of law or government departments, show a tendency to allocate the property rights directly to the party who will use the property most efficiently, thus eliminating the need for this party to acquire the right from a less efficient user.

THE RENT-SEEKING SOCIETY

It is opportune to discuss here a possible normative application of Posner's principle. According to this principle, the economic justification of metamarket institutions is to be found in their contribution to optimum resource allocation in the market. Hence, the principle can be used to support criticism of institutions when they do not perform this function. We have progressed enormously in the study of this question since Bentham's original delineation of the inconveniences for society in reducing the guarantees of private property, or since Bentham's explanation that any such violation of the guarantee of private property would be consented to if the public interest is something other than the sum total of individual private interests.

Karl Brunner, in an article entitled "Reflections on the Political Economy of Government: The Persistent Growth of Government," sets out an economic theory of the state based on the role of what I have called the institutions of the metamarket in furthering market efficiency. He begins by distinguishing between two basic types of social activity: trading activity, which he defines as a positive sum game, since all the participants in the game benefit, and plundering activity, which he defines as a negative sum game, since the benefits that accrue from plundering to one party produce a net loss for society. Wealth can be acquired through productive effort or voluntary interchange, or by extorting an income from the rest of society by the use of force.

The state is for Brunner an ambivalent institution, a two-edged social weapon. By putting an end to anarchy, the state cuts down on negative sum games such as piracy, banditry, and civil war. But the state monopoly of coercion necessary for ridding society of parasites makes the state in turn a tempting prize for those who like to live at others' expense.

So widespread is this kind of extortion in society that Professor Anne O. Krueger titled an article published in 1974, "The Political Economy of the Rent-seeking Society." In it she gave as a dominant characteristic of our world social competition to obtain rents. Professor Krueger explained that the use of the powers of the state by pressure groups for their own benefit in order to obtain rents constituted a negative sum game for two reasons: first, because the concession of protection or exclusivity in itself reduces economic efficiency, and second, because the granting of a legal privilege to an individual or to a group incites others to use scarce resources in order to obtain a similar privilege, or at least to supplant those first favored with it. Professor Krueger came to these conclusions as a result of her studies on quotas in Turkey: they reduced the economy's competitiveness and unleashed competition between other groups in society seeking to obtain the same prizes.

As Professor Krueger's study was being published, Professor Posner was writing an article entitled "The Social Costs of Monopoly and Regulation," published in the Journal of Political Economy. In this article Posner precisely defined the nature of the two kinds of costs of state protection of or extension of privileges to a specific group. Ten years previously Arnold C. Harberger had attempted to show that monopolies were not as harmful to society as was usually thought, since in a large part their effects were only those of a transfer. To this end he drew a diagram in which "Harberger's triangle" appeared as the representation of the net loss to society of a monopoly, which corresponds to Professor Krueger's first effect. If we assume that the state increases by means of a tariff the price of a good produced by a local monopolist from P_c to P_m, the product will be reduced by Δ Q. The loss of consumers' surplus is L + D, but for Harberger the rectangle L is only a transfer to the monopolist and does not give rise to a net social loss. D is Harberger's triangle, which he takes as the sum total of net social loss. Posner nevertheless maintained that Harberger's result did not remain in equilibrium. The income L obtained by the legally privileged monopolist would incite other pressure groups to devote resources to obtaining a similar income. Finally, L would be squandered in bribes, political elbowing, or electoral competition and the net transfer would be zero. Thus, the game for society would result in a negative sum represented by Harberger's triangle plus Posner's rectangle.

FIGURE 1. Harberger's triangle and Posner's rectangle.

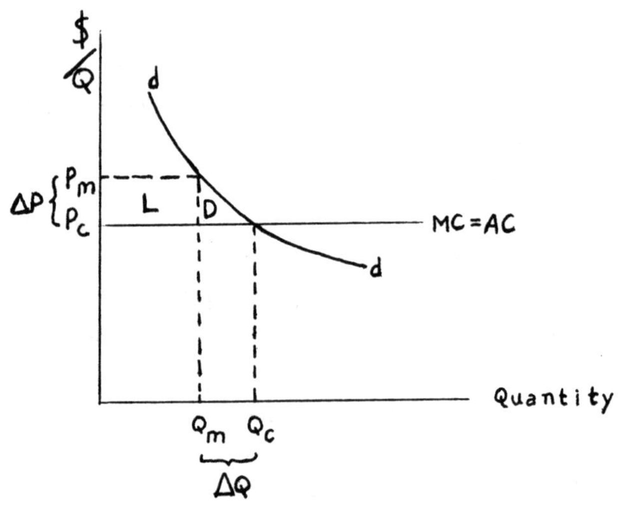

Much has been written on the importance of those institutions which protect production and free exchange from the extraction of rents by commercial, political, or military means. Recent research by American economic historians (North and Thomas 1971; North 1974) attempts to attribute the economic progress of the West to the appearance of institutions that protected the zero sum game of production and exchange from rent extractors.

SUMMARY

The object of this chapter has been to summarize a new, and in my opinion, particularly fruitful development in economic thought--the economic theory of property rights. Although economists have been concerned with property rights and the legal organization of society since the eighteenth century, it is only recently that they have begun to try to define with precision the relationship between the institutional metamarket and the economic market.

The starting point of the new analysis of property rights is a study by Ronald Coase published in 1960. Posner's hypothesis provides the analytical instrument to ascertain to what extent legal institutions promote economic productivity. The metamarket shows a tendency to redefine property rights continually, as technological conditions in supply, or tastes in demand, change. Also when transaction costs are high, the metamarket tends to grant property rights to those who will use them most productively.

Implicit in this positive analysis is a critique of the growing government intervention in the economic market which has taken place in the twentieth century. This analysis seems to indicate that the market works well enough if left to its own devices and that the spontaneous evolution of the nonpolitical institutions of the metamarket is favorable to the growing mercantilism of society. In a world of scarcity, efficiency is a moral virtue.

NOTES

1. A complement to this paper is Erik Furubotn and Svetozar Pejovich's article, "Property Rights and Economic Theory: A Survey of Recent Literature," Journal of Economic Literature x, 4 (December, 1972): 1137-62. Particularly interesting, apart from the summary of the development of the economic theory of property rights up to 1972, is the way in which the authors of this article apply Coase's theorem to the theory of the firm. Nevertheless, they make no effort to relate Coase's conditions to those necessary for perfect competition. In the field of the economic theory of law and the workings of the metamarket, they make only a few brief references to the theory of the state. Nor is there any discussion of rent-seeking or of normative welfare theory. A more up-to-date treatment may be found in the March, 1979, issue of The Journal of Legal Studies, especially in the introduction by Henry G. Manne, where attention is brought to Paul H. Rubin's contribution to explaining the mechanism behind what I have called Posner's hypothesis: the economic logic of law is explained as the result of a quasi-natural selection process.

2. With reference to the Chivirla School, see John Burton, "Externalities, Property Rights and Economics" in Cheung 1978.

3. Hume 1751/1975. R. Coase suggested that I give explicit attention to Hume on property.

4. Hume 1751/1975, p. 204. "It is entirely agreeable to the rules of philosophy, and even of common reason; where any principle has been found to have a great force and energy in one instance, to ascribe to it a like energy in all similar instances. This indeed is Newton's chief rule of philosophising."

5. Even those economists who insist on the need to take into account "state defects" before recommending public intervention continue to speak of "market defects" as an independent category, without seeing that all defects in the economic market exist for some good reason, either as a result of defects in the institutional metamarket, or because the cost of correcting these institutional defects is such that one is prepared to tolerate any repercussion they might have in the market. This omission of any reference to the scientific consequences of Coase's theory is to be seen, for example, in Wolf 1979.

6. As a result of the studies of Nobel prize winner Kenneth Arrow and other mathematical economists such as Professor Amartya Sen, it has become clear that a market without a legal framework, that is to say, without a metamarket, can produce contradictory effects of the kind described by Fred Hirsch in his book Social Limits to Growth (1977) if one pushes the application of the Paretian criterion to its final consequences. The importance of the metamarket, however, lies precisely in the need for established rules that provide a channel for the individual's pursuit of his profits. This is not the place to pursue any further this

line of research, but any economist interested in the problems described might consult Harsanyi 1979, together with Dworkin 1978.

REFERENCES

Bentham, J. 1802. Traités de législation civile et pénale. Published in French, by E. T. Dumont. 3 vols. Paris.

Brunner, K. 1978. Reflections on the political economy of government: The persistent growth of government. Rochester, N.Y.: University of Rochester.

Cheung, N. S. 1978. The myth of social cost. London: Institute of Economic Affairs.

Coase, R. 1937. The nature of the firm. Economica n.s. 4. Reprinted in G. J. Stigler and K. E. Boulding, Readings in price theory. AER, 1953.

------. 1960. The problems of social cost. Journal of Law and Economics 3.

Dworkin, R. 1978. Taking rights seriously. London: Duckworth.

Engels, F. 1884. Der Ursprung der Familie, des Privateigentums und des Staats.

Harberger, A. C. 1954. Monopoly and resource allocation. American Economic Review 44/(May):77-87.

Harsanyi, J. C. 1979. Bayesian theory, rule utilitarianism, and Arrow's impossibility theorem. Pp. 289-317 in Game theory, social choice and ethics, compiled by H. W. Brock. Dordrecht, Netherlands: D. Reidel.

Hegel, G. W. F. 1821. Grundlinien der Philosophie des Rechts.

Hirsch, F. 1977. Social limits to growth. London.

Hume, David. 1751/1975. Enquiry concerning the principles of morals. 3rd ed. 1777. Re-edited by L. A. Selby-Bigge and P. H. Nidditch. Oxford, 1975.

Knight, F. 1924. Some fallacies in the interpretation of social cost. Quarterly Journal of Economics 582.

Krueger, A. O. 1974. The political economy of the rent-seeking society. American Economic Review 64 (June):291-303.

Manne, Henry G. 1979. Introduction. Journal of Legal Studies 8, no. 2 (March).

Mill, J. S. 1848. Principles of political economy. Book II. London.

------. 1965. Collected works. Book II. Toronto.

North, Douglass C. 1974. The rise of the Western world: A new economic history. Cambridge University Press.

North, Douglass C. and R. P. Thomas. 1971. The rise and fall of the manorial system: A theoretical model. Journal of Economic History 47, no. 4 (December):777-803.

Posner, R. 1973. Economic analysis of law. 2nd ed. 1977. Boston and Toronto.

------. 1975. The social costs of monopoly and regulation. Journal of Political Economy 83, no. 4 (August):807-27.

Robbins, Lionel. 1848. The theory of economic policy in English classical political economy. London.

Rubin, Paul H. 1977. Why is common law efficient? 6 Journal of Legal Studies 51.

Wolf, Charles, Jr. 1979. A theory of non-market failure. Journal of Law and Economics 22, no. 1 (April):107-39.

Chapter 3

THE LIMITS OF ECONOMIC POLICY

By

Karl Brunner*

ALTERNATIVE APPROACHES TO ECONOMIC POLICY

Academic analysis of economic policy and associated normative conclusions exhibits two distinct traditions. The historical evolution of policy and policy conceptions reflects over the past 200 years shifting influences from both traditions. One addresses an open-ended field of specific actions potentially available to government and explores the consequences of these measures. More importantly, this tradition justifies an action-oriented approach aimed at a wide range of specific results over a loosely limited or practically unlimited range. This policy conception envisions government as an active agent at least approximately concerned with the optimization of some social welfare function. This concern would require a wide array of policy instruments in order to allow the policymakers an unobstructed play in the policy game. The analysis of economic policy examines under the circumstances the relation between

---

*K. Brunner is professor of economics at the University of Rochester. Reprinted by permission from <u>Schweizerische Zeitschrift für Volkwirtschaft und Statistik</u>, Vol. 121, 1985.

instruments and goals expressed by a social welfare function and the useful range of possible instruments. It investigates in particular the dependence of the choice of instruments and their setting on the prevailing state of affairs in view of the desired goals of policymakers. A substantial literature followed this line exemplified by Tinbergen's (1952) "Theory of Economic Policy" and the work on optimal control (Chow 1975). Most of the discussions directed by academicians to the public arena address the policy problem in a similar vein. They concentrated on specific actions, choices of instruments or their setting in the past, at the present or in the future.

The second tradition is more attuned to classical political philosophy and classical economics. It rejects the action oriented approach with its characteristic desire to mold the world in some detail and its emphasis on choices of specific instruments or their level of application. The classical tradition emphasizes by contrast the proper choice of rules governing the socio-political or socio-economic game. The difference between the two approaches may be usefully explained with the metaphor of a football game. The policymakers would be represented by the commissioner of the football league and the players represent agents in the socio-economic game. The classical tradition with its constitutionalist thrust limits policymakers to formulate, monitor and enforce the general rules controlling the detailed plays of the game. The choice of strategies, tactical procedures, and all the varied details of the play are left to the players. The other tradition empowers the commissioner to shape both the general rules and much detail of the play in a shifting pattern in accordance with the state of the play. The classic approach to policy analysis thus understands policy not as a choice of specific actions but as a choice of general rules usually embedded in a set of institutions. We may juxtapose it under the circumstances as an "institutional policy" to "specific action policies." Analysis of economic policy means in this case an examination of alternative sets of rules. Variations in the rules yield in general different patterns in the socio-economic game. Any normative concern requires thus some careful analysis of the consequences associated with different sets of rules. Opportunities and incentives are in general affected by the choice of rules. The resulting modification of behavior influences unavoidably the broad pattern of the outcome produced by the social process. An evaluation of this outcome guides the analyst's choice of rules.

THEORISTS, PRAGMATISTS AND UNDERSTANDING POLICY

The discussion of policy is ultimately guided by a desire to provide an understanding of its role and consequences. It should contribute in particular to a reliable assessment of the alternative traditions. Academic contributions, whether made in academia or offered to the public arena, do not exhaust however the public discussions. We also encounter the comments, views, and proposals made by the media, suggested by officials or politicians and advanced by policymakers. Some components in this second strand of the discussion interact quite closely with the academic discussion. But major components evolve according to their own "logic" and with their own momentum. The discussion surrounding the U.S. budget deficit demonstrates this aspect with remarkable force. The media and other participants in the political process recognize this state and typically reflect it by juxtaposing the pragmatist or practical men of affairs to the academic "theoreticians." This juxtaposition involves more than a simple description of facts. It occurs with a peculiar epistemological thrust. It conveys a subtle sense about a difference in the state of knowledge. Practical men of affairs directly immersed in the reality of the policy problem experience somehow an immediate absorption of the relevant knowledge. The academic by contrast approaches reality indirectly via the construction of theories. The underlying message suggests moreover that the epistemological quality of such theories hardly compares with the acquisition of knowledge based on "direct exposure to reality." This more or less implicit theme embedded in the cliche represented by the juxtaposition suffers however under a fatal illusion. It thoroughly misconceives the nature of human knowledge. All potential knowledge appears in the form of theories or hypotheses about various aspects of our physical or social environment. This holds for academics and equally for "practical men of affairs." The latter are full of theories about matters concerning them. They are however rarely aware of the essentially theoretical nature of their perceptions of reality. They fail consequently to appreciate that perceptions about reality occurring in the form of some general conceptions (i.e. theories) are not automatically true simply because they were motivated somehow by "exposure to reality." They still need to be critically assessed against observations. Most of these ideas would hardly survive this process. An analysis of the remainder reveals moreover that they yield almost no information about the range of important consequences to be expected under different sets of policy actions or under various policy institutions. We encounter here the crucial focus of a minimal understanding of economic policy. A rational evaluation and choice of policy actions or institutions requires some more reliable knowledge of the probable consequences. This knowledge defines in an important sense the relevant limits of economic policy. But such knowledge can only be supplied in form of theories which survived some first rounds of critical assessment. The "practical men of affairs," geared for other and quite important functions in life, frequently demanding high levels of intelligence, are in general, with remarkable exceptions however, not equipped for this task.

The crucial point which needs to be made on occasion is the existence of a professional core expressed by economic analysis and represented by the best accumulated work of the profession. This core guides our exploration of "the limits of economic policy."

LIMITS OF ECONOMIC POLICY

General Remarks

The relevant limitation on policymaking emerges once we examine the consequences of policies and the nature of the policymaking process. The implications of the constraints imposed by the social opportunity set and the prevalence of perennially incomplete information about the detailed working of the private and public sector determine the range of issues to be examined in this context. The term "economic policy" is used here in a very inclusive way. It subsumes social policy, regional policy, housing policies, labor market policies, etc. It subsumes in a sense all government actions conditioning the use and development of (human and nonhuman) resources.

Implications of Constraints Characterizing the Social Opportunity Set

The notion of a social opportunity set

The range of possible states of affairs is not unlimited. Physical nature and the patterns of social interaction constrain the feasible set of states potentially realizable. This limitation has been recognized and analyzed for a long time by economic analysis under the label of a set of social possibilities or a social opportunity set. It should be noted for our subsequent discussion that the concept of the social opportunity set is not confined to standard goods and services. It can usefully include any dimension of our environment valued positively or negatively.

The social opportunities, whatever the dimensions subsumed, remain limited and the frontier imposes trade-offs with unavoidable choices or associates social costs with all actions. Policymakers can only move the economy (in the longer run) along the frontier trading off one good for another good. The opportunity set is moreover not just the reflection of a physical environment. It is crucially determined by socioeconomic and socio-political institutions. Changes in admissible forms of organizing activities or changes in the admissible range of contractual arrangements modify in general the social opportunity set. We also learned over the past fifteen years that variations in policy regime also influence this set. This means that some social costs imposed by policies appear as a contraction of the social opportunity set. This contraction occurs however relative to the expansion produced by economic growths and possible social benefits of policy. Other welfare losses occur as so-called distortions in the use of resources expressed by deviations between marginal social and private costs or deviations between marginal social costs and private relative evaluations (marginal rates of substitutions) expressing the agent's preference system.

The recognition or acknowledgment of such limitations is frequently difficult for "political entrepreneurs," policymakers or a politically committed intelligentsia. They will resent an analysis emphasizing inherent limitations and the reality of trade-offs or of social costs. The pursuit of policies which disregard inherent limitations produces unavoidably new problems not expected by the policymaker and wrongly attributed to a variety of irrelevant conditions. A further round of policies is then introduced to cope with the new problems. They will be quite ineffectual however. They do not, in general, address the crucial conditions and further problems result.

The reality of trade-offs

The general characterization needs some illustrative exemplifications. Two sets of policies based on recent experience and discussions will be adduced. The first set refers to monetary problems. Central Bank officials and politicians attempt (or profess to attempt) on occasion to pursue simultaneously a policy of exchange rate control and a monetary control policy. But this combination is not within the feasible set of possible combinations. An exchange rate policy implies that monetary growth reflects all the random shocks operating on exchange markets. "Sterilization" or "desterilization" operations may for a short period appear to reconcile the two goals. This reconciliation cannot persist over the longer-run. A monetary control policy on the other hand is consistent with interventions in exchange markets. It is however inconsistent with interventions guided by longer-run exchange rate targeting. The experiences of the past fifteen years and most particularly the experience of the Swiss National Bank confirm this point. Monetary authorities and politicians need to recognize the basic facts. They are confronted with a trade-off and they must choose between controlling exchange rates or controlling monetary growth. It is noteworthy that this issue determined Dr. Schiller's resignation as Minister of Economic Affairs from the German government in 1972. The German government chose to disregard Dr. Schiller's warning about a trade-off and was subsequently confronted with the hard facts. We note in passing that the same limitation extends to any attempt to combine a monetary control policy with a policy of controlling some real variables (say, e.g., interest rates).

This means also that the constraints imposed by reality exclude the simultaneous realization of a policy avoiding persistent inflationary or deflationary episodes and a monetary policy addressed to control some real variables.

The policy debates of the European Parliament in Strasbourg erupted on occasion with demands for a persistently expansionary monetary policy ("eine monetäre Vorwärtspolitik") substantially raising monetary growth. It seems that advocates of this policy expect with its aid to lower permanently unemployment and to revive permanently the growth or level of output. The reality of the social opportunity set precludes however this option. Its pursuit beyond a deep depression actually reflecting a contraction in aggregate nominal demand involves a serious illusion. Such a policy would under the present circumstances yield at best a very temporary effect on output and ultimately produce a pattern of rising inflation. The same impossibility obstructs the wishful dreams of many politicians who propose to lower interest rates by an accelerated monetary growth.

Other examples drawn from agricultural policy, housing policy, tenancy protection, risk regulation, etc. abound. A survey of the range addressed by policy in any country offers a rich menu of possible cases.

Labor market policies pursued in Europe over the past decades yield some particularly important examples. The goal of job security or economic security in a more general sense found increasing favor over the past twenty years in the political arena. The goal was pursued with little recognition of, or concern for, inherent limitations. Such limitations do exist, however, and we can easily appreciate that committed advocates of more (and more) economic security resent being confronted with the reality of such limitations. The limitations impose trade-offs involving economic security, employment, real wages and real fringe benefits. They also impose a trade-off between economic security and economic growth with rising standards of living. The policies addressed to job security or to economic security in general varied between countries. Their gradually expanding implementation within each country proceeded, moreover, with a variety of measures. All these measures, whatever their detail, directly or indirectly raised the real cost of employment. This implies that either employment, real wages, or real fringe benefits fall. The inherent nature of the social process thus imposes a trade-off. Its reality exists irrespective of ideological commitments or theological dreams and this reality ultimately confronts us with a choice. Employment will fall or stagnate with an insistent maintenance of real wages. Employment levels can be maintained, on the other hand, with trading off of real wages. It might appear that these unpleasant choices can be avoided with subsidies to business firms offsetting the increase in the real cost of employment. But such subsidies must be financed, either with taxes or money creation. In the first case, net real wages or net real income from investment will be lowered. And the latter effect discourages investment and lowers growth. The recourse to money creation generates inflation. The political reality of inflation determines moreover a highly erratic inflation with pervasive uncertainty lowering investment and growth. Similarly, an increasingly rigid or demanding policy of economic security impedes economic growth. It obstructs adjustments in the pattern of resource use and lowers incentives to explore new possibilities or opportunities. Most European nations moved along a course trading off employment and stagnation for economic security. But this implicit choice is not recognized in the political arena. The loss in employment imposed by the political choice is insistently attributed by the media and most politicians to the evolution of modern technologies. Any politician who dares to recognize the crucial issue is usually ridiculed and vilified in the public arena. But the professional core of economics informs us that "technology" is an opportunity for rising general welfare and not the problem asserted. It does become a problem within the institutional arrangements characterizing an ossified or petrified society.

The reality of social costs

The reality of the social opportunity set with the economy's inherent drive to settle in the neighborhood of the production frontier confronts policymaking with another important dimension. This dimension involves a significant limitation almost systematically neglected in the politics of economic policy. This neglect substantially distorts the balance of social benefits and social costs associated with policy decisions. It encourages economic policies with social benefits less than their social costs. These costs may involve a decline in welfare expressed by a relative compression of the social opportunity set whenever resources are allocated to socially nonproductive investments in the political process encouraged by distributional gains associated with the policymaking process. The costs may also reflect larger inputs ("rent seeking") in the production process required per output unit. But welfare losses also occur whenever policies distort the pattern of resource uses relative to the prevailing preference system within a given opportunity set. In either case, social costs reflect a sacrifice in some dimensions of the social process positively valued by some members of society. Social costs are not an abstract entity beyond human concerns. They ultimately represent underlying human valuations by the only source of human values, i.e. the individual persons in a society.

The regulation of pharmaceutical products initiated in the USA in the early 1960s offers a remarkable example of the consequences associated with the neglect of this particular limitation. The traumatic impact on public impressions made by the tragically crippled and deformed babies resulting from the use of thalidomide by pregnant women influenced new legislation and tougher regulatory policies. Public attention became fixed on a single goal: to lower the risk to zero of admitting new pharmaceutical products with potentially dangerous side effects. The measures implemented for this purpose substantially raised the costs of development for new products by a large factor. Other measures shortened at the same time the expected pay-off period of new drugs and thus lowered the potential return. Regulatory policies quite generally obstructed the flow of inventions and innovations. Innovation consequently declined by a wide margin and the appearance of new drugs sharply contracted. It would be difficult to dispute that new legislation and regulatory policy provided no benefits. They most probably offered some useful effects. But they also impose some heavy burdens on the members of society. They obstructed the creation and use of new and effective drugs for a wide array of health problems. Avoidable illness and death due to unavailable but potentially producible drugs increased. Illness and death unrecognized by legislators and regulators forms the social cost of a well-meant endeavor. A detailed research of this problem concluded that the social cost of the new policy vastly exceeded the social benefits it provided to the public. The single-minded obsession with the minimization of risk attached to new drugs failed to recognize the unavoidable alternative risk associated with a lower innovation of useful and health or life preserving drugs. A policy addressed to minimize the probability of bad pharma products maximized at the same time the probability of <u>not</u> having useful drugs.

The Swiss Federal Council's report on regional policy presenting arguments for a proposed legislation is quite indicative. It diligently lists the benefits and here especially the number of jobs saved or created in some regions as a result of the policy. The reader finds however no allusions to any potential social cost. Legislators are not warned that regional policy also means ossification of inherited inefficient structures. It also means that more efficient jobs in other regions are destroyed or thwarted. And it means lastly, that some nonhuman resources will be used less efficiently in a social sense. All this implies that the social opportunity set is contracted for the benefit of some "regional balance or restoration."

The same argument extends to protectionism and cartel legislation. Benefits and beneficiaries are easily recognized. But these benefits are hardly ever <u>social</u> benefits. They usually involve redistributions of income and are matched by corresponding losses elsewhere. The establishment of a privileged position by means of protectionist measures, cartel legislation and its implementation, or on the basis of other monopolizing actions requires substantial investment of resources in the political process. These investments also contract the social opportunity set. "Rent-seeking behavior" thus absorbs socially valuable resources and imposes a welfare cost on society. The <u>social</u> cost of these policies is usually overlooked in the political process whereas some <u>private</u> benefits are much touted as <u>social</u> gains.

The central proposition of this section emphasizes the comparative blindness of the political process to social costs typically associated with economic policy. Political debate centers on the private gains and losses, i.e. on redistributional aspects, and rarely considers the significant limitation expressed by relevant social costs. It is noteworthy that academia suffers under a similar blindness. The standard discussion of market failure resolves the associated welfare problem with suitable interventions by the government. These interventions are moreover supposed to involve no social costs. This is particularly remarkable as many cases of alleged "market failure" are attributable to the operation of neglected social costs also affecting governmental interventions. It follows that this analysis offers little guidance for rational policymaking.

The Problem of Information

Legislation and regulatory rules and ordinances encounter a compliance problem. There is no automatic compliance. The norms established by policymaking must be monitored and enforced. The investment in the apparatus required for this purpose imposes also a social cost on society. Compliance is however linked with another problem involving limitations on economic policy. We need to recognize that the mode of operation of both private and public sector produces a substantial uncertainty about the detailed pattern of outcomes. The nature of this problem will be explored in the following two sections.

Uncertainty in the private sector

Government interventions confront members of society with a challenge. These measures modify private opportunity sets and thus induce various responses. Many of these responses address an imaginative search to lower the impact of government intervention. This search by many smart operators eventually produces an array of devices, arrangements and procedures which more or less legally at least partly circumvent the government's intervention. The extent of these activities depends on private costs imposed by intervention and search relative to expected private gains. The very nature of these activities implies moreover that many detailed adjustments made in response to an intervention are quite unpredictable. Important longer-run consequences to complex policies remain thus essentially unknown at the time the policies are under consideration. Even the most rational legislator or policymaker fully devoted to the mythical entity called the "public interest" suffers under very incomplete information about the detailed ramification of policies. Every intervention tends to produce unintended and unexpected consequences which eventually affect the evaluation and usefulness of the intervention. This uncertainty confronts economic policy with another dimension of possible limitations which need to be considered in rational policymaking.

It may be useful to develop the argument in a more general context. The social process governed by spontaneous interaction between agents in market economies operates as a vast system continuously creating and disseminating new information. Acquisition and interpretation of these flows of new information modifies private opportunity sets and expectations of future market conditions. These revisions induce pervasive adjustments in behavior. The detailed nature of outcome patterns produced by the social process continuously changes as a result. By the very nature of the process conditioned by the dissemination of new information (i.e., essentially unanticipated), the evolving outcome patterns are unpredictable in their full detail. Economic analysis thus explains quite successfully the nature and characterization of the social process. But this understanding of the spontaneous order created by the social process also implies that no analysis can predict beyond the broad contours the detailed outcome of the uncertainty. This uncertainty confronts policymakers with a serious problem. The correlation between actions or policies and intended outcome or desired results is burdened with shadows of doubt. Some components of the total outcome may be quite predictable but many other evolving effects remain unpredictable. The full consequences of policies are thus hidden behind the veils of an uncertain future.

This theme emerges in the range of stabilization policies with particular force. A wide gulf separates the reality of stabilization policy from the official claims and academic rhetoric. The latter proceed as if we possessed detailed and reliable information about the economy's response structure. Once again this information is not available and the information problem confronts any ambitious stabilization policy with a severe and fundamental limitation. Incomplete information about the economy's detailed response structure lowers the correlation between desired or intended and actual performance level produced by "stabilization policies." The unknown detail of the response structure conditions ultimately the outcome of the best meant policy. Attempts at "stabilization" proceed under the circumstances in contrast to a general belief without any guarantee of stabilization.

The operation of the public sector

Policies emerge from a political process which contributes to a last dimension of the limitations encountered by economic policy. The inherent nature of the process conditions policymaking into patterns poorly correlated with well meant and sensible proposals measured in terms of general welfare. Politics is not dominated by consideration of public interest or vague feelings of good will. Self-interested political entrepreneurship affects the resulting pattern of legislation and executive actions. An examination of environmental or regional policy in Switzerland reveals, for instance, that proposals for efficient (i.e. welfare raising) solutions to underlying problems do not survive successfully in the political process. The outcome is usually controlled by a redistributional conflict associated with any measure to cope with the problem.

The crucial aspect to be emphasized in this context addresses the pervasive uncertainty about the detailed pattern of legislation, executive actions and court decisions unleashed by some intentions or proposals. The previous section considered the uncertainty produced by the searching and coping responses of agents to policy measures. A similar phenomenon occurs within the political process. Legislation passed influences but does not determine the outcome. The implementation of the legislation by the state's apparatus with the aid of rules, ordinances or regulatory actions frequently enjoy a wide field for the crucial detail of policies. The U.S. experience with a pattern of legislation appearing more and more in the form of general mandates offers some important examples. The independent power of implementing agencies tends to rise with the complexity of the material addressed by the legislators' intentions and the generality of the mandate legislated. Implementing agencies acquire thus some range of operative opportunities. They will exploit this range according to their own political interests and perceptions, searching and coping with their own opportunities. It follows under the circumstances that the translation of legislation into specific actions conditioning socioeconomic evolution is a highly uncertain process. This uncertainty is heightened by the fact that implementing agencies often change their interpretations and rules guiding their actions. Various sections of the same agency often proceed moreover according to different interpretations of the same rules. The result is a pervasive uncertainty built into the policymaking process. The ramifications and consequences of policy at the original plane of intention, planning, and proposals remain somewhat obscure. This is quite consistent with the fact that immediate beneficiaries suffer little doubt, and correctly so, about their <u>private</u> advantage in the matter. Not the least among the beneficiaries are the implementing agencies themselves.

ALTERNATIVE POLICY CONCEPTIONS, ONCE MORE

The Reality of the Political Process

The chapter opened with the juxtaposition of two basically different policy conceptions. An institutional policy was distinguished from an open-ended action-oriented policy. We may also characterize the alternatives as the choice of a set of general rules monitored and enforced by the government on the one side and an activist intervention over an open-ended range on the other side. The two traditions involve thus an essentially limited, or constitutionalist policy conception and an unlimited, open-ended policy. The issues associated with these two policies still need to be clarified. The discussion of the limits confronting economic policy provides the basis for my assessment. The reality of the social opportunity set imposes trade-offs and social costs associated with policy actions frequently disregarded in the political process. An analysis of this process explains some reasons for this neglect and the role of incomplete information in this context.

The Classic Policy Conception as a Cooperative Solution to a Prisoners' Dilemma Problem

The reality of the political process explains the systematic neglect of objectively existing "limitations of economic policy." The bias is inherent in any loosely limited or essentially unlimited policy process. The incentives embedded in a more or less open-ended policy process unavoidably produce a pattern with a low feedback from social costs of policy programs. The political process provides no incentives and no mechanisms for a realistic representation and assessment of the _social_ trade-offs and _social_ costs associated with economic policymaking. No incentives operate, moreover, to foster a recognition bearing on the consequences occurring over a _longer_ horizon. The immanent characteristics of the political process produce an externality problem usually overlooked in "market failure" and welfare discussions. The parties involved assess their strategies in terms of their _perceived private_ gains and costs related to the redistributional consequences of the policy game. These perceived private gains and costs are quite generally poorly correlated with the relevant social benefits and social costs. The latter involve aspects beyond the direct redistributional consequences perceived as the relevant costs and gains by agents in the social process. Social costs are thus not sufficiently "internalized" by political operators. We encounter here a sort of prisoners' dilemma problem. The activist and open-ended policy game contracts the social opportunity set and lowers general welfare. The members of society as a group are worse off as a result of their prevalent behavior. The game promises, however, to individuals and subgroups, separately substantial advantages. These advantages are acquired of course at the expense of other members of society. Our previous discussion indicates, moreover, that this game is not a zero sum game with little effect on _general_ welfare. The crucial problem goes beyond the redistribution of wealth produced by the game. The reality of social costs associated with the game reminds us that we encounter here a _negative_ sum game compressing the social opportunity set. The costs imposed by active rent seeking behavior form in this context a major portion of the relevant social burden of the game.

This analysis of the policy process provides the basis for the classic policy program. It should be understood as an attempt to break out of the prisoners' dilemma. It offers essentially a cooperative solution to this dilemma. A constitutionalist approach expressed by a set of general rules severely constraining the government's admissible range of actions would moderate the game by a large margin. But such a set of rules is not unique and its choice would have to be carefully examined. The accumulated discussion in various fields of economics indicates quite clearly the nature and thrust of rules extending the social opportunity set. The choice of rules proceeds however not beyond the political process. It would appear however that the conflict bearing on the choice of general rules is less intense and protracted than the conflict surrounding the redistributional schemes proceeding under any label (cartel legislation, agricultural policy, trade policy, housing policies, export risk guarantees, etc.) The discussion of general rules is moreover more likely to direct attention to their effect on the social opportunity set than the conflict-loaded disputes generated by specific schemes of wealth redistribution.

Objections to the Classic Program

The classic program is often characterized by academic critique as a "retreat from potential opportunities to raise welfare." Tinbergen's "Theory of Economic Policy" developed formal arguments representing this vision. The traditional argument on behalf of an activist stabilization policy may illustrate the prevalent attitude. This argument emphasizes that a pattern of discretionary interventions offers opportunities to offset a range of exogenous shocks and produce consequently a much better performance of the economy. Such a policy pattern, not confined by general rules, can sensitively adjust to all contingencies. Such adjustments are bound to raise the economy's over-all performance level. But this means that the social opportunity set is actually expanded under the circumstances.

The fallacy of this argument has been demonstrated at another occasion (Brunner 1981). It is based on two conditions which deny the two dimensions of the information problem confronting any adequate analysis of the policy problem. This problem seems rarely recognized by advocates and is implicitly discarded with the assumptions built into their analytic demonstration of the activist case. The first condition invokes full and reliable information by the policymaker about the economy's dynamic response structure. The possession of such knowledge would certainly guarantee the possibility for an effective application of activist policy sensitively adjusted to evolving contingencies. But a survey of our state of knowledge denies the existence of this condition. The detail required for the rational guidance of an activist policy is not available. It is moreover inherently impossible to ever acquire this information level. We noted before that market processes also function as mechanisms perennially producing new information to agents. This implies a persistent evolution in a random pattern of an economy's detailed response structure. It follows that this detailed response structure is not constant over time to be approximated even more closely by clever econometric estimation. The information problem destroys the case for an activist and contingent policy pattern. The execution of such policies in spite of inadequate and unreliable information contributes with substantial probability to the opposite of the desired stabilization.

The other condition of the activist case pertains to the political economy of policymaking. The activist argument implicitly assumes a public interest or goodwill theory of government. Government is supposed to pursue policies only guided by a general interest summarized by some social welfare function. But this (romantic) vision hardly describes the reality of policymaking. Politicians, policymakers, and bureaucrats interact with constituencies in a context of incomplete and non-uniform information. They are moreover motivated in the light of an essentially self-interested appraisal of their opportunities. The characterization of policymakers as optimizers of a social welfare function expressing a social consensus is thus remarkably irrelevant. The policy process actually produces, under the circumstances described above, a pattern of uncertain drift reinforcing the pervasive information problem. The reader is reminded in particular that under the incentives controlling the political process "stabilization policies" usually appear as a camouflage for redistributional activities with minor, if any, real concern for aggregate stabilization. Examples supporting this point may be observed in any country.

The Irrelevance of Academic Objections and the Actual Driving Forces of the Political Process

The complex of neo-mercantilist interests engaged in the exploitation of the political process cannot provide a full explanation of the driving forces at work in contemporary western democracies. We need more fully to recognize the role of ideology and ideological beliefs in this context. Their motivation contains a component which is separate and independent from wealth. This motivation involves basic and radical restructuring of society. The ideological beliefs express a commitment to "a new socio-economic order" requiring foremost a complete political control over the socio-economic process. The realization of the "new order" does not rely on revolutionary strategies. It is approached via an "incrementalist tactic." Active participation in the policy process is the essential instrument in this game. An unlimited economic policymaking offers thus the necessary field of operation for ideological beliefs. Any potential issue and any measure can be exploited for the purpose of an expanded political control. This "incrementalist tactic" yields moreover some important benefits. The measures adopted by the political process or executed by policy agencies under the combined influence of neo-mercantilist interests and ideological beliefs frequently create a new pattern of social conditions which can be problematized. The evolution of labor market institutions in Europe exemplifies the point. The various measures of "job security" raised the real cost of employment. Unyielding real wages impose adjustments on employment and unemployment. Thus emerges a new opportunity for further tactical exploitation. Work-sharing forms the next claim to "solve the problem." But once again it will impose a new problem. It will lower the social opportunity set and thus strengthen the incentives for politically engineered wealth redistribution. The more problems the policy process generates along a road influenced by the interaction of neo-mercantilist interests and ideological beliefs the more attractive become the opportunities for "the incrementalist tactics."

The experiences with environmental and health policies in the U.S. offer a wide range of illustrative material for this theme. Environmental and health problems assuredly deserve our careful attention. But they can be approached in very different ways. This field of concern suffers most particularly from the illusion that no deviation from some imagined ideal can be tolerated. Any consideration of social costs imposed by the realization of the absolutist goal is scorned. This implicit refusal to recognize social costs reflects either ignorance of an elitist or authoritarian attitude. The social costs associated with a given course shaping the use of resources mirror the values attached by members of society to goods and services sacrificed by using resources in this particular manner. A deliberate unwillingness to consider such costs reveals thus a refusal to recognize other people's values. This pattern is unavoidably associated with the role of ideological beliefs in the policy process. The deliberate disregard of social costs in the ideological approach to economic policy is typically supplemented by another pattern. The proposals emanating and issues raised are hardly addressed to the _substance_ of a genuine problem requiring serious attention. The proposals and issues formulated are dominated by the ideological motivation directed to an encompassing socio-political vision.

CONCLUDING REMARKS

Economic policy does not occur in a socio-political vacuum. It forms an essential component of an ongoing fundamental conflict about the future order of Western civilization. Questions bearing on the possible "limits of economic policy" thus ultimately involve decisions about alternative policy conceptions with substantially different institutional approaches. These differences imply over the longer run divergent social, economic, and political evolutions. But the implicit denial of any "limits of economic policy" expressed by one of the alternative policy conceptions does not suspend their reality. Their neglected operations will increasingly burden societies and moderate our opportunities.

REFERENCES

Brunner, Karl 1981. The control of monetary aggregates. Patrolling monetary aggregates III. Federal Reserve Bank of Boston.

Chow, Gregory C. 1975. Analysis and control of dynamic economic systems. New York: Wiley & Co.

Efron, Edith, 1985. The Apocalyptics: Cancer and the big lie. New York: Simon and Schuster.

Tinbergen, Jan. 1952. On the theory of economic policy. Amsterdam: North Holland Publishing Company.

PART TWO

SOCIALISM: PHILOSOPHICAL ISSUES

Chapter 4

IS SOCIALISM INEVITABLE?

HISTORICAL PROPHECY AND THE POSSIBILITIES OF REASON

By

Hans Albert*

THE POSSIBILITIES OF SCIENCE AND THE PROBLEM OF PROPHECY

Before the end of World War II two important books were published that considered the current tendency toward socialism: Joseph A. Schumpeter's _Capitalism, Socialism, and Democracy_ (1942) and Friedrich A. Hayek's _The Road to Serfdom_ (1944). The first tries to demonstrate the inevitability of socialism and the other denies inevitability but tries to show that socialism can be avoided only if the possibility of a development in this direction is recognized and if one is prepared to adopt political measures against it.

The conflicting views of the two authors--both coming from the Austrian school of economics, which was engaged in very early debates on Marxism--involve a problem of the philosophy of history that has epistemological aspects as well. The thesis of the inevitability of socialism

*H. Albert is professor of philosophy at the University of Mannheim.

has its origin in the thought of Karl Marx. It is the core of the historical prophecy included in his doctrine (cp. Schumpeter 1942, 1, Marx der Prophet; Popper 1944, ch. 18-21. Marx's prophecy, pp. 324-384). Karl Popper, in his analysis of historicism, criticized in principle the possibility of historical prophecy as a rational undertaking and later changed his criticism to a strict refutation.[1] This refutation is based on two simple premises, namely, the propositions that the "course of human history is strongly influenced by the growth of human knowledge," and that we "cannot predict, by rational or scientific methods, the future growth of our scientific knowledge." Presumably, it will not be necessary to know the details of Popper's argument to accept these statements and their implications that the future course of human history cannot be predicted. To a great extent, the growth of scientific knowledge consists of unexpected or accidental discoveries. Technological progress and economic and social development are dependent on these discoveries. That is sufficient to come to Popper's conclusion.

The growth of knowledge not only opens up new technological possibilities, but also leads to changes in human needs, attitudes, and norms and to consequences that cannot be predicted (cp. Lepsius 1971). But even apart from the growth of knowledge there often arise new ideas, which lead to new problems and solutions, which in turn will have an impact on the behavior of people. The unpredictability mentioned by Popper is therefore valid for all cultural and creative achievements, whether they occur in science or in other realms.

From this it follows that it is impossible to predict the course of history and that advances in science cannot remove this impossibility because science itself is an important cause of this unpredictability. As it were, the development of human culture is the continuation of biological evolution by other means. Instead of mutation we have innovation; instead of endosomatic hereditary transmission we have a kind of exosomatic evolution by tradition, that is, "by the transfer of information through non-genetic channels from one generation to the next" (cp. Medawar 1957, p. 141). Just as we cannot predict mutations in detail, even if we have all necessary information about the relevant mechanisms, we are not able to predict genuine innovations, even if we have sufficient theoretical and historical knowledge about the problem-solving behavior of the individuals and about the social mechanisms involved. The processes in question are dependent on the laws concerned and on initial and boundary conditions, and some of the conditions are society's information, needs, and values, which will change unpredictably. The claim that historical prophecy is impossible with rational means is, as Popper has emphasized, compatible not only with the existence of theoretical knowledge in the social sciences but also with the possibility of predictions of a particular kind, namely with conditional predictions that can have technological relevance.

Thus, new ideas that may lead to new problem-solutions in all social and cultural areas belong to the autonomous factors of our sociocultural development.[2] They are not predictable, but only understandable, and, in spite of this, they can be called upon to explain the processes that have been influenced by them. Institutional arrangements and the social mechanisms resulting from them may be very different with regard to new problem-solutions. They may promote their invention, their examination, and their application and diffusion or they may more or less hamper them or even suppress them. We cannot expect to use theories about social systems and mechanisms to predict the details of future developments. At best they can help us explain how such systems and mechanisms function in principle (cp. Hayek 1976a, pp. 3ff., esp. pp. 11ff; also Albert 1976b, p. 152f.), for instance, how they would incorporate innovations if these occur somewhere and how they would promote or prevent the occurrence of such innovations.[3]

If one accepts our argument against historical prophecy, one must conclude that the thesis of the inevitability of socialism is refuted and I could end my examination of the case. But Joseph Schumpeter has formulated this thesis with greater caution than Karl Marx. He has made the attempt to transform it into a scientific proposition. He tells us explicitly that no economic or other analysis could ever contain more than the identification of the <u>tendencies</u> inherent in an object of observation and that these tendencies tell us not what <u>will</u> happen to the object but what <u>would</u> happen if they continued to work as they did in the period of our observation if no other factors intervene. In his opinion, "inevitability" and "necessity" could never mean more than that (cp. Schumpeter 1942, p. 105).

However, there exist still more qualifications in his argument. He points to the fact that the social process is a function of so many variables that not only the prognosis but even the bare diagnosis of a given state of affairs is an ambiguous undertaking. Nevertheless, in his opinion, one is justified to say that the dominant features of the picture he has drawn support some interesting conclusions. And the most important of these conclusions is that the statement that it is precisely the accomplishments of capitalism--not its failures--that lead to socialism. He claims that the success of the capitalist system alone undermines the social arrangements that protect this system and is "inevitably" leading to conditions under which it cannot survive and which point emphatically to socialism as its legitimate heir (cp. Schumpeter 1942, p. 106).

It is extraordinarily difficult to gain from these remarks a clear picture of the methodological views in the background of Schumpeter's analysis. Obviously, by formulating the reservations I have mentioned above, he wants to protect himself against the accusation of indulging in historical prophecy; he seems to concede here that historical trends depend on conditions which are apt to change. That fact has been used by Popper to show that there is no theoretical basis for predictions of this kind.[4] On the other hand he perhaps wants to deter possible critics who, for the reasons he himself has formulated, might deem long-term projections of this kind pointless. As it were, he wants to demand the advantages of prophecy without bearing its costs. At the same time, he uses within his analysis so much historical and theoretical knowledge that the reader gains the impression that his prediction has been supported by it. But that is of course an illusion. This prediction is by no means better supported than Karl Marx's, which Schumpeter himself has characterized as a historical prophecy claiming to express "the logic of the dialectical process of history (Schumpeter 1942, p. 22). In the writings of Marx as well, we find some interesting theoretical and historical analyses and attempts to explain social phenomena, which must be taken seriously. But they are embedded in a philosophical framework that goes back to the eschatological conception of Judeo-Christian thinking (cp. Löwith 1953;

Topitsch 1968a, 1968b) and meets with the same criticism this conception does.[5]

In my view it is very interesting that Schumpeter displays as a genuine accomplishment a feature of the Marxian conception that seems to support his own prognostications. It is the fundamental idea connected with this analysis, namely, the idea of a theory that is not only a set of models that are unrelated to each other or to a logic of economic quantities in general, but which contains the factual succession of these models or of the economic process as it is developing in historical time, where every state is produced endogenously by the preceding state (Schumpeter 1942, p. 78). A theory of this kind being permitted to determine the course of history is obviously regarded by Schumpeter as the ideal aim of economic theorizing. As I have shown before, this ideal has been refuted by Popper's criticism of historicist thinking, just as the idea of historical prophecy is legitimized by such a theory. In this respect Schumpeter appears to have given too much epistemological credit to Marx.

Thus, the thesis of the inevitability of socialism seems to be refuted, even in its more cautiously formulated version. At best one can identify _tendencies_ toward socialism and state, with the help of appropriate theories, these being conditions in which such tendencies are to be expected. Mises already had hinted at such tendencies in the 1920s.[6] In this respect there is also agreement between Hayek and Schumpeter. However, Schumpeter, like Marx, believes that the development of capitalism inevitably produces conditions sufficient to destroy the capitalist system and to lead to the establishment of a socialist society, so that the intentions of the individuals involved in this historical process could not change its direction. Mises and Hayek, on the other hand, see the possibility of countermeasures, by first elucidating for these individuals the relevant facts and causal relationships and by appealing to self-interest. Mises and Hayek believe that the ideas and interests of the individuals concerned belong to the essential conditions of social development and that the current tendencies toward socialism are therefore determined to a considerable degree by prevailing ideas and interests, with ideas being used for the interpretation of the actual problem-situation. Whereas Schumpeter's analysis would appropriately cause resignation with regard to politics, the views of Mises and Hayek contain clues for political action. In my view, a rational politics will not capitulate in the face of a thesis of inevitability which can be defended only on the basis of an untenable philosophy of history, but it will take warnings seriously and attempt to influence the historical development so that the dangers announced can be avoided. We will return to this problem in the last section of this chapter.

THE THESIS OF THE IMPOSSIBILITY OF SOCIALISM

The strongest contrast to the thesis of the inevitability of socialism is contained in the thesis of the impossibility of socialism, which is connected with the name of Ludwig von Mises. With respect to the central point of his argument Mises has made the following statement: "To prove that economic calculation would be impossible in the socialist community is to prove also that Socialism is impracticable" (Mises 1981, p. 117). And the section of his book about the impracticability of socialism (Mises 1981, pp. 186-94) ends with the statement: "Capitalism is the only conceivable form of social economy. . . ."[7] If this is the case, the thesis of the inevitability of socialism is untenable on theoretical grounds, apart from the methodological reasons mentioned above. It is untenable then not only because it is impossible to predict historical developments of this kind, but because a social system of this kind could not exist at all. Thus, all attempts to bring about a socialist society are doomed to failure. At best they might lead to chaos.[8] Of course, this would be a good reason to warn against all such endeavors and to recommend a policy to counteract them.

To assess the validity of Mises' thesis, we must first concede that it is often possible to exclude on theoretical grounds, that is, on the basis of appropriate nomological hypotheses, the factual possibility of certain (logically possible) events, states, or developments.[9] Natural laws leave, as it were, a range of possibilities of factual occurrences such that all events outside this range are excluded. Thus, whoever commands an appropriate nomological knowledge can deduce some theses of impossibility, which may also be interesting according to technological viewpoints and, as far as social science is concerned, for politics, for "it is one of the most characteristic tasks of technology to point out what cannot be achieved" (Popper 1957, p. 61) and a very important task of political thinking to destroy the illusions fondled by utopian social philosophers. Obviously, the question that immediately emerges here is whether we really have, perhaps in theoretical economics, the nomological knowledge to deduce the thesis of the impossibility of socialist systems. The nomological statements in question then would be falsified by one counterexample, that is, by identifying an existing, true socialist system.[10]

Of course, one can point out that socialist systems exist today, so that the impossibility thesis seems to be refuted by statements of fact. But the case is not quite so simple, for some of these facts were well known to Mises, who considered them fully. If one looks at his arguments more closely, one finds that he has attached to his thesis some qualifications that do justice to these facts. He has by no means denied that a socialist system could exist as long as it has a connection to a capitalist environment from which it could take clues for its calculations.[11] And today that of course is always the case. In fact, Mises has denied only the possibility of a closed socialist system, and such a system, as far as I can see, does not exist anywhere today.

How can we characterize such a system? "Under socialism all the means of production are the property of the community. The community alone disposes of them and decides how to use them in production. The community produces, the products accrue to the community, and the community decides how those products are to be used" (Mises [1922] 1981, p. 110). In such a community, he points out, "the unitary expression of the common will, which is the essential object of the socialization of the means of production, necessarily implies that all offices entrusted with the supervision of different affairs shall be subordinate to one office. This office must have supreme authority to resolve all variations from the common purpose and unify the executive aim" (Mises [1922] 1981, p. 112). Thus, the socialization of the means of production is connected to the central direction of production and distribution. That means that the community in question is a society without any market, which can be seen as one large organization. However, "where there is no market there is no price system, and where there is no price system there can be no economic calculation" (Mises [1922] 1981, p. 113). And without calculation, as Mises tries to show in his analysis, such a community cannot exist. That is the core of his argument.

How can we assess this argument today? To begin with, it refers to a limiting case: to a pure, centrally planned economy, that is, <u>pure socialism</u>.[12] To refute the thesis of impossibility of pure socialism one could try to show that a price system without markets, or calculation without a price system, or a planned economy without calculation may be possible. Attempts at the first two have been undertaken; the question of their success I would like to leave unanswered here. That a planned economy can exist without <u>any</u> calculation nobody has seriously asserted, as far as I can see. Of course, there may arise the question of the extent to which economists are inclined to connect conceptually the facts under consideration in such a way that the three components of Mises' thesis appear to be acceptable by definition. To the extent that this is true, the thesis would lose its substance, so that finally a planned economy in which calculation is based on shadow prices is not acceptable as a counterexample. Such an immunization of the thesis would, of course, render it completely uninteresting with respect to the problem concerned. I shall assume, therefore, that it has substance. This means that the negations of some of the components at least involve logical possibilities, which are factually excluded on the basis of corresponding nomological statements.

The problem of economic calculation in a planned economy has been neglected by socialists for a long time, and the most important contributions to its solution have been furnished by critics of socialism. In analyzing this problem most of the theoreticians, the advocates of socialism included, have assumed that the relevant values for this calculation must correspond to those values which would arise in a market system under ideal conditions. It has been assumed that a planned economy, at least to a certain extent (above all, with respect to the determination of an adequate production on the basis of the needs accepted), must simulate the results of an ideal market economy, apart from the fact that the objectives, and therefore the final demand, may be partly different.[13] These values (prices) would have to be determined without recourse to markets. Perhaps an institutional analogy to the market system would have to be established so that an adequate price system and an appropriate calculation would be available.

Thus, a planned economy and a market economy were compared as methods for attaining social objectives such as the satisfaction of human needs and a just distribution of income and wealth, in other words, a comparison between alternative institutional arrangements and their effect on the situations of individuals. Therefore, to characterize the central question involved as a problem of calculation is not sufficient and, indeed, a bit misleading.

The argument of Mises refers, as I have mentioned above, to a pure planned economy, which, following Hayek, can be seen as "the limiting case of a long series of systems which are centralized in a lesser degree" (cp. Hayek 1952b, p. 173). By introducing elements of a market, to create freedom of choice in consumption and employment, for instance, forms of impure planned economies can be constructed with a decreasing degree of central regulation up to a pure market economy, where there is no regulation whatsoever. Here we come to the other limiting case, that of a pure market society, such as is defined and defended as ideal by the advocates of radical capitalism (Rothbard 1973; Friedman 1973). It would be a system without a central coercive apparatus, that is, without even the minimal state of liberalism. But this case will, presumably, just as the other limiting case of pure socialism, never occur in fact because the system of laws which is necessary for markets to function in a complex society could not be maintained without at least a minimal state. We are therefore entitled to contrast Mises' thesis of the impossibility of pure socialism with the thesis of the impossibility of pure capitalism (formulated and defended by Alchian and Nozick[14]), and we can even do that by arguing that without a system of law enforced by the state, there could be no economic calculation because under these circumstances, no markets and therefore no market prices would arise. If one accepts Alchian's statement that "Government is socialism, by definition,"[15] then one must conclude that a minimal socialism will be indispensable. That statement is, of course, compatible with and even included in Mises' conception, for the capitalism he defends is not the pure capitalism of our market anarchists.

This shows, at least, where the argument on limiting cases can lead us. Such cases may be constructed logically, but they cannot be expected to occur factually. It may be useful to think about them, to mentally experiment with them, and to refute their factual possibility on the basis of our nomological knowledge--also useful to criticize utopian thinking for political reasons. But the discussion must pass over to the "impure" cases. With respect to them, it will usually be more difficult to defend "strong" theses, as we have done up to now, because the existence of such cases can be supported mostly by historical evidence, so that their possibility is indisputable. The most interesting question, also in political terms, will then be whether social systems of a certain kind are more or less successful with respect to certain hypothetical objectives or criteria (see notes 7 and 8). If different objectives are assumed or the criteria concerned are weighted differently, the results of the analysis will be more or less different.[16]

With respect to the "impure" cases that are interesting in themselves, it may be useful to make some historical commentary. Schumpeter has drawn our attention to the fact that matters which today are seen exclusively as objects of public administration were in feudal societies administrated by a kind of system in which these functions seem to have been made objects of private property and sources of private profit (cp. Schumpeter 1942, p. 320f.). Later on these administrative functions were "socialized," that is, placed under the command of a central authority that gradually developed and became "the state" in our modern sense of the word. Even in the sixteenth and seventeenth centuries the conduct of wars was one of the most lucrative industries in Europe, one of the few that were run on a larger scale under the profit principle, with the profits sometimes used as a basis for banking transactions (cp. Caspary 1932, pp. 45ff.; also Weber 1924b, p. 500f.). The military entrepreneurs, Wallenstein, for instance, invested their capital in armies and made contracts with princes for military services. Even in the eighteenth century the colonels were entrepreneurs who had to hire soldiers and make their own profit by offering their military services. This "industry" was gradually "socialized" at the end of the eighteenth century. As Max Weber has stated, in this time the conduct of war as private business was seen as quite normal, in contrast to our modern view of the matter. On the other hand, the provision of cereals in the towns of the Middle Ages, as in ancient Rome, was usually a task of the public administration. As Weber has shown, the question of which goods were to be supplied by private markets and which goods by the public administration has been answered in various ways throughout the course of history.

If we consider modern times, we notice that the systems of the socialist nations of the world too are interspersed to varying degrees with market elements. The abolition of the market system, which for Marx was one of the essential features of socialism (Craig and Stephenson 1973, p. 24), has never been wholly accomplished, not even in the Soviet Union (cp. Roberts 1971). That means that not even the Soviet system has attained the properties of a pure planned economy. The attempts to achieve this aim have broken down in the time of the so-called "war communism" (cp. Roberts 1971, pp. 70ff.). The steering of such a complex social system by central planning has proved to be a utopian undertaking. The real function of the planning bureaucracy has been described as "to act as supply agents for enterprises in order to avoid free price formation and exchange on the market," as it appears to be necessary on ideological grounds to avoid the appearance of "commodity production." This leads to obvious nuisances on the supply side, however (Roberts 1971, p. 80f.). This bureaucracy seems to be occupied primarily with overcoming difficulties caused by its own existence. There is a plan, but no steering based on this plan in the usual sense, so that one can characterize this system as an _administrative_ economy, the operation of which is veiled by an _ideology of planning_.[17] The operation of this kind of system is, as is well known, facilitated by the official toleration of free markets, in the agrarian sector, for example, and by the fact that there is a shadow economy the extent of which can barely be estimated.[18] Apparently, the lacunae of the system are used by "entrepreneurs" to establish market relationships that are officially forbidden, but more or less tolerated to some extent (Nove 1980, p. 78). Where the control by the official authorities is loose enough, markets arise spontaneously and are better able than the official regulated markets to serve the needs of the consumers.

If we take these facts seriously, we cannot be concede that the problems raised by Ludwig von Mises are important not only for pure socialism but also for the attempts to attain pure socialism, which will fail because they have a utopian aim and will stall in an administrative economy with inefficient central planning. Obviously, Mises has also hit a sore point of systems remote from the limiting case of pure socialism. The problem then is not that of the impossibility of pure socialism but of the operation of systems in which a central authority attempts to steer the economy in accordance with a comprehensive plan. The question is: to what extent do such attempts lead to counterproductive effects with respect to certain supposedly relevant criteria? In other words, the question to be analyzed is that of the comparative efficiency, in a broad sense of the word, of systems with dominant socialist features.

THE PROBLEM OF EFFICIENCY IN THE DEBATE ON THE SOCIAL ORDER

How can we assess the comparative efficiency of social (or economic) systems? It is difficult to avoid an analysis of the problem-situation with respect to this question, which presupposes some special ideas connected with "the economic viewpoint." From the outset the economic critics of socialism have put the problem of calculation at the center of their analysis. Thus, they have created the impression that the central problem of socialism--and of the economic order in general--is a problem of calculation. If this problem could be solved, the possibility of a rational socialism could be shown and, assuming certain criteria, also its preferability, "rationality" meaning nothing more than "efficiency" in the usual sense. With that we would have a specific economic point of view as opposed to an ethical point of view. Whereas production, and therefore the allocation of the means of production, would have to be evaluated according to a standard implied by this point of view, for the evaluation of distribution the ethical viewpoint of justice could be decisive.

The background of this view is the idea, deeply rooted in economic thought, that the aim of production is the attainment of a maximum of goods, which serves to meet the needs and wants of the members of society. To this claim is usually connected the idea that production, as a means to achieve this satisfaction, can only be evaluated instrumentally with respect to consumption. It seems to follow that there is a possibility of evaluating the results and arrangements of a social realm--the sphere of production which is, almost by definition, ethically neutral and is based exclusively on economic thinking. On the basis of an objective which is self-evident (because it is inherent in the meaning of economic activity, or, if we follow Mises, of human action in general) it appears to be possible to assess the processes and the institutional arrangements of the sphere of production by a purely instrumental evaluation, according to a standard of efficiency, a view that at first glance is quite plausible.

This manner of perceiving the problem-situation was severely criticized in the thirties by Gunnar Myrdal.[19] Later on he analyzed and criticized to a greater depth the kind of thinking involved.[20] At the same time we find a criticism by Lionel Robbins of Pigovian welfare economics, which had operated with economic aggregates on the basis of the untenable idea of interpersonal utility comparisons (cp. Robbins [1932] 1935), an analysis which partly yields the same conclusions as Myrdal's analysis. There then came into fashion the new welfare economics of Paretian origin, which tried to take into account the objections of Robbins and to restrict the evaluation of a market system to the thesis of the Pareto-optimality of perfectly competitive equilibria. Finally, there have been attempts to overcome this restriction by constructing social welfare--functions allowing the evaluation of social states by recourse to individual preferences.

This is not the appropriate milieu for a detailed review of these developments (cp. Albert 1978, ch. 5). In any case, the mode of thinking that is the basis of such attempts is faced with a simple but fundamental objection, namely, that the construction of a uniform scale of values for a society with different needs, aims, and values and with conflicting interests is a meaningless enterprise. The "communistic fiction" connected with this idea[21] is, incidentally, incompatible with the individualistic presuppositions of the economic tradition. If we stick to these presuppositions, we have to give up this fiction and with it the whole manner of thinking which is incorporated in the tradition of welfare economics.[22]

If this is accepted, then there is no basis for either a purely economic evaluation of social aggregates and social states of any kind or for an efficiency argument of the kind usually applied in the context of the problem of economic calculation.[23] The common point of reference of the debate on this problem is the idea of the optimality of the state of equilibrium under conditions of perfect competition, that is, the idea of ideal production in this state. The calculation is adequate because and insofar as the economic process is steered by it in the direction of this state. Even Schumpeter, one of the most forceful critics of the idea of perfect competition, has founded his argument for the possibility of socialism on the "fundamental logic of economic behavior" (cp. Schumpeter 1942, p. 276f. and passim), as expressed in Barone's solution of the problem. Thus, he has in fact referred back to this idealization of neoclassical thinking to give a positive answer to the question against Mises.

It seems clear that the model characterized by this idealization gives a picture of market processes in which decisive features of this kind of social mechanism, for instance, the function of the entrepreneur, have completely vanished. The market is operating here like a computer, selecting from given alternatives one which is optimal for allocative efficiency. The fact that imagination is indispensable for detecting or developing possible alternatives, that a certain kind of motivation (e.g., an achievement motive) may be necessary to take the risks involved,[24] and that certain institutional arrangements, offering incentives to perform certain actions, belong to the social framework of market processes--all these facts are neglected in this model. That means that the causal connections relevant for the functioning of the market processes are completely removed from the analysis. In fact, a logic of decision is projected into social reality in such a way that the creative aspects of these processes--of the human problem-solving behavior involved--have vanished.[25]

But it is obviously possible that market processes which never attain the state of general equilibrium may produce social states that are not allocatively efficient but nevertheless are preferable to equilibrium states attainable under other conditions, because in the former case there are alternatives developed by innovation which are not available in the second case. That means that the absence of allocative efficiency may be <u>compensated</u> for by the use of productive imagination, by the emergence of new productive combinations in Schumpeter's sense. If that is the case, the question whether allocative efficiency is more attainable in socialism or in capitalism may be a secondary one.[26]

If we take into account the facts mentioned above, the usual idea of consumer sovereignty can be shown to involve an overstatement. Propositions such as the following cannot be taken at their face value if they are to describe the reality of competitive markets: "The producer only directs production towards the goal set by the consumers," or "The entrepreneurs . . . conduct production according to the direction set by the consumers" (Mises [1922] 1981, pp. 30, 31). They implicitly deny the existence of genuine entrepreneurs making autonomous decisions without which economic development would not be possible. The power of the consumers in a market society does not consist in giving orders for the solution of problems in the sphere of production, but in testing the solutions adopted by the entrepreneurs and in influencing the future activities in the sphere of production indirectly by accepting or refuting these solutions. Of course, Mises had enough knowledge of the facts to see the difference, but he was in favor of strong formulations in spite of their unacceptable implications.[27]

In my view it is a bit paradoxical that the attempts to show the impossibility of economic calculation in a socialist community by recourse to the "fundamental logic of economic action" regularly lead theoreticians engaged in this undertaking to consequences which will demonstrate conversely that a market economy is operating under ideal conditions as if it would follow a common plan, a plan aimed at the welfare of all its participants, which is fulfilled by competition. This manner of reasoning is liable to suggest to the defenders of the opposite thesis the idea that it must be possible to effect this kind of planning directly without making a *detour* by the market, in other words, to substitute the communist fiction of economic thinking by a corresponding communist reality.

THE SIGNIFICANCE OF FREEDOM FOR THE SOCIAL ORDER

Concentrating on the problem of allocative efficiency has led to a discussion which has neglected other possible values, above all, the various kinds of liberty. But whoever examines the development of socialism in all parts of the world since the Russian revolution will probably consider the most striking property of such systems to be their despotic character. They are all more or less totalitarian societies.[28] Can this feature of socialist systems be accounted for by doing an economic analysis?

First of all, liberty, or a particular kind of liberty, could be classified as a good, and insofar as it is appreciated directly, as a consumer good. It would be difficult, however, to treat this kind of good analytically as you would other goods since it is an aspect of the social system, the sphere of production included (although it is of course possible to analyze the problem of to what extent individuals are prepared to sacrifice other goods to increase their liberty in a particular dimension of the social system).[29] As Robbins has pointed out, the classicists have already seen consumption as the only aim of production, but they have conceded that "the satisfactions associated with particular types of production, the pleasures of workmanship, the enjoyment of certain ways of life, were to be counted, as it were, as pleasures of consumption, and if a man preferred them to the increased consumption of other things which he could obtain by working elsewhere, there was no presumption whatever that this was in any way undesirable" (Robbins 1961, p. 7f.). And, surely, the classicists have particularly emphasized the value of freedom, characteristic of the social system they preferred (cp. Robbins 1961, p. 11), and in their analysis they have brought this freedom into connection with the performance of the market system with respect to the aims of its participants, with the incentive and the steering function of the market mechanism. But, as Robbins is eager to point out, "the claims of the Classical Economists for competition and the market do not rest upon any very precise mathematical or semi-mathematical conceptions of static equilibrium."[30]

In any case, freedom as an aspect of the social system cannot be incorporated into a kind of analysis in which this system is only evaluated with respect to its allocative efficiency. Of course, this does not mean that freedom of any kind can be attained without costs, but only that these costs cannot be introduced into the usual calculation for allocative efficiency without difficulties. In this respect there is a similar problem for other goods of this kind, such as security, peace, and justice, which belong to the social capital contained in institutional arrangements that are connected with the social order (cp. Buchanan 1975, ch. 7).

Thus, even if it could be shown that it is possible to establish a pure socialist system with an adequate calculation and corresponding regulation of production, a system in which allocative efficiency in the usual sense is attained, there were good reasons to criticize this system if it had despotic features, as is probable, even if it were a case of benevolent despotism--a despotically organized welfare state. From the liberal point of view such a system had to be repudiated, even if most or all of its members were adapted to it to such an extent that they would not be ready to question it.[31]

As is well known, Marxism has adopted an anarchistic variant of the idea of freedom, taking the "withering away of the state" as a necessary condition of the communist society of the future. At the same time, it has strictly repudiated recourse to the market mechanism to solve economic problems and has operated on the concept of planning, which in fact must lead to the establishment of an omnipotent state.[32] In fact, everywhere where advocates of Marxist views have tried to realize their conceptions, the socialist components have dominated. Socialism/anarchy has turned out to be paradoxical; socialism/despotism is realizable, almost unavoidable even. The authoritarian form of control which is usual in these systems is not even compatible with the accomplishments of the bourgeois age.

The idea of a planned economy dominant in socialism is a genuine child of classical rationalism--of constructivism, in Hayek's terminology--which has tended toward technocratic solutions of political problems.[33] It can be made plausible in the following way: By scientific research we are able to know the laws of nature and of society so that they can be used to steer social processes. To warrant an adequate use of this knowledge we need a scientific-technological elite. For this elite the steering of social life is reducible to the solution of problems of efficiency, for it is only a question of the adequate use of the available means. So the central problem seems to be a problem of calculation.

This view fails to recognize that efficiency problems can be formulated only with respect to aims and that the selection of aims, just as the evaluation of the means available, presupposes values which are not derivable from scientific knowledge, except when one relies on a utilitarian answer. If such an answer is accepted, the "commonweal" or the "general welfare" becomes decisive for all evaluations. Then we can think of a technocratic solution to the problem, one amounting to a benevolent dictatorship of the scientific elite, which, however, also has to be an elite in the moral sense. Socialism then would boil down to a modern version of the Platonic ideal state.[34]

Today we have some reasons for judging this solution to be utopian. First, there is no reliable means for recruiting the elite required. Secondly, even if this problem could be solved, there would be no way of identifying the "commonweal" or the "welfare" of the community.[35] But there is a further difficulty caused by the nature of our knowledge. Do we have at our disposal a kind of knowledge that permits us to treat society as a machine that can be steered to fulfill the aims identified by a minority? And would the functioning of such a machine be any more capable of satisfying the basic needs of the members of society?

With this question we come back to a problem already touched upon in our analysis of the inevitability thesis. To begin with, there is always only imperfect knowledge at our disposal, "conjectural knowledge," as Popper has characterized it. Further, the consequences of our knowledge can never be overlooked completely. And new problems and new solutions unexpectedly arise all the time. This renders the technocratic solution utopian, because the information problems involved cannot be solved. We must assume that the elite are as fallible as all other people with respect to scientific, political, and moral problems. The technocratic ideal seems to be counterproductive with respect to most problems in a community, and this fact is strongly related to the lack of freedom in such a society.

The more society is removed from the ideal type of machinery steered by a minority of power holders, the more it is appropriate to use the knowledge and the abilities of all its members and also to further the production and the diffusion of new ideas and problem-solutions in all spheres of culture, as long as it has an order warranting to a sufficient extent its own stability and the security of its members. But in an order of freedom opposed to this ideal type, one must put up with the fact that correct prognoses with respect to details of the social process may not be available. This order must have properties such that its functioning does not depend on these predictions.

It should be clear, moreover, that the members of a society with such an order can never make the conditions of their lives equal to any desired degree. Thus, the existing inequalities may lead, on the basis of social comparison processes, to relative deprivation of individuals and groups (cp. Festinger 1954, pp. 117ff.; Merton and Rossi 1957a; Runciman 1961, pp. 315ff.; cp. also Duesenberry 1949 and Albert 1965), and to attempts to overcome this deprivation by individual or collective actions. That may be an incentive to seek and to find new problem-solutions, that is, an incentive to creativity, but also, on the other hand, an incentive to break through the limits set by the law, that is, an incentive to criminality,[36] and finally an incentive to organize political movements aimed at the reduction or elimination of certain inequalities. Movements of this sort will always be able to operate with the idea of justice, for the element of equality contained in this idea can be interpreted in different ways.[37] The determination of the relevant dimensions to which the demand for equal treatment can refer is a question of interpretation, to which political entrepreneurs may give different answers with different consequences for society. Thus, it should be clear that an order of freedom is not without costs and that the readiness to support it cannot be taken for granted. It may depend on fulfilling other requirements that make this order attractive in the eyes of the members of society.[38]

THE TENDENCY TOWARD SOCIALISM AND THE POSSIBILITIES OF LIBERAL POLITICS

I now come back to the initial point of this chapter, to the future of our social order. The question is no longer one of speculating about the historical inevitability of a certain development, but of analyzing the possibilities of a kind of politics that will preserve and increase freedom in our society. To show that a social order fulfilling certain requirements, for instance, an open society with an extensive market economy and with a democratic organization of the state, is possible in principle may be interesting. But it is quite another task to show, in a particular historical situation, possibilities of bringing about or maintaining such an order. For political considerations there is always an "institutional a priori" that must be taken into account, or, as Buchanan has pointed out: "Any proposal for change involves the status quo as the necessary starting point" (cp. Buchanan 1975, p. 78). And, obviously, for a policy aimed at conservation to be successful, an analysis of the status quo is required.

Ludwig von Mises has emphasized how important enlightenment, that is, the elucidation of the fact, is for a liberal policy and that a liberal order is useful not only for a particular class, for entrepreneurs or for capitalists, but also for all members of society, so that one need not appeal to the special interests of a particular class to motivate endeavors to maintain such an order (Mises [1922] 1981, p. 418). And, in his view, enlightenment involves the unmasking of Marxism as "a doctrine of salvation which rationalizes their [the workers'] resentment and transfigures their envy and desire for revenge into a mission ordained by world history" (Mises [1922] 1981, p. 417). But in his reliance on enlightenment he has, in my view, too much taken as self-evident the harmony of interests in society and has underrated possible conflicts of interest between its members. He has presupposed that the enlightened interests of the workers--those interests they would have, if they had sufficient insight into the relevant causal relationships--would induce them to desist from socialist demands.

Now Marxism has indeed contributed a great deal to the underestimation of the factual and even more the possible accomplishments of capitalism with respect to the situation of the workers. On the other hand, the programs and propaganda of political entrepreneurs inspired by Marxism have been able to refer to features of capitalism--to characteristics of the life situations of its workers--which have been plausible motives for relative deprivation (e.g., the want of security in case of illness, invalidism, unemployment, and old age), which has been gradually alleviated or eliminated in Germany since the time of Bismarck by a corresponding legislation, that is, the nature of work and the authoritarian rules governing people in many enterprises.[39]

Of course, one can have different opinions about the question of whether the solutions found for these problems till now are adequate or if they have been counterproductive in some way. But that the situation of the workers had led to problems that had to be solved can hardly be denied. In our treatment of problems of the social order we must make allowances for the factual circumstances and, therefore, also for the fact that in general "freedom . . . is only a secondary need in relation to the primary need for security" (cp. de Jouvenel 1972, p. 404 and passim, esp. pp. 402, 424ff.). This fact has been neglected by Mises, in contrast to Hayek, in his assessment of the situation of workers and his evaluation of socialism. Whoever wants to let an order of freedom appear _attractive_ to the members of society, therefore, has cause to take into account the need for security, especially among people who, because of their social situation, appreciate the advantages of freedom less than the disadvantages of the insecurity connected with it.[40] Anyone who wants to counteract today's tendencies toward socialism cannot be content with enlightenment. Rather, he must consider the real roots--the "material basis"--of these tendencies in the life situations of the people.

Thus, politics, in its attempts to get support for particular measures, must take into account the ideas and the interests of the individuals in concrete situations. That means it must refer to the problem-situation as it is _and_ as it is seen by the people involved. Only the perception of the situation can be influenced by enlightenment; beyond that political measures are necessary, and that means gradual reforms following a program of legislation with corresponding objectives.

Anyone who wants to change the existing order to push it in the direction of an order of freedom must bear in mind that there are often alternative solutions for political problems which differ significantly with respect to freedom.[41] One kind of attempted solution--the liberal one--aims at the extension of the individual autonomy of the people concerned. It is designed to enable them to help themselves. The other kind aims at assistance by the state and, as a consequence, leads to increased dependence on the state.[42] Because of the existing constellation of power and interests, one must, perhaps, sometimes practice both kinds of problem-solutions. But in certain circumstances one is at least able to give precedence to encouraging independence. The point is to increase the chances of autonomy and of freedom and to decrease the chances of getting advantages by redistributive measures, so that it will become attractive for people to improve their life situation by autonomous activities.[43]

Incentives to independent activities would have to be produced by corresponding institutional arrangements, by legislation that would not increase the power of functionaries or promote the bureaucratization of society, but increase instead the range of possibilities open to individuals. Every move in that direction is appropriate as a means of enlarging the social basis for a further liberalization of this kind because the number of individuals who learn to appreciate the advantages of independence is increasing. Thus, it becomes possible to mobilize to a greater extent interests in favor of a liberal policy. That means that any political measure and any law must also be judged with respect to the question of how it shall affect the balance of freedom in a society. In other words, apart from considering the question of how far the measure or the law contributes to the solution of the concrete problem that has motivated it, in every case the consequences of the policy concerned for the freedom of the members of society must be taken into account.

In spite of this, perhaps certain redistributive measures must be taken, for instance, by a corresponding revision of the system of taxation, because extreme differences in income and wealth can endanger the stability of the social order and therefore do not appear to be politically bearable. It seems hopeless to me to exclude the possibility of redistributive measures by an argument based on the doctrine of natural law, as Nozick has tried to do. That rights of any kind exist "as such," independent of any social constellation, is a metaphysical assumption that is no longer acceptable.[44] But it seems reasonable to admit redistributive measures only insofar as they have no counterproductive effects, above all with respect to the structure of incentives.[45] It cannot be in the interest of liberal politics to endanger the stability of an order of freedom by entirely excluding redistribution.

Thus, whoever wants to counteract the tendencies toward socialism in our time must take into account the interests of those who could be mobilized for the support of corresponding policy measures and legislation suitable for this purpose. He must attempt to let the order of freedom aimed at them appear as attractive as possible by offering acceptable problem-solutions. To do that successfully, an analysis of the political problem-situation is necessary--an examination of the constellation of interests and of possible problem-solutions, which is based on historical and theoretical knowledge. For this, a sociotechnological use of our knowledge is required, rather than misuse of it to support historical prophecy.

NOTES

1. Cp. Popper 1944-45 and Popper 1957. His first attempt at a strict refutation of historicism and of the possibility of historical prophecy is to be found in Popper 1950-51. An improved version is contained in Popper 1982, cp. esp. p. 20. Historical Prediction and the Growth of Knowledge, pp. 62ff. In an abbreviated form the argument is included in the preface to Popper 1957, p. Vff.; cp. as well Popper 1944, p. 63.

2. Cp. note 6 for Mises' view on the role of ideas.

3. Cp. Schumpeter (1911) 1926, where the attempt is made to take the occurrence of innovations as the basis for the explanation of economic development.

4. Cp. Popper 1957, p. 115f., about the differences between laws and trends: "But trends are not laws. A statement asserting the existence of a trend is existential, not universal. . . . And a statement asserting the existence of a trend at a certain time and place would be a singular historical statement, not a universal law. The practical significance of this logical situation is considerable: while we may base

scientific predictions on laws, we cannot (as every cautious statistician knows) base them merely on the existence of trends," and later, p. 116, n. 1: "A law, however, may assert that under certain circumstances (initial conditions) certain trends will be found."

5. Cp. as well Mises 1981, pp. 249ff., where the author points to the chiliastic sources of Marxism, and where he is making a sharp contrast between this kind of philosophy of history and scientific thinking. In this book we find also a reference to the eschatological interpretation of the Christian message (pp. 373ff.) and to the questionable character of every interpretation which wants to draw positive conclusions with respect to a social order of any kind and tries to legitimate the attempts of the churches to adapt themselves to it. All attempts of this kind belong to the realm of ideological thinking.

6. Cp. Mises 1981, p. V. Destructionism, pp. 413ff., where he tries to show that not only the socialist parties but also all other "present day parties are saturated with the leading socialist ideas" and that even "the stoutest opponents of Socialism fall within its shadow." This is in Mises' view a decisive condition for the tendency toward socialism. For, as he states in his epilogue: "The history of mankind is the history of ideas. For it is ideas, theories and doctrines that guide human action, determine the ultimate ends men aim at, and the choice of means employed for the attainment of these ends" (1981, p. 518). And, as he says at the end of his analysis of "destructionism": "The world inclines to Socialism because the great majority of people want it. They want it because they believe that Socialism will guarantee a higher standard of welfare. The loss of this conviction would signify the end of Socialism."

7. Cp. Mises 1981, p. 194. In the original German of his book, Die Gemeinschaft. Untersuchungen über den Sozialismus (1922), (2nd German ed. 1932, reprinted 1981), p. 197, the last sentence of this section is: "Der Kapitalismus ist die einzig denkbare und mögliche Gestalt arbeitsteilender gesellschaftlicher Wirtschaft." This strong statement has been weakened in the English edition by the following qualification: "(Capitalism is the only conceivable form of social economy) which is appropriate to the fulfillment of the demands which society makes of any economic organization." In this chapter I first examine the original strong thesis. The weaker formulation of the English edition may have been motivated by the discussion about the possibility of calculation in a socialist economy provoked by the original thesis.

8. Cp. Mises (1922), p. 117: "Der Versuch, die Welt sozialistisch zu gestalten, könnte die Zivilisation zertrümmern, er wird aber nie zur Aufrichtung eines sozialistischen Gemeinwesens führen können." If we look in the English edition, we again find a change in the direction indicated in note 7: "It would never set up a successful socialist community" (p. 118). It seems to be clear that the insertion of the word "successful" amounts to a weakening of the original strong claims about the impossibility of socialism. Judgments about the success of a social system obviously permit gradation and may depend on multiple criteria.

9. Cp. Popper (1935) 1959, p. 69 and passim; cp. also Popper 1957, p. 138f., in his discussion with Hayek, who at that time seemed to believe that the "negative" character of theoretical knowledge is a specialty of the social sciences.

10. In my opinion, many economists are questioning the nomological character of theoretical statements in economics. And even economists with an explicitly theoretical orientation sometimes practically capitulate to historicism, as can be shown for instance in Walter Eucken's methodological views; cp. my article (Albert 1984a, pp. 42-47). Indeed, one often has difficulties detecting genuine nomological statements in economic models. Sometimes the problem is minimized in spite of its connection with the question of how theoretical explanations are possible in economics, and whether they are possible at all. Without recourse to nomological statements of some kind the impossibility of socialism could not be shown. For, on purely logical grounds the possibility of a socialist society obviously cannot be excluded; cp. for instance Bernholz and Breyer 1984, where the authors show how one could conceive of a functioning socialist economy. Besides, the weaker thesis of Mises could not be established without lawlike statements.

11. Cp. Mises (1922) 1981, p. 18: "Without the basis for calculation which Capitalism places at the disposal of Socialism, in the shape of market prices, socialist enterprises would never be carried on, even within single branches of production or individual countries"; cp. also p. 206.

12. In Hayek 1952, p. 168f. Friedrich von Hayek makes the distinction between "planned economy" as method and "socialism" (in a stricter sense) as designation for a certain objective, namely, the improvement of the situation of the classes without property by a redistribution of unearned income. I don't make this distinction here because in the argument of Mises, only the practicability of the method is in question.

13. There are two questions involved which have puzzled me since the early 1950s: (1) To what extent is the logic of allocation involved valid for every economy and why? (2) To what extent is it realized at all in a market economy? See Albert (1954) 1972. Maybe I have overstated the case in criticizing the positive answers to these two questions in that book, but the results of the debates in welfare economics seem to justify my mistrust in neoclassical solutions.

14. Cp. Nozick 1974, pt. I, where we find an argument that amounts to establishing this thesis, which is in fact a counterpart to Mises' thesis.

15. Cp. Alchian and Allen 1971, pp. 627-28: "Without government, a system of private property and market-oriented exchange and production would be impossible on any significant scale." We have to take notice of the qualification "on any significant scale" because this impossibility thesis is valid only for complex societies, just as the thesis of Mises is. If population is small, as in primitive societies, custom and trust,

connected with the kinship structure, are sufficient to maintain a fairly stable exchange economy. Cp. Sahlins 1974, and Brenner 1983.

16. Cp. Bernholz and Breyer 1984, where an analysis of this kind is attempted with respect to four main ideal-typical systems and some variants of them.

17. But cp. Nove 1983, pp. 79ff., for a defense of the thesis that there is central planning in this system against criticism. The author concedes, however, "that the deficiencies and imbalances, and distortions due to group interest too, are the inescapable accompaniments of the endeavor to plan centrally," when "central planning is the inescapable consequence of trying to organize a socialist economy along non-market lines." So it is planning, by definition, but the facts connected with such planning do not seem to be controversial to the participants in this discussion. Maybe we should distinguish between "market economy" and "administrative economy" in order to open up the question of the functioning of central planning in our terminology.

18. Cp. the partly amusing description in Hauer 1980, pp. 109ff. and passim.

19. Cp. Myrdal (1930) 1953. A German edition of this work had been published in 1982.

20. Cp. Myrdal 1933. I don't agree with the methodological conclusions of Myrdal; cp. Albert 1958, p. 335f. But it has to be conceded that Myrdal has at least discovered an unsolved problem in economic thinking. To put it into a formula as simple as possible and well known in ethics: Does the end sanctify the means? The merit of Myrdal's analysis is to be _identified_ this problem _within_ economic thought; cp. Albert 1978, ch. 5.

21. That is Myrdal's term for the fiction of a society with a common aim and a common value scale based on it, as it is implicitly assumed very often in economic thinking; cp. Myrdal (1930) 1953, p. 54 and passim. On pp. 149-54 he refers to Wieser's theory of natural value; cp. Wieser 1889, pp. 59-63, where this author has tried to show that the values referred to in the doctrine of marginal utility are really values as they would arise in an ideal communist state. As Myrdal has shown, Wieser has not seen the problematic character of this fiction, for even in such a state, conflicts of interests would be possible.

22. Cp. also James Buchanan's criticism (e.g., 1960b, pp. 78ff.), which points to the same defect of neoclassical thinking; cp. also Vining 1956, pp. 16ff. and 34ff., where the fact is emphasized that society is no task-oriented group with a well-defined common objective, so that the idea of an efficient use of its resources with respect to such an objective is not meaningful; cp. also Hayek's criticism of the concept of social justice in Hayek 1976, Vol. II, _The mirage of social justice_, pp. 62ff., which has the same background, but another target. All these criticisms are, as far as I can see, convergent, as they call into question the whole

tradition of welfare economics. That they are also valid with respect to socialist systems is acknowledged in Nove 1983, p. 104.

23. In his argument against the possibility of economic calculation in a socialist economy, Ludwig von Mises has presupposed that the harmony of interests postulated by him renders such a calculation in a modern society principally possible, if not under the conditions of socialism. He seems to have assumed that the idea of an economic calculation, valid for a society as a whole--as a community of ends, as it were--is compatible with the individualistic assumptions which he has in common with the other representatives of marginalism. In his writings one finds no hint that he has seen the problem of the "communist fiction" in economic theorizing; cp. Mises (1922) 1981, pp. 95-109. Yet, one can find indications for his opinion that economic calculation, possible in a market economy and established there under competitive conditions, leads to a result that is optimal for the members of society. The point is not that individual enterprises are able under these conditions to calculate and to act profitably, that is, efficiently, but that the money calculation taking place here has optimal steering effects for the whole economy with respect to individual needs. It is not a question of some kind of calculation but of a calculation adequate with respect to a particular goal because of its <u>steering effects</u>. Thus, even Mises, probably like all other participants in the debate on calculation, was not able to make his point without recourse to the "communist fiction."

24. In his theory of economic development, Schumpeter himself developed very interesting ideas about the motivation of entrepreneurs that later influenced the research about achievement motivation in psychology; cp. Schumpeter (1911) 1926, pp. 131ff., 138ff., and McClelland 1961, pp. 233ff. and passim; cp. Albert 1968, pp. 43ff. In Schumpeter's thinking we find a strange mixture of neoclassical views and insights into the dynamic character of economic reality, incompatible with these views.

25. It is to the credit of the Austrian economists, e.g. Schumpeter and Hayek, that the creative and innovative aspects of economic development have been emphasized and that the reduction of economic reality to some of its features has been criticized, compatible with a logic of choice neglecting these aspects.

26. Cp. Böhm 1983, pp. 149ff., esp. pp. 153-56, where the differences between modern general equilibrium theory and the ideas of Adam Smith are emphasized and the practical irrelevance of the former is exhibited.

27. There is an interesting analogy between the neoempiristic logic of science and neoclassical economics, for in both areas static aspects of the subject have been accentuated and problems of imagination and heuristics have been excluded in general. In both cases, one of the reasons seems to be that these aspects are easier to treat by formal methods.

28. It was, above all, Hayek's The road to serfdom that drew the attention of the public to the problem of freedom and gave a new turn to the debate about the social order.

29. For the application of value theory to such problems, cp. Boulding 1956, pp. 1ff., esp. p. 11f.

30. Cp. Robbins 1961, p. 16; he continues: "Indeed, I cannot help suspecting that if they had been confronted with the systems of this sort which have been developed since their days, they would have had some hesitation in acknowledging a near family relationship. Their conception of the mechanism of the System of Economic Freedom was surely a conception of something more rough and ready, something much more dynamic and real than these exquisite laboratory models. Their claim, in essence, was not so much that the system of markets was always tending to some refined equilibrium adjustment, but rather that it provided a rough pointer and rough discipline whereby the tumultuous forces of self-interest were guided and held in check"; cp. also Böhm 1983.

31. Let us assume for a moment that a monopoly of information and interpretation by a minority has led to habits of thinking and feeling which have made the adaptation acceptable and even pleasant for the members of this society. In my view we are then not obliged to withhold criticism on the basis of the assumption that the system is legitimized by the consensus of its members. We need not accept the value judgments of these individuals as authoritative for the evaluation of the system. But in our analysis of social systems it is not even necessary to formulate any value judgment about such a system. The comparative analysis of social systems can be carried through as a purely social-technological enterprise as it has been claimed by Max Weber for the theory of economic policy. To assess the performance of such systems we have only hypothetically to assume performance criteria and to find out to what extent the systems analyzed or compared with each other fulfill these criteria. That is obviously a factual analysis. Therefore, in this respect I cannot agree with the views expressed in the book by Peter Bernholz and Friedrich Breyer (1984, pp. 16ff.). It is not difficult to show that the core of their analysis consists of the assessment of the extent to which certain systems factually fulfill certain criteria, in other words, to what extent they have properties of a certain kind.

32. About the contradiction between the anarchist and the socialist component of Marxism, cp. Kelsen (1930) 1965, pp. 78ff.

33. Above all, Saint-Simonism, which has influenced Marxism in this respect, very early produced such solutions; cp. Fehlbaum 1970, where the scientistic features of this kind of thinking are emphasized, which, by the way, are in opposition to the fallibilism of John Stuart Mill's analysis of liberty. Where advocates of Marxism came to power, the Saint-Simonism contained in it came into the open, whereas the neomarxist critics of Western capitalism were able to indulge in ideas of romantic anarchism.

34. For a criticism of this ideal cp. Popper 1944, ch. 18-21, where even the view of the problem-situation connected with it is subjected to a devastating criticism.

35. Cp. the criticism by Schumpeter (1942, pp. 397ff.) of the idea of a uniquely determined "commonweal."

36. Cp. Brenner 1983, where a certain kind of relative deprivation is used to explain some features of modern complex societies.

37. Cp. Ross 1958, pp. 268, 269: "All wars have been fought by all parties in the name of justice, and the same is true of the political conflict between social classes"; p. 270: "The demand for equality must therefore be understood in a relative sense, that is, as a demand that like shall be treated in a like manner. This means that as a prerequisite for the application of the norm of equality, and independent of it, there must be some criteria to determine what is to be considered as equal."

38. Therefore we cannot expect the maximization of freedom to be a reasonable aim of politics. "Blanket arguments about maximizing freedom can lead to the advocacy of social and economic policies detrimental to democracy and to freedom itself," as Dan Usher points out (1981, p. 91); cp. also Albert 1978, pp. 156ff.

39. Cp. Hayek 1944, pp. 119-33, where in contrast to Mises, Hayek takes the problem of security very seriously. Walter Eucken, one of the leading German Neoliberals, has put into the center of his analysis of the problem of the social order questions of social security; cp. Eucken 1959, p. 10 and passim.

40. Cp. Berlin 1969b, p. 124f., where he states that some people "need medical help or education before they can understand, or make use of, an increase of their freedom," and continues with the question: "What is freedom to those who cannot make use of it?" and, what is for them "the value of freedom"? For many people freedom may be a luxury good.

41. Cp. Hayek 1981, Vol. 3, Freiheit im Wohlfahrtsstaat; cp. also the interesting historical analysis of the different policies of Tiberius and Gaius Gracchus in ancient Rome in de Jouvenel 1972, pp. 392ff. The older of both, Tiberius, wanted to solve the problems by trying to let every citizen be a landed proprietor, whereas the younger, Gaius, instituted a law with the aim to give every citizen his ration of grain at a modest price and later, even free of charge. The policy of the older Gracchus thus aimed at greater independence of the individuals, the policy of the younger at their greater dependence on the state. As an interesting modern counterpart de Jouvenel (1972, pp. 394ff.) points to the political measures of the older and the younger Roosevelt in the United States.

42. To do justice to some socialists it has to be mentioned that the kind of solution which I have characterized as a "liberal" one is to be

found also in the program of the German "freiheitlicher Sozialismus," primarily in the writings of Gerhard Weisser.

43. Cp. Schelsky 1976, pp. 13-48, where the author is developing a program for the increase of independence and freedom, referring to the social structure of modern societies. It is connected with an analysis of the meaning of independence in modern industrial society, which comes to the conclusion that today three properties are relevant in this respect: (1) the fact that a person has a certain freedom of disposal in his work situation, (2) that he is able to develop satisfaction in his activity ("berufliche Tätigkeitsfreude"), and (3) that he is able to realize an individual plan of life. Schelsky obviously did not want to base his definition on the usual purely legal characteristics because he thought that these often are not decisive.

44. Insofar as I agree with Dan Usher, cp. Usher 1981, p. 7.

45. Cp. the distinction between "redistribution" and "reassignment" made by Usher (1981, p. 34); cp. also p. 122f., where the author points to the possible effects of redistribution in making capitalism acceptable.

REFERENCES

Acham, Karl, ed. 1983. Gesellschaftliche Prozesse. Graz.

Albert, Hans. 1958. Das Wertproblem in den Sozialwissenschaften. Schweizerische Zeitschrift für Volkswirtschaft und Statistik.

------. 1965. Zur Theorie der Konsumnachfrage. Jahrbuch für Sozialwissenschaft 16.

------. 1968. Erwerbsprinprinzip und Sozialstruktur. Jahrbuch für Socialwissenschaft 19.

------. (1954) 1972. Ökonomische Ideologie und Politische Theorie. 2nd ed. Göttingen.

------. 1976a. Aufklärung und Steuerung. Hamburg.

------. 1976b. Macht und ökonomisches Gesetz. Der Gesetzesbegriff im ökonomischen Denken. In Albert 1976a.

------. 1978. Traktat über rationale Praxis. Tübingen.

------. 1984a. Modell-Denken und historische Wirklichkeit. In Albert 1984b.

------, ed. 1984b. Ökonomisches Denken und Soziale Ordnung. Tübingen.

Alchian, Armen, and William R. Allen. 1971. University economics. Elements of inquiry. 3rd ed. Belmont, Calif.: Wadsworth Publishing.

Bartley, W. W., III, ed. 1982. The logic of scientific discovery. London.

Berlin, Isaiah. 1969a. Four essays on liberty. London: Oxford University Press.

------. 1969b. Two concepts of liberty. In Berlin 1969a.

Bernholz, Peter, and Friedrich Breyer. 1984. Grundlagen der politischen Ökonomie. 2nd rev. ed. Tübingen.

Böhm, Stephan. 1983. Das Beispiel der "unsichtbaren Hand." In Acham 1983.

Boulding, Kenneth E. 1956. Some contributions of economics to the general theory of value. Philosophy of Science 23.

Brenner, Reuven. 1983. History--The human gamble. Chicago and London: University of Chicago Press.

Buchanan, James. 1960a. Fiscal theory and political economy. Chapel Hill: University of North Carolina Press.

------. 1960b. Social choice, democracy, and free markets. In Buchanan 1960a.

------. 1975. The limits of liberty. Between anarchy and leviathan. Chicago and London: University of Chicago Press.

Caspary, Adolf. 1932. Wirtschaftsstrategie und Kriegführung. Berlin.

Duesenberry, James. 1949. Income, saving and the theory of consumer behavior. Cambridge, Mass.: Harvard University Press.

Eucken, Walter. 1959. Grundsätze der Wirtschaftspolitik, ed. Edith Eucken-Erdsiek and Paul K. Hensel. Hamburg.

Fehlbaum, R. P. 1970. Saint Simon und die Saint Simonisten. Vom Laissez-Faire zur Wirtschaftsplanung. Basel/Tübingen.

Festinger, Leon. 1954. A theory of social comparison processes. Human Relations 7:117ff.

Friedman, David. 1973. The machinery of freedom. Guide to a radical capitalism. New York: Harper and Row.

Hayek, Friedrich von. 1944. The road to serfdom. Chicago: University of Chicago Press.

------. 1952a. Individualismus und wirtschaftliche Ordnung. Erlenbach-Zürich.

------. 1952b. Sozialistiche Wirtschafrechnung I. Natur und Geschichte des Problems. In Hayek 1952a.

------. 1971. Die Verfassung der Freiheit. Tübingen.

------. 1973, 1976, 1979. Law, legislation and liberty. 3 vols. London and Henley.

------. 1976a. Degrees of explanation. In Hayek 1976b.

------. 1976b. Studies in philosophy, politics, and economics. London.

de Jouvenel, Bertram. 1972. Über die Staatsgewalt. Die Naturgeschichte ihres Wachstums. Freiburg.

Kelsen, Hans. (1930) 1965. Sozialismus und Staat. Eine Untersuchung der politischen Theorie des Marxismus. 3rd ed. Wien.

Lepsius, M. Rainer. 1971. Soziale Konsequenzen von Technischen Fortschritten. In Wirtschaftliche und gesellschaftliche Auswirkungen des technischen Fortschritts, VDI. Düsseldorf.

Löwith, Karl. 1953. Weltegeschichte und Heilsgeschenen. Die theologischen Voraussetzungen der Geschichtsphilosophie. Stuttgart.

McClelland, David C. 1961. The achieving society. Princeton, N.J.: Irvington Books.

Medawar, Peter B. 1957a. Tradition: The evidence of biology. In Medawar, 1957b.

------. 1957b. The uniqueness of the individual. Edinburgh.

Merton, Robert K., and Alice Rossi. 1957a. Contributions to the theory of reference group behavior. In Merton 1957b.

Merton, Robert K. 1957b. Social theory and social structure. Rev. ed. Glencoe, Ill.

Mises, Ludwig von. (1922) 1981. Socialism. An economic and sociological analysis. Indianapolis, Ind. Orig. published in 1922 as Die Gemeinschaft. Untersuchungen über den Sozialismus. 2nd ed. 1932, reprint Munich, 1981.

Myrdal, Gunnar. 1933. Das Zweck-mittel-Denken in der Nationalökonomie. Zeitschrift für Nationalökonomie 4 (1933). Reprinted and translated in Gunnar Myrdal, Value in social theory: A selection of essays on methodology, ed. Paul Streeten (London, 1958), pp. 206-30.

------. (1930) 1953. The political element in the development of economic theory. London.

Nove, Alec. 1983. _The economics of feasible socialism_. London.

Nozick, Robert. 1974. _Anarchy, state, and utopia_. Oxford.

Popper, Karl. 1944. _The open society and its enemies_. Rev. ed. Princeton, N.J.: Princeton University Press, 1950.

------. 1944-45. The poverty of historicism. _Economica_ n.s. 11 (1944), 12 (1945).

------. 1950-51. Indeterminism in classical physics and in quantum physics. _British Journal for Philosophy of Science_ 1:117-33, 173-95.

------. 1957. _The poverty of historicism_. London.

------. (1935) 1959. _The logic of scientific discovery_. London.

------. 1982. The open universe. An argument for indeterminism. Postscript to Bartley 1982.

Robbins, Lionel. (1932) 1935. _An essay on the nature and significance of economic science_. 2nd ed. London.

------. 1961. _The theory of economic policy in English classical political economy_. London.

Roberts, Paul Craig. 1971. _Alienation and the Soviet economy. Toward a general theory of Marxian alienation, organizational principles, and the Soviet economy_. Albuquerque: University of New Mexico Press.

Roberts, Paul Craig, and Matthew A. Stephenson. 1973. _Marx's theory of exchange, alienation and crisis_. Stanford, Calif.: Hoover Institution Press.

Ross, Alf. 1958. _On law and justice_. London.

Rothbard, Murray N. 1973. _For a new liberty_. New York: Macmillan.

Runciman, W. G. 1961. Problem of research in relative deprivation. _European Archive for Sociology_ 2.

Sahlins, Marshall. 1974. _Stone age economics_. London.

Schelsky, Helmut. 1976. _Der selbständige und der betreute Mensch. Politische Schriften und Kommentare_. Stuttgart.

Schmidt-Häuer, Christian. 1980. _Das sind die Russen_. Hamburg.

Schumpeter, Joseph. (1911) 1926. _Theorie der wirtschaftlichen Entwicklung_. Munich.

------. 1942. Kapitalismus, Sozialismus und Demokratie. 2nd rev. ed. Munich, 1950.

Topitsch, Ernst. 1968a. Entrefremdung und Ideologie. Zur Entmythologisierung des Marxismus. In Topitsch 1968c.

------. 1968b. Marxismus und Gnosis. In Topitsch 1968c.

------. 1968c. Sozialphilosophie zwischen Ideologie und Wissenschaft. Neuwied/Berlin.

Usher, Dan. 1981. The economic prerequisite to democracy. Oxford.

Vining, Rutledge. 1956. Economics in the United States of America. Paris.

Weber, Max. 1924a. Gesammelte Aufsätze zur Soziologie und Sozialpolitik. Tübingen.

------. (1918) 1924b. Der Sozialismus. In Weber 1924a.

Wieser, Friedrich von. 1889. Der natürliche Wert. Wien.

Chapter 5

SOCIALISM: DO THE ENDS JUSTIFY THE MEANS?

By

Roland Vaubel*

"Das Gegenteil von 'gut' ist 'gut gemeint.'"
- Bert Brecht

INTRODUCTION: MEANS AND ENDS

Many socialists are people of goodwill who cannot resign themselves to the misery and imperfections of this world. They are appalled by the poverty of the unfortunate and by the "squandermania" of many who are rich. They are alarmed by humiliating working conditions, and they are sad about the greed and the lack of cooperative spirit among many of their peers. Socialists want to eliminate these evils. But the same is true of most classical liberals, be they humanists or Christians. These aims of socialism are perfectly consistent with classical liberalism, so the conflict between socialists and classical liberals is over the means of achieving their common goals.

Socialists believe that their aims can and should be achieved by collective action. This action includes reduction of differences in income

---

* R. Vaubel is professor of economics at the University of Mannheim.

and wealth by taxation and transfers, a mandatory social insurance system, collective wage bargaining and governmental price controls, socializing the means of production, or a combination of these. A socialist system to improve working conditions would include socialization, codetermination, collective bargaining or protective government regulation, or a combination of these. The cooperation needed to achieve these goals or socialism would be fostered with governmental moral suasian and an educational system run or at least regulated by the government. To the extent that the government controls the economy, it must develop and enforce a consistent overall plan: that enlightened collective planning is to replace the apparently arbitrary, or at least unsatisfactory, outcomes of decentralized decision-making in the market.

Socialists are prepared to use the coercive power of the state to attain their goals. They justify such coercion with the belief that government acts in the public interest. Dissenters must be either wicked or ignorant; they must be forced by the enlightened majority (Rousseau) or by the enlightened (self-appointed) vanguard of the majority (Marx).

For the classical liberal, neither (actual or presumed) majorities nor laudable intentions are sufficient to justify coercion. The main purpose of government, in this view, is to prevent coercion of citizens. It should not use coercion except on the basis of constitutional agreement because coercion prevents individuals from pursuing their own goals. However disliked the wishes of others may be, the classical liberal respects them, believing that the individual is likely to be the best judge of his own interest (Bentham) or at least has the strongest incentive to act according to his own interest (James Mill). In what concerns oneself, an individual knows better and acts better than the "collective spirit" (Hegel's _Weltgeist_) or its operational equivalent, which is the average politician and the median (or decisive)--rationally ignorant--voter. The role of the political and economic order is to coordinate the wishes of independent individuals, not to change them.

If the classical liberal is concerned about poverty and humiliation (which is likely to be the case), he will offer his help and appeal to the altruistic feelings of others who could help. If he is concerned about greed and "squandermania" (also likely to be the case), he will try exhortation and persuasion. He will welcome and support a religion or system of ethics that can act as a psychological counterweight to the competitive spirit of the market. He will encourage voluntary giving as long as it increases the happiness of all. However, even if these means do not succeed, he will not use or advocate others' use of force, not even by the majority or the politicians it has elected. Government, in his view, should be based on consent, not coercion. It must not overrule minorities, especially if the latter are to pay the bill. In the classical liberal's view government should act in the common interest of all rather than in the "social" interest of the majority.

Classical liberalism specifies the political means which must be avoided at all costs; socialism specifies the political aims which must be attained at all costs. While liberalism is consistent with any noncoercive individual aims, socialism is consistent with (almost?) any collective means.

Both of these themes are consistent with Christian (notably Catholic) social teaching, as long as the principle of subsidiarity is not operationalized. However, socialism is much more ambitious than Christian social teaching or classical liberalism. Christian religion prescribes goals but is vague on means. Classical liberalism rejects certain means but is silent about goals. Both can agree on a division of labor and clear boundaries that facilitate social peace.[1] Socialism, by contrast, prescribes goals as well as specifies means (i.e., collective means) to achieve them. Hence, the situation is bound to create divisiveness. Socialism is a worldly religion.

Religions have little to say about the logical derivation and the empirical implementation of their values. The values are regarded as given (through revelation); they do not require a philosophical foundation. There is little if any interest in the choice among alternative means of implementation. Only the simplest and most direct approach tends to be considered. The scientific, particularly the economic, foundations of religious social teaching are usually very weak.

Is this also true of the worldly religion of socialism? Three fundamental questions must be raised: (1) Does socialism establish the desirability of its ends? (2) To what extent can these ends be attained? and

(3) What is the cost of approaching them? These questions set the agenda for this chapter.

REDISTRIBUTION

Why should politicians be empowered to redistribute income and wealth? Three types of reasons have been given: (1) efficiency, (2) utilitarian maximization of collective happiness, and (3) distributive justice. We shall examine them in turn.

Redistribution is Pareto-efficient if conditions improve for some but worsen for no one. Redistribution may be efficient in this sense if voluntary transfers generate external effects. Voluntary transfers may be due to various motives:

a. the donor enjoys giving for its own sake
b. the donor enjoys being seen giving
c. the donor gives in order to be given
d. the donor enjoys seeing the recipient happy
e. the donor cares about the distribution of income and wealth
f. the donor cares about the welfare of the society in which he lives.

Socialists believe that the utility functions of individuals are highly interdependent, either because of compassion or because of envy (keeping up with the Joneses or relative income hypothesis). Hence, with respect to charity, socialists emphasize cases d, e, and f, where voluntary transfers generate positive external effects for others without compensation for the donor. However, if the donor is universally benevolent (f), he will allow for the altruistic feelings of others. He is as likely to do so as the average politician or the median voter. If the donor's benevolence is confined to the recipient (d), he knows better than the average politician or the median voter to whom he wants to give how much. He will also be more efficient in effecting the transfer he desires. Thus, if the donor attaches little importance to the positive third-party effects of his giving, the optimal solution is not redistribution by governments but tax benefits for those who donate to private charity. Redistribution by governments, on the contrary, eliminates the incentive for this giving to private charity.[2]

With respect to envy, socialists argue that redistribution reduces the probability of crime and social unrest; they recommend it as a way of purchasing social peace. If the individual donor does not obtain compensation from the other beneficiaries, he is likely to give too little to the poor.

This argument is short-sighted because it ignores the incentive and information effects. Pacifist redistribution rewards envy and encourages blackmail. It draws attention to income differentials, generating demands for greater redistribution. Since the appeasers nourish expectations of acquiescence, the cost of resistance is likely to grow the longer it is delayed (witness the outbreak of World War II). From a strategic (instead of myopic) point of view, pacifist redistribution tends to be an explosive process.

Is redistribution efficient if government guarantees a minimum income? The answer depends on whether such an assurance is a natural monopoly and whether government is the most efficient producer of natural-monopoly goods. If all citizens believe that these conditions are satisfied, they will unanimously agree to a constitutional provision that guarantees a minimum income. Do they? Consensus among the participants is the only test of whether such redistribution is Pareto-efficient or merely utilitarian.

Socialist redistribution may be justified on _utilitarian_ grounds only if income has a higher marginal utility for the low-income earners than for the high-income earners. This condition is by itself not sufficient reason for redistribution because coercive redistribution may have undesirable side effects. Moreover, the case for governmental redistribution from the high-income earners to the low-income earners does not follow from utilitarianism as such; it follows only in conjunction with certain empirical assumptions about human psychology and the social cost of coercive transfers. These empirical assumptions are not self-evident.

Utilitarian value judgments involve interpersonal comparisons of cardinal (e.g., marginal) utilities. Such comparisons are neither logically meaningless nor incapable of being supported by empirical evidence (the behavior of human beings). But we know that behavior can be feigned, and a reliable utilometer has yet to be invented. It follows that the empirical content of utilitarian value judgments cannot be conclusively falsified, let alone verified. Thus, the only safe procedure for maximizing collective happiness is to let individuals peacefully maximize their own happiness. Cooperation between individuals then takes the form of voluntary contracts. When politicians or a majority of voters decide on collective action, we can never be sure that such action will increase collective happiness. When two or more individuals voluntarily conclude a contract, we know that each of them feels better off.

The problem is not only that empirical assumptions of utilitarian coercive redistribution cannot be conclusively (i.e., scientifically) tested; they also rest on implausible premises. It is usually assumed that, on average, low-income earners have a higher marginal utility of income than the high-income earners because (1) the marginal utility of income tends to diminish and (2) all individuals have, or should be assumed to have (Lerner), the same utility function. But is it not likely that the utility functions of the higher-income earners differ systematically from the utility functions of the lower-income earners? Many of those who work hard and earn high incomes are likely to do so because they feel a particularly strong need of security or prestige (which money may provide) or because they happen to have some minority taste which is particularly costly to satisfy. To take income away from them and to give it to lower-income people who may value leisure more highly can easily reduce collective happiness. The rich who suffer from rapidly diminishing marginal utility of consumption are likely to solve their problem by giving more voluntarily.

Justice

In view of the difficulty of deducing egalitarianism from utilitarianism on the basis of "secure" empirical assumptions, many socialists prefer to derive their precepts from the concept of social or distributive justice. This merely shifts the question: From what premises can the aim of distributive justice be derived?

Distributive justice is often contrasted with commutative or civil justice, which is the justice of property rights. It is enforced by the protective state. Commutative justice consists of three principles: (1) inviolability of property, (2) compensation for damage, and (3) freedom of contract. Its logical structure is that of negative rules, that is, of rules that prohibit certain actions that infringe upon the liberty of others, but do not require positive action.

Distributive justice is the justice of giving in collective organizations (e.g., the family, the tribe, the state). It is typical of the welfare state. It prescribes positive actions toward a certain pattern of distribution. What is just does not depend on the rules according to which the end-state pattern came about, but on whether the end-state pattern conforms to criteria such as need, merit, effort, or marginal product.

At first glance it must be highly surprising that two so contradictory moral precepts have both been subsumed under the heading of justice. Distributive justice, when pursued by the state, interferes with commutative justice. The classical economists saw this problem; they solved it by delegating distributive justice to the second rank, where it served to exclude arbitrariness in unrequited transfers of private property.[3] Socialists tend to reverse this order. What is their justification?

Surprisingly, there is an easy transition from commutative justice to distributive justice. The connecting link is retributive justice. Retributive justice is a device to protect property rights and individual liberties in general, for if those who violate the rights of others are not consistently and promptly detected, compensation for damage (including the cost of detection and trial) tends to be an insufficient deterrent. Penalties imposed by the judicial branch of government will be required. Penalties will be geared to the severity of damage, as well as the personal circumstances of the criminal; a mentally ill person such as a kleptomaniac is granted extenuating circumstances and punished less severely. Retribution allows for the possibility that the criminal may not be fully responsible for what he has done. This can be rationalized on utilitarian grounds: to the extent that a person is mentally unsound, punishment is not a deterrent.

What holds for punishment (disincentives) may by analogy be applied to rewards (incentives). People are not responsible for the natural and circumstantial endowments with which they begin life. What moral right do they have to such "windfall gains"? The utilitarian would agree: inequality of endowments serves no useful purpose. It ought to be abolished if that is feasible at tolerable cost. Thus, the argument from responsibility can lead to the demand for equal opportunity and a distribution according to merit or effort in using one's endowments. Is it conclusive? There are several problems.

If causation is all-pervasive, there can be no responsibility at all. In a deterministic setting, the distinction between endowments and the efficient use of endowments breaks down: everything is endowed, and the argument from responsibility leads to complete egalitarianism. There are two possible ways of meeting this objection. One may either exempt human action (or parts of it) from the principle of causation ("free will") at the cost of philosophical dualism and the associated borderline problems, or one may rationalize the notion of responsibility in terms of the utility of maintaining appropriate incentives and disincentives even in a deterministic world. In that case, however, there is no independent argument from responsibility; it reduces to a variant of utilitarianism, and the question arises whether a broader utilitarian perspective would not be preferable.

If the argument is ultimately utilitarian, the information problem has to be recognized. With the exception of pecuniary bequests, there is no operational way of measuring the value of the initial endowments. This is inevitable because nobody can know beforehand to what use the endowments can be put. On the other hand, if government tries to infer their value from their use, efficient endowment use is discouraged. There is a sort of Heisenberg effect: any attempt at measurement alters the quantity to be measured.

Instead of trying to measure the value of endowments directly, one may treat them as the residual that remains when effort has been accounted for. However, rewards according to effort raise the same problem: everybody obtains an incentive to choose the job for which he is least suited, for this gives him the opportunity to try hardest. The problem is that differences in income may have nothing to do with differences in the value of endowments: they may merely reflect differences in age or in preferences between work and leisure, risk and security, present and future consumption, procreation and childlessness, that is, rational voluntary choices among opportunities intended to maximize individual self-fulfillment. The socialist does not know whether and to what extent poverty (or low income) is due to bad fortune.

In view of these difficulties, socialists tend to adopt the following fallback position: they accept the failure to fully equalize resource endowments as "instrumentally justified," but they insist that inequalities of opportunity must be reduced to some extent through ex post income redistribution, however imperfect this method may be. This position is not conclusive, unless some redistribution is worth any cost.

The cost of socialist redistribution is not only the cost of political error and economic discouragement. If politicians are given the power to redistribute as they or the majority think fit, they can, and often will, abuse this power. Since the information problem is insurmountable, there is no operational limit to political discretion. Discretion for politicians means risk for citizens. The mere possibility of coercive redistribution opens a battle either to obtain government transfers ("aggression") or to avert them ("protection"). These costs, in terms of largely offsetting redistributive efforts by politicians, bureaucrats and an ever-growing multitude of pressure groups, are a deadweight loss to society, comparable only to the arms race at the international level (see Tullock 1971). The redistributive "class struggle" leads to a "new Hobbesian dilemma" (see Gray 1984). It erodes the democratic consensus. Its ultimate consequence is the decomposition of democracy and society. As Mises (1922/1981, p. 40) has pointed out, "Our whole civilization rests on the fact that men have succeeded in beating off the attack of the redistributors."

Alternatively, one may try to derive the concept of distributive justice from contractarian premises. Rawls (1972) has explicitly done so. Buchanan (1975), too, has employed the contractarian approach to define the limits of governmental redistribution; he is indifferent on whether to use the concept of justice in this context. Both authors regard governmental redistribution as justified only to the extent that it can be viewed as explicitly or implicitly agreed upon in a voluntary constitutional contract of all citizens. Rawls (1972, p. 274) emphasizes that his conception of justice is also applicable to a socialist economy.

In Rawls's theory the relevant constitutional contract must be viewed as concluded "behind a veil of ignorance" about individual endowments. Such a setting for the constitutional contract can never have existed. Thus, Rawls's social contract cannot be more than a philosophical artifact designed to derive and describe what he believes we mean by justice. It is a logical exercise (methaethics), but not a basis for ethical prescription. Since the contract is fictitious, the crucial advantage that contractarianism can have over utilitarian collectivism is lost: its ability to offer an operational procedure of ascertaining preferences. Buchanan, who starts from a "natural distribution" in "anarchistic equilibrium," avoids this pitfall and criticizes Rawls for falling into it.[4]

Rawls argues that the social contract which individuals would conclude behind the veil of ignorance would contain two principles: (1) equal rights to the most extensive liberty compatible with a similar liberty for others (p. 60), and (2) the so-called "difference principle" concerning the pattern of just distribution. The first principle has priority over the second and guarantees the right to hold personal property (p. 61). Rawls indicates that, in his view, a market economy is more likely than a command economy to be consistent with the first principle (p. 272f.), but he does not exclude the latter. The difference principle implies that "the minimum (income) is to be set at that point which, taking wages into account, maximizes the expectations of the least advantaged group" (p. 285).

This maximin rule may be rational behind a veil of complete ignorance; it is not rational for any social contract to be concluded in the real world. In the real world, the rational, utility-maximizing individual does not simply choose the distribution characterized by the highest minimum expected rate of return, but will take into account the whole range of possible rates of return (each weighted with its probability) as well as the mean expected rate of return. Since the optimal choice depends on one's risk aversion and since people cannot be assumed to possess the same degree of risk aversion, unanimous agreement on the desired distributional pattern is likely to be even ex ante impossible, unless the contract provides for compensation to those whose preferences deviate from the average. This, however, means that, contrary to Rawls's view, the just distribution is no longer independent of who gets what; the social contract no longer produces an anonymous pattern of just distribution.

The difference principle is to take into account the welfare of the least advantaged groups in all living and future generations (p. 285). This requires precisely the utilitarian interpersonal comparisons of cardinal utility which the maximin rule was supposed to avoid despite a patterned conception of justice (p. 91f.). Once more, Rawls gives away the crucial advantage which contractarianism has over utilitarian collectivism: its ability to do without dubious interpersonal utility comparisons.

Though the contractarian has good reason to reject this theory of justice,[5] Rawls's difference principle is useful in defining the limit to which a rational socialist would want to push coercive redistribution by governments. If, under socialism, "each individual will receive less than the poorest receives today" (Mises 1922/1981, p. 454), then the classical liberal has no difficulty in accepting the difference principle either. In any case, the difference principle defines a set of outcomes which neither the liberal nor the social desires: immiserization of the poorest as a result of redistribution. But this common ground on what to reject is of little help in agreeing upon goals. Neither the utilitarian liberal nor the contractarian liberal is prepared to welcome all redistribution that makes the poorest better off. Both refuse to be guided by a few group interests rather than by the interests of all. Would both agree with each other?

For many contractarians, the ultimate starting point of their ethical and political theories is the inviolable autonomy of the individual (see, e.g., Buchanan 1975, p. 6). This type of individualism is at a crucial disadvantage. As Frank Knight put it (1923, p. 580),

> social policy must be based on social ideals. An organized system must operate in accordance with a social standard. This standard will of course be related in some way to the values of the individuals making up the society, but it cannot be merely identical with them; it presupposes some process of organizing the various individual interests, weighing them against each other and adjudicating conflicts among them.

With regard to justice, we may quote David Hume's "Enquiry Concerning the Principles of Morals" (1752; 1965): "The rules of equity or justice . . .

owe their origin and existence to that utility which results to the public from their strict and regular observance" (p. 39). "The necessity of justice to the support of society is the sole foundation of that virtue" (p. 53; see also p. 112f.). Ethical and political discourse is about the well-being of a group, not that of the individual. The logic of our ethics is not such that deliberately sacrificing the interests of one member of the group is immoral as a matter of logical necessity, not even at the constitutional level. It is possible to regret this, but it cannot be otherwise. To start from individualist premises, therefore, is to miss the logical level of moral argument. It is bound to be ineffective.

This means that contractarianism must be derived from utilitarianism or from some other conception of the public interest. Since this derivation must be empirical, it cannot be conclusively verified, but it can achieve its purpose, unlike the vain attempt to prejudge the outcome at the logical level. The missing link is the utilitarian's need for an operational method of ascertaining preferences. Utilitarian collectivism does not have such a method. Contractarianism provides it. It makes utilitarian individualism possible.

Application

On a contractarian basis, governmental redistribution is free of coercion only if it has been unanimously agreed to in a constitutional contract or if it is the result of rules that have been unanimously agreed to in this way. The contractarian principle requires that a minority of citizens must be able to repeal or restrict the constitutional powers of government--also in the field of redistribution. This condition is not satisfied in present-day democracies.

Even in the absence of a contractarian legitimation, the economist may try to appraise the comparative efficiency of alternative methods of coercive redistribution by governments. There is widespread agreement among nonsocialist economists that the only efficient way of redistributing income and wealth is an integrated system of taxation and explicit transfers. Redistribution through a mandatory social insurance system is inefficient because it requires government to have an insurance monopoly in this field; competition and individual choice are suppressed. Collective bargaining and governmental price controls are also inefficient because the result is excess supply (unemployment, agricultural overproduction, etc.) or shortages (e.g., a shortage of housing because of rent controls). Even worse, collective bargaining and price controls tend to be counterproductive, hitting the weakest: those who are not yet established (the young) or those who are not well organized (the unemployed). How about socializing the means of production to stop the "exploitation of workers"? Socialization is a blunt weapon of redistribution because recipients of capital earnings need not be rich and recipients of labor income need not be poor. The functional distribution of income and the interpersonal distribution of income are logically entirely distinct concepts and empirically highly imperfect substitutes. Moreover, socialization cannot be a more efficient instrument of redistribution than a tax-cum-transfer system, unless socialized factories produce more efficiently than private enterprises. Even socialists hesitate to make that assumption; if they believed it, they would have no reason to suppress competition from private producers. The socialized means of production would be able to prevail in conditions of perfectly free entry.[6]

Given that the philosophical and economic foundations of socialist redistribution are weak, why is it so widespread and why is it advocated even by parties that do not call themselves socialist? One explanation is the movement toward noncontractarian majority rule, which, however, implies redistribution to middle- rather than low-income earners. Moreover, growth of real income per capita may have stimulated generosity, but it does not explain why coercive redistribution by governments has expanded at the expense of voluntary private charity.

Historically, the roots of socialist redistribution may be traced back to the French revolution. The battle cry "liberté, egalité, fraternité" underwent a remarkable transformation. "Fraternité" was no longer interpreted as a voluntary affair among brothers, but as the proper task of coercive government. "Egalité" was no longer interpreted as political equality or equality before the law, but as economic equality, more precisely, the equality of economic outcomes in terms of income or wealth.[7] "Liberté" was no longer interpreted as freedom from government interference, but as freedom from economic necessity[8] and as freedom to obtain, with the help of government coercion, the material means for individual self-fulfillment.

Such freedom to take is for others a compulsion to give. What the recipients gain is a loss to those who are forced to pay the bill. Thus, redistribution cannot increase total freedom in the socialist sense, and it must reduce total freedom in the liberal sense. Freedom in the liberal sense is a genuine and independent goal; freedom in the socialist sense either is not an independent goal (if it merely means more economic equality [cf. Hayek 1944, p. 26]) or is not attainable by socialist means (if it means more prosperity for all).

WORKING CONDITIONS

The working conditions in modern industry may be regarded as humiliating or "alienating" for several reasons. One is that, owing to the increasing division of labor, the individual worker cannot see, let alone "appropriate," the final product to which he has contributed. This type of alienation is unavoidable if modern industry and prosperity are to persist. However, the market economy allows everybody to choose a less alienating activity in exchange for a sacrifice of income. The same is true in the case of working conditions that are unpleasant because of noise, dirt, or repetition. In a centrally planned economy, for example, a worker is less likely to have that choice.

Another reason working conditions may be regarded as humiliating is the hierarchical organization of large, modern enterprises and the lack of worker participation in company decision-making. Once more, hierarchical organization is unavoidable if economies of scale are to be exploited. Since the work to be done cannot be described in full detail in the labor contract, the worker gives the employer some leeway in implementing the contract; within the limits of the contract, the employer obtains the right to give orders and to monitor the performance of the worker. Again, the market economy allows people to reject work in a hierarchy, and they are not likely to have that choice in a centrally planned economy. Is the "joy of labor" greater in a government bureaucracy?

Central planning and even public ownership of the means of production have grown less popular with many socialists. Their modern substitute is worker participation (or "codetermination"). Worker participation has the advantage of being attractive to the labor unions; moreover, since it can be depicted as "industrial democracy" (which it is not[9]), it appeals to the democratic sentiment of the median voter.

Worker participation in decision-making at the plant and company level might not only reduce alienation. It might also improve the quality of the decisions. The worker representatives may dispose over information to which the owners or their managers have no access. The workers also have an interest in good decisions. Management errors have adverse effects on the workers' wages and job security. If the company fails, they are likely to suffer losses as well: they may not find a suitable job for some time. Since some of their skills were company-specific, their human capital depreciates and new investments in human capital become necessary. If they have to move, they are likely to incur additional transaction costs and capital losses (especially if they have to sell real property). Thus, there might be a case for worker participation. At least, the issue at stake cannot be decided by theoretical arguments. It is a matter of empirical testing.

If worker participation improves the quality of management decisions, that is, efficiency, the entrepreneur will be keen to implement it because it would increase his income. If worker participation reduces the efficiency of the enterprise, the workers can try to compensate the entrepreneur by accepting a corresponding reduction of their wages. If the reduction of alienation is worth more to the workers than it costs the entrepreneur (and his managers), codetermined companies can reduce their wage costs to such an extent that they gain a competitive advantage over other firms. In other words, if worker participation were Pareto-efficient, it would have prevailed in the market. It would not have to be introduced by governments. Since it has not prevailed in the market[10] (although there have been no legal obstacles to it), the result of the empirical test is negative: worker participation is not a Pareto-improvement but a form of redistribution. What is being redistributed is power of disposition, a form of wealth.

The socialist would not be impressed by this conclusion. The socialist wants redistribution. But is worker participation, imposed by government, an efficient means of redistribution?

As has been noted above, collective interference with the individual's freedom of contract is a less efficient method of redistribution than a progressive tax-transfer system. In the case of worker participation, this is easy to see. If the benefits of worker participation are worth their cost, workers can use the government's cash transfers to compensate their employer for the cost of admitting worker participation. If they prefer to use the money for some other purpose, they are also free to do so. If, by contrast, the government introduces mandatory worker participation, redistribution is in kind, and the workers have no choice but to consume their benefits in this form. The governmental imposition of worker participation, therefore, is not an act of worker emancipation. It is a method of redistribution that treats the workers as incapable of making their own choices.

CREATING A BETTER PERSON

Most socialists believe that the political and economic order affects the character and the tastes of the people who live under it. Classical liberals need not deny this. Some of them have expressly voiced their agreement.[11] But they insist that it is not the task of government to judge and alter the preferences of the citizens (as long as they do not wish to impose their will on others).

Most socialists believe that the competitive market economy fosters selfish greed and base materialist tastes. Once more, this belief is compatible with classical liberalism. Classical liberals who share it are likely to advocate a cooperative and antimaterialist, Christian or humanist, system of values, which serves as a counterweight. But as long as agreement on ends cannot be attained, they do not want to use government to administer their ethics. And, if agreement on ends became possible, there would be no need for government propaganda.

If competition has made people greedy and uncooperative, social policy must take this into account, at least for the time being. This means that social insurance, public assistance, and the other outlets of the welfare state must contain safeguards against abuse. However, the socialist rejects such precautions and denies the probability of abuse. This is a contradiction.

Can the "new man" be created? There is another contradiction: if capitalism has corrupted people, how can they establish a socialist order?[12] Moreover, would the socialist order really reduce conflict and encourage cooperation?

Working class solidarity is likely, but not certain, in the struggle with the class enemy. However, as soon as the capitalists are expropriated or stripped of their power, the distribution of positions and incomes among the workers becomes all the more important. The distributional conflict is likely to become even more bitter. First, there is less income to be distributed. Second, the distribution is the result of governmental coercion rather than voluntary contracts. Third, the distribution is settled not by impersonal market forces but by identifiable politicians and officials.

Is there any empirical evidence that supports the socialist's prediction? As Alex Nove (1983, p. 61) argues, it "obviously owes nothing to the study of the actual experience of the Russian revolution." On the contrary, the discrepancy between socialist ideology and socialist reality in the East engenders hypocrisy, cynicism, and corruption. Is socialist taste and culture superior to what develops under a liberal order?[13] To paraphrase Samuel Johnson, the socialist's prediction is a triumph of hope over experience.

The new man whom the socialist wants to create is not only cooperative and cultured but also emancipated. The young Marx wrote in 1844:

> The emancipation of society from private property, etc., from servitude, is expressed in its political form as the emancipation of workers, not as though it is only a question of their emancipation but because in their emancipation is continued universal human emancipation [p. 299]. . . The position of communism . . . is for the next stage of historical development, the necessary actual phase of man's emancipation and rehabilitation [p. 314].

In the nineteenth century, socialists were on the side of those who fought for their civil rights, who were discriminated against and suppressed by the state. Socialists championed the emancipation of workers, women, and minorities and helped liberate them from unjustified legal restrictions. They even hoped that the state would ultimately fade away. This emancipatory drive has largely disappeared and turned into its opposite. Today, socialists are on the side of the state. They do not hesitate to restrict citizens' choices. They regard them as incapable of taking care of themselves. They are notorious for ignoring the interests of minorities. Examples are legion:

- Socialists favor a strong expansion of government expenditure. As a result, the relation of government expenditure to gross national product (GNP) is today a multiple of what it was a few decades ago. What this has meant for taxpayers and government debt need not be spelled out.
- Socialists favor government monopolies. If government provides some service (e.g., mail delivery, telephone service, public broadcasting and television, domestic air transportation, social insurance, labor exchanges, etc.), private concerns may not compete to provide that service. In the case of natural monopolies, socialists are so opposed to privatization (by franchise) that they do not even want to find out whether private suppliers would be cheaper.
- Socialists prescribe the extent of social insurance coverage. They do not permit the citizen to choose more or less coinsurance.
- Socialists restrict choice in public education by prescribing the school to be attended. They deny an adequate education to the minority consisting of exceptional talents.
- Socialists impose minimum wages, rent controls, notice conditions, and other "protective" regulations that favor the majority of the "haves" at the expense of the minority of "have-nots," the employed at the expense of the unemployed, attractive tenants at the expense of families with small children and other "handicaps," and so on.
- Socialists hinder the emancipation of women by enacting motherhood laws, shop acts, and high marginal tax rates for double-income earners.
- To please the unions, socialists not only limit the opening hours of shops but also the working time of all workers. They restrict the choice of the individual worker by declaring bargains between unions and employers to be mandatory and by imposing codetermination.
- Socialist demand management treats the citizen as incapable of forming rational expectations. It rests on the assumption that, with regard to their own market decisions, most people can be fooled most of the time.
- Individual ignorance is rational where collective decisions have to be taken by many voters. By substituting collective decisions for individual decisions, socialism weakens the citizen's incentive to collect information or generate knowledge about many circumstances

> that affect his life. Socialism lowers the quality of education and weakens the feeling of personal responsibility.

Emancipation means more self-fulfillment as a result of greater and more equal liberty for all. It is inconsistent with an increasing degree of collective coercion. The tragedy of the socialist is that he does not seem to see this inconsistency. Not only does he use means that are ineffective or inefficient for his purpose, but his means are even incompatible with one of his most important aims. Socialism has become an obstacle to emancipation. This is probably its greatest contradiction.

Most classical liberals doubt that the new man can be created, let alone by socialist means. As long as the new man does not prevail, they prefer an incentive system that, like the market, favors emancipation and operates efficiently regardless of whether people are selfish or altruistic. To abolish the market before the new man has been created seems to them to put the car before the horse. The socialist may object, saying that perhaps coercive collective control is a necessary condition for the creation of the new man.

Is there any empirical test to decide this issue? The classical liberal can make an offer that the socialist cannot easily refuse. Let all socialists of the world unite. Let them set up any system of coercive collective control on which they can voluntarily and unanimously agree. But do not force those who have not agreed. Do not mistake power or majorities for consensus. Do not impede exit. Let socialism freely compete with the liberal order.

To reject this test would be to admit that socialism is a religion.

EPILOGUE: THE PSYCHOLOGICAL FOUNDATIONS OF SOCIALISM

The foundations of socialism are not primarily philosophical or economic. They are psychological. What makes socialism emotionally attractive?

1. Socialism recognizes and criticizes the imperfections of this world.
2. Socialism promises to overcome these imperfections.

3. Socialism recommends the simplest and most direct approach to attack these problems: no detour via the price mechanism--the visible hand of government instead of the invisible hand of the market.

4. Socialism does not elaborate in tedious and vulnerable detail how the socialist alternative is to work.

5. Socialism ignores or denies trade-offs: while the classical liberal freely admits that the market generates economic inequality, the socialist tends to deny that his recipe is a threat to freedom and prosperity.

6. Socialism concentrates on the short term at the expense of the long term.[14]

7. Socialism appeals to atavistic instincts[15]: the hunter's habit of sharing an ownerless prey, the dominant role of the tribal chief, or the search for security in the group.

8. Socialism appeals to religious feelings: solidarity with the poor and punishment of the wicked (rich); the omniscient and benevolent dictator (government) modeled after the image of the omniscient and benevolent creator; the prophecy of paradise (even on earth).

Socialism is extremely popular with low-income earners, intellectuals, government officials, and the young. It is easy to show that each of these groups is likely to benefit from socialist redistribution and the growth of government, at least, relative to the other groups.

Moreover, in Schumpeter's words, "Whether a free lance or a party executive or a civil servant, the individual socialist looks upon the advent of socialism, naively but naturally, as synonymous with his advent to power. Socialization means to him that 'we' are going to take over" (1943/1966, p. 205). If it were not so, the intellectuals in particular might have second thoughts, for they must know that collective provision of uniform, standardized products is not likely to satisfy their minority tastes.[16] The young meet the conditions for socialist enthusiasm to the highest degree:

1. They are at a stage of life where ends ("the meaning of life") rather than means have to be defined. Socialism, like religion, offers

ends. Classical liberalism leaves them open, or, rather, to the individual. The question is confined to the means.

2. The young are interested in goals that will mean change. They do not want to consider themselves the lucky heirs of a perfect society; they want to make their own contribution. They are looking for a missionary task and an ideology that promises to overcome the imperfections of this world. They want to strengthen their moral position vis-à-vis the older generation. They are aggressive rather than defensive.

3. The young are less used to the discipline of patient rational argument. They are more likely to follow their natural instincts and spontaneous emotions.

4. The life of the young has been dominated by the experience of collective organizations: the family and the school. Their notions of morality and especially of justice have been molded by this experience.

5. The young have less experience in life and less knowledge of human nature. They know little about means, efficiency, and trade-offs in the economy and in public-policy matters.

6. The young are have-nots. They have nothing to defend. They do not know what it means to pay taxes. They have enjoyed a free education and many other government subsidies.

7. For the young, the future is wide open. They do not feel squeezed into some bourgeois pigeonhole. They are not yet highly specialized and have not found their place in society. Why should it be so improbable that, when their time has come, they will run the government, or at least be assistants to a benevolent dictator?

The proportion of young people is diminishing in most industrialized countries. The average age of the population is rising. But at the same time, classical liberalism is gradually losing one of its allies: religion. Classical liberalism cannot be defended unless it is complemented by some vision of human ends. But classical liberalism cannot be more than a theory about means. Therefore, classical liberalism is not enough. The individual liberal must also be able to propose respectable ends and show that he takes the ends of the socialist seriously.

In the contest over means, the ultimate test is success. To be recognized by a majority of voters, the success must be outstanding. Classical liberalism must produce results that are substantially different from the results of socialism. But to produce substantially different results, the adherents of classical liberalism would have to pursue substantially different policies.

NOTES

1. Christian religion is more at ease with a social theory that, like liberalism, is limited to the instrumental sphere and requires a spiritual complement that confines itself to the choice among goals. As the nineteenth century has shown, the "division of labor" between Christian religion and liberal social theory can be fairly harmonious and to mutual advantage. A division of labor between the ends-specialists and the means-specialists facilitates the integration of minorities, for it permits them to accept the means but not the ends, or vice versa. The integration of minorities facilitates social peace and the advancement of knowledge on which economic progress rests. Moreover, only a religion that is vague about ideal social order can prevail in very different circumstances over time and space.

2. See the econometric study by Paqué (1982).

3. Consider for example the following quotation from Adam Smith's Wealth of Nations (1776/1976): Man "is at all times surrounded by unknown enemies from whose injustice he can be protected only by the powerful arm of the civil magistrate" (Smith 1976, p. 232). "Distributive justice consists in proper beneficence, in the becoming use of what is our own, and in applying it to those purposes, either of charity or generosity, to which it is most suitable" (p. 269f.). "Society may subsist, though not in the most comfortable state, without beneficence; but the prevalence of injustice must utterly destroy it. . . . Society . . . cannot subsist among those who are at all times ready to hurt and injure one another" (p. 86).

4. "We start always from here, not from an original position" (Buchanan 1972, p. 127).

5. Buchanan (1976) tries to save Rawls's difference principle by reinterpreting it as a condition for social peace. Quite apart from its short-run nature, this argument generates a different conclusion: it does not justify redistribution in favor of the "least advantaged" (Rawls) but in favor of the most powerful pressure groups of potential criminals and revolutionaries.

6. Of course, the aim of socialization need not be redistribution. The political aim may be to gain the support of the labor unions or to weaken the financial basis of the political adversary and to identify a

personal enemy (the entrepreneur), who must be liquidated (expropriated). The economic aim may be to establish central planning or industrial democracy (to be discussed later in this chapter.)

7. Okun (1977) has suggested that this was not only inevitable as a matter of fact but also correct as a normative inference: "If . . . a preference for equality operates in the social and political realm, it must apply to the economic realm as well. . . . Egalitarian preferences do not--logically cannot--stop abruptly at the boundary line between economic and non-economic institutions. The case for economic egalitarianism can be inferred from the equality of sociopolitical rights" (p. 16).

The problem about arguments by analogy is that they are never of a purely logical nature; they have to substantiate empirically that the cases to be compared satisfy the relevant (here, ethical) criterion. Is it a logical inconsistency to advocate, for example, military conscription for men but not for women?

8. "The realm of freedom only begins, in fact, where that labor which is determined by need and external purposes ceases" (Marx, 1893/1956, p. 259).

9. Present forms of codetermination are not democratic because they violate the principle of one-man, one-vote. Since they allot fixed quotas of votes to the owners of equity capital (the capitalists) and to the owners of human capital (the workers), they are corporativist.

10. For explanations of why it has not prevailed see, for example, Pejovich 1978.

11. See most notably Knight 1982, p. 592.

12. As a consequence, the legitimation of socialism is independent of the views of the people and of actual events. This, too, makes socialism a religion.

13. "The wealth of the 'bourgeois' civilization is not spent on base enjoyments alone. . . . There never has been a time when art was closer to the heart of large circles of people. It is no phenomenon peculiar to our time that coarse and vulgar amusements appeal more to the great mass of the people than nobler forms of enjoyment. It was always so. And we may take it that in the socialist community good taste will not always predominate" (Mises 1922/1981, p. 395).

14. Capital accumulations is hampered by, for example, high taxes on "unearned" income and wealth, government borrowing, pay-as-you-go social security programs, inflation, socialist wage policies, and codetermination. Other symptoms of a high-time preference are the preoccupation with short-term Keynesian demand management rather than long-term supply side economics, the prevalence of antisaving theories, pacifist and other types of redistribution, and the increasing leniency of criminal punishment in the face of a rising crime rate, which itself represents a destruction of public security capital (Buchanan 1975, pp. 135, 107ff.)

15. This has been stressed, in particular, by Hayek (e.g., 1976, p. 149f.).

16. As Buchanan (1970) and others have emphasized, socialists like to assume similarity of tastes.

REFERENCES

Buchanan, James M. 1970. Notes for an economic theory of socialism. Public Choice 8: 29-44.

------. 1972. Rawls on justice as fairness. Public Choice (Fall): 123-29.

------. 1975. The limits of liberty: Between anarchy and leviathan. Chicago.

------. 1976. A Hobbesian interpretation of the Rawlsian difference principle. Kyklos 29: 5-25.

Gray, John. 1984. "The road to serfdom: Forty years on. Pp. 27-24 in Hayek's serfdom revisited. London: The Institute of Economic Affairs.

Hayek, Friedrich von. 1944. The road to serfdom. Chicago.

------. 1976. Law, legislation, and liberty. Vol. 2, The mirage of social justice. London and Henley.

Hume, David. 1752/1965. An enquiry concerning the principles of morals. Pp. 23-156 in Hume's ethical writings, ed. A. MacIntyre. New York.

Knight, Frank H. 1923. The ethics of competition. Quarterly Journal of Economics 37: 578-624.

Marx, Karl. 1844/1967. Economic and philosophic manuscripts. Pp. 283-337 in Writings of the young Marx on philosophy and society, ed. Lloyd D. Easton and Kurt H. Guddat. Garden City, N.Y.

------. 1893/1956. Capital Vol. 3, quoted from Karl Marx, Selected writings in sociology and social philosophy. ed. T. B. Bottomore and M. Rubel. Harmondsworth: Ringwood.

Mises, Ludwig von. 1922/1981. Socialism. Indianapolis.

Nove, Alec. 1983. The economics of feasible socialism. London, Boston and Sydney.

Okun, Arthur M. 1977. Further thoughts on equality and efficiency. Pp. 13-34 in Income redistribution, ed. Colin D. Campbell. Washington, D.C.

Paqué, Karl-Heinz 1982. Do public transfers "crowd out" private charitable giving? Some econometric evidence for the Federal Republic of Germany. *Kiel Working Papers*, No. 152. Kiel: Institute of World Economics.

Pejovich, Svetozar. 1978. Codetermination: A new perspective for the West. Pp. 3-21 in *The codetermination movement in the West*, ed. S. Pejovich. Lexington, Mass.

Rawls, John. 1972. *A theory of justice*. London, Oxford, and New York.

Schumpeter, Joseph A. 1943/1966. *Capitalism, socialism and democracy*. London.

Smith, Adam. 1776/1976. *The wealth of nations*, ed. Edwin Cannan. Chicago.

Tullock, Gordon. 1971. The cost of transfers. *Kyklos* 24: 629-43.

Chapter 6

HAYEK ON LIBERTY AND THE RULE OF LAW: THE ROAD TO SERFDOM REVISITED

By

Dieter Schmidtchen*

The Road to Serfdom was written more than forty years ago, under the shadow of impending catastrophe in Western Europe. According to Hayek it was "designed almost exclusively for English readers," particularly "as a warning to the socialist intelligentsia of England" (Hayek 1967, pp. 216-17). Since "advanced" views on social matters were to be found in all parties, among friends and colleagues too, Hayek dedicated it "To the Socialists in all Parties." During those days the belief was widespread that national socialism represented a specific German capitalist reaction against socialist exaggerations of the Weimar republic. In contrast to that, Hayek took the position that national socialism was nothing but the further development and manifestation of socialism (collectivism) as fascism and communism. Because of the fairly obvious socialist tendencies in English public opinion, Hayek feared that ". . . it is Germany whose fate we are in some danger of repeating" (Hayek 1944, p. 2). It was this

*D. Schmidtchen is professor of economics at the University of the Saarland.

that Hayek tried to counteract; therefore he wrote Road to Serfdom, admittedly a political book (Hayek 1944, p. xvii). Since Road to Serfdom is a product of a specific historical setting we may well ask ourselves whether Road to Serfdom has any relevance today. Does it contain issues and findings of lasting value, things which would make it a classic? Or is it a milestone afflicted with the inevitable characteristics of milestones, meaning is it forever doomed to remain in one place?

One way open to answer these questions would be to find out whether there are still "Socialists in all Parties" around the world. To expound on this would be beyond the scope of this work, however. Furthermore, this procedure could run the risk of begging the question, for the content of the book would have to be accepted as unquestioned. But there are problems, a fact confirmed by Hayek himself several times. So I would like to confine myself in the first part to showing how Hayek himself assesses his early and most famous book.[1] This self-appraisal does not seem to me to have always been sufficiently taken into account in assessments of Road to Serfdom.[2] This is followed by an analysis of Hayek's concept of freedom, that is, in light of his most recent publications. The discussion is concluded by the question of whether the concept of the Rule of Law, which in a sense is the center of gravity in Road to Serfdom,[3] is actually suitable as the institutional safeguard of a regime of individual freedom against the perils of socialism.

ROAD TO SERFDOM: THE FIRST ATTEMPT IN A NEW DIRECTION

If Road to Serfdom is to be adequately assessed, it must not be forgotten that it was simply the starting point of work in a new field (Hayek 19844, p. xix). On the one hand it contains all the ideas around which Hayek's thoughts revolved during a forty-year period.[4] But it is only the "first sketch" with its inevitable shortcomings, a judgment which is confirmed by Hayek himself: "I could not free myself from the feeling . . . that much that I had said in my first sketch needed clarification and elaboration. When I wrote the book I had by no means sufficiently freed myself from all the prejudices and superstitions dominating general opinion, and even less had I learned to avoid all the prevalent confusions of terms and concepts of which I have since become very conscious."[5]

Machlup is correct when he states that "The Road to Serfdom did not satisfy Hayek's scholarly standards."[6] This especially applies to the analysis of the consequences of a socialist policy as well as the nature of an order of freedom and the requirements to be met by an appropriately run market order. Wrote Hayek, "It was the latter problem that the further work I have since done in the field was mainly devoted. The first result of these efforts of explaining the nature of an order of freedom was a substantial book called The Constitution of Liberty."[7]

This also did not satisfy Hayek: "After its publication, I found there were certain gaps in the traditional expositions that became the subject of the three-volume discussion of constitutional problems, Law, Legislation, and Liberty."[8]

The significance of Road to Serfdom is not diminished by stating that it has imperfections.[9] It poses the correct central questions with respect to the future of man under freedom. It cannot be said that these questions are answered incorrectly. But the theoretical and sociophilosophical foundation is only hinted at. In particular, a systematic theory of freedom is lacking, a theory we have come to know from Hayek's later work, formulated in a comprehensive and sophisticated manner and integrating findings from such distinct fields as economics, law, philosophy, anthropology, evolutionary theory, systems theory, and epistemology. However, one need not be a prophet to realize that the message Hayek was trying to get across would not have been conveyed in such an extensive and clear way had he chosen the manner of representation which is common in his later writings. And one can only agree with Hayek when he says, "I could never again produce as short a book covering as much of the field; and it seems to me whatever other merits it may have, its relative brevity is its greatest" (Hayek 1967, p. 223).

Yet there is another problem which is commonly overlooked. Road to Serfdom was mainly directed against "hot socialism"--the "organized movement towards a deliberate organization of the economic life by the state as the chief owner of the means of production."[10] And it was specifically asserted "that fascism and communism are merely variants of the same totalitarianism which central control of all economic activity tends to produce. . . ."[11] This is stated in his chapter 7, "Economic Control and Totalitarianism," in an emphatic and convincing manner, unequaled in its terseness. It is headed by the motto "The control of the production of wealth is the control of human life itself" (Hilaire Belloc). Indeed, it is a mistake to assume that central planning affects only our economic interests, but does not seriously adversely affect the more basic values of life: "Whoever controls all economic activity controls the means for all our ends and must therefore decide which are to be satisfied and which not. This is really the crux of the matter. Economic control is not merely control of a sector of human life which can be separated from the rest; it is the control of the means for all our ends" (Hayek 1944, pp. 91-92).

But who supports the ideas of "hot socialism" in the Western world today? Hayek himself realizes that "hot socialism" is dead (Hayek 1967, p. 220), having been replaced by a less dogmatic, less doctrinaire, and less systematic "cold socialism."[12] He asks whether "an argument applicable solely against those clear-cut conceptions of social reform which characterized the socialist movements of the past might today well appear as tilting against windmills" (Hayek 1967, p. 220).

Some are sure to agree with the latter. But this only indicates that they have not understood the true argument of the book and the real purpose Hayek was pursuing when he wrote it. To be sure, Road to Serfdom is concerned with painting a picture of hell. For example, one needs only to consider chapter 11, "The End of Truth," which most certainly influenced Orwell when writing his novel 1984. Admittedly in many places only implications are discovered, those of the "application of the engineering technique to a whole nation" (Hayek 1944, p. 125). But the title as well as unbiased reading make it overwhelmingly clear: the central theme is the road to serfdom. The disturbing message itself was that one could unwittingly end up in hell as the result of actions which were not intended for this purpose.

The idea of consequences--positive as well as negative--that are the result of human actions but not of human design is a notion frequently encountered in Hayek's economic and sociophilosophical writings. Road to

Serfdom can be viewed as his first systematic attempt to show how a series of thoughtless and often well-meant actions can undermine the foundations of a free social order.[13] Using an example, he demonstrates what happens if people believe that freedom and hot socialism can be combined.[14] A belief which in Hayek's opinion is substantially nurtured by the fact that the difference between the meaning of "new" or "material" freedom[15] and freedom in a "formal" sense ("negative" concept of freedom) is not sufficiently borne in mind. Who would want to deny that today many still espouse the idea of material freedom (power, wealth) being compatible with formal freedom (negative freedom)? They surely do not want hot socialism, and their belief that (cold) socialism will result in "real" freedom may be genuine. "But this would only heighten the tragedy if it should prove that what was promised to us as the Road to Freedom was in fact the High Road to Servitude."[16] This warning is as urgent today as it was when it was first written down.

No one can seriously claim that we in the Western world have fallen afoul of totalitarianism. Thus, it is often reasoned that the claims made in Road to Serfdom have proven wrong. But Road to Serfdom does not claim for example that England really has to take the road to serfdom. Road to Serfdom contains not prophecies but conclusions based on a theoretical framework. Thus it was analyzed, for example, what happens to freedom when the Rule of Law is dispensed with. It was not postulated that a totalitarian system would inevitably be established in England, but that this danger exists if certain liberal principles, that is, the Rule of Law, are not heeded. This was illustrated by experiences in countries which had a head start of thirty or forty years by disregarding liberal principles. Therefore in Hayek's opinion, the book actually contained a warning. Thus, he writes: "It has frequently been alleged that I have contended that any movement in the direction of socialism is bound to lead to totalitarianism. Even though this danger exists, this is not what the book says. What it contains is a warning that unless we mend the principles of our policy, some very unpleasant consequences will follow which most of those who advocate these policies do not want."[17]

Hayek does not do his critics complete justice. The book actually treats both problem areas. The impression could very well be created that any movement in the direction of socialism gives birth to a totalitarian system; in any case, Hayek does not mention any limiting conditions. Also, the observance of the "principles of our policy" does not constitute such a condition, for this above all things is supposed to prevent movement in the direction of socialism. On the whole it can be said that Road to Serfdom does not contain any unconditional prophecies, but rather conditional prognoses based on theories about the functioning of market economies and centrally administered economies.[18]

But what are the principles we should mend, if we want to prevent the unpleasant consequences Hayek warns of and preserve a regime of freedom? After Road to Serfdom was published, Hayek became aware of the fact that he could not get around a restatement of these principles.[19] He would need two attempts. Were they successful?

THE FIRST RESTATEMENT: THE CONSTITUTION OF LIBERTY

Hayek makes his first comprehensive restatement of the principles of a liberal order in The Constitution of Liberty. Personal freedom is defined there as "the state in which a man is not subject to coercion by the arbitrary will of another or others."[20] But when does coercion occur? "Coercion," Hayek continues, "occurs when one man's actions are made to serve another man's will, not for his own but for the other's purpose" (Hayek 1960, p. 133). Coercion does not imply the absence of choice. A person who is being coerced still chooses. But in a coercive situation one does not choose what one would like to do, but rather what the coercer wants.[21]

The concept of freedom Hayek developed in The Constitution of Liberty, however, cannot fulfill the function it was intended for. It leads to conceptual muddles:

1. Does coercion occur when person X under a regime of "hot socialism" receives a command from a central authority to perform activity A at place B at time C? What amount of choice does he have?

2. When someone is subjected to physical force, so that he can no longer act, then, according to Hayek, coercion does not occur. So he would have to be regarded as free according to Hayek's definition.[22]

3. One is free as long as no one manipulates his range of action to such an extent that an action (or sequence of actions) is chosen which is of any use to him. The problems are obvious: "Unqualified, this definition is useless, since under it the overwhelming preponderance of human interactions could be shown to be coercive" (Hamoway 1978, p. 288). The actual problem lies in distinguishing coercive manipulations from the conditions or terms under which others are willing to make a trade.

Hayek dealt with this problem and attempted to solve it as follows: "So long as the services of a particular person are not crucial to my existence or the preservation of what I most value, the conditions he exacts for rendering these services cannot properly be called 'coercion'" (Hayek 1960, p. 136). But how can someone else determine "what is crucial to my existence" or what "preserves what I most value"?[23] This can be done only in a purely subjective way.

4. A concept which requires such subjective criteria is hardly suitable as the basis of an objective Constitution of Liberty, for coercion disappears and freedom results by narrowing the set of things which someone feels to be crucial to his existence or values most. By altering one's order of preference one can transform a "coercive act" into a "noncoercive" one and vice versa.[24]

5. When the deprivation of person X of the things he values most can be called coercion and the abolishment of freedom, then freedom of person X demands that others act in a certain way. Thus, a concept of negative freedom can surreptitiously be transformed into a concept of positive freedom.[25] At any rate, the dividing line becomes fuzzy.

Summing up, we see that the concept of coercion plays a decisive role in the statements of The Constitution of Liberty. However, an attempt is made to define it without recourse to a theory of rights.[26] But all attempts to define freedom as an antipode to coercion result, as Hamoway states, ". . . in hopeless conceptual muddles without such a theory."[27] If that is correct then a Constitution of Liberty essentially has to contain statements concerning the specification and personal assignment of rights. The legal system would define what coercion is and is not.[28]

THE SECOND RESTATEMENT: LAW, LEGISLATION, AND LIBERTY

Hayek's second attempt to outline the fundamentals of a Constitution of Liberty steers clear of the conceptual muddle mentioned above. The trilogy Law, Legislation, and Liberty contains in volume I "Rules and Order," a concept of freedom which is rooted in law right from the beginning. The central chapter is entitled "Nomos: The Law of Liberty." It deals with the "inseparable trinity" of law, liberty, and property (Hayek 1973, p. 107).

The concept of "protected domain" is of fundamental importance here. By delineating protected domains, individual freedom, which is understood as "a state in which each can use his knowledge for his purpose" (Hayek 1973, pp. 55-56), and conflict-free behavior are to be reconciled with one another. This is to be accomplished via property, whose extent and personal assignment are to ensue from a system of rules of just conduct, which is why law, liberty, and property are an "inseparate trinity." Because of the abstract character of the passages in the volume "Rules and Order," however, it is not easy to reconstruct the relevant structure within this trinity. Based on the idea of the compossibility of rights, Hillel Steiner has now developed an analytic framework which is not only compatible with Hayek's line of reasoning but even makes a deeper understanding of the same possible in some respects.[29] Therefore, a brief statement of the basic idea of this structural theory of rights will be given.

A right denotes the set of actions which its possessor may perform. Further, it implies the duty of nonpossessors not to perform actions which may interfere with or prevent those actions. "Rightful actions--actions that are exercises of rights--are thus both permissible and inviolable" (Steiner 1977, p. 767). Actions which interfere with rightful actions or prevent their execution are themselves impermissible. A set of rights is now said to be "compossible" if "it is logically impossible for one individual's exercise of his rights within that set to constitute an interference with another individual's exercise of his rights within that same set."[30] "Compossibility of a set of rights" therefore prevents conflicts in actions from arising and thus assures the peaceful coexistence of man.[31] "Incompossibility of rights" implies logical contradictions and thus the possibility of conflicts of action. If nomos, the right of freedom, is characterized by the reconciliation of individual freedom with the avoidance of conflicts, then it necessarily must satisfy the criterion of "compossibility."

Now there arises the question of how the actions of two persons can be mutually obstructive. Each action consists of making use of objects, which also includes the body of the individual performing the action. By necessity, movement through space is also linked with this. Steiner calls the material and spatial components of an action its physical components. Interference of one individual's actions with another's can occur only when at least one of the physical components necessary for these actions is identical. "It follows that one individual's action cannot interfere with another's if and only if none of their respective physical components is identical" (Steiner 1977, p. 769). This is of logical necessity. It is satisfied when rights of exclusive use or possession (property rights) are assigned to each physical component by way of property rules.[32] Property rules make possible the formation of well-founded expectations as to which actions are permissible and inviolable. The fact that such expectations can take shape is central to Hayek's concept of the protected domain:

> (T)he only method yet discovered of defining a range of expectations which will be thus protected, and thereby reducing the mutual interference of people's actions with each other's intentions, is to demarcate for every individual a range of permitted actions by designating (or rather making recognizable by the application of rules to the concrete facts) ranges of objects over which only particular individuals are allowed to dispose and from the control of which all others are excluded. The range of actions in which each will be secured against the interference of others can be determined by rules equally applicable to all only if these rules make it possible to ascertain which particular objects each may command for his purposes. In other words, rules are required which make it possible at each moment to ascertain the boundary of the protected domain of each and thus to distinguish between the *meum* and the *tuum* (Hayek 1973, p. 107).

According to Hayek, not only is this the process on which all known civilization is founded, but property is also the only solution which man has developed to date for dealing with "the problem of reconciling individual freedom with the absence of conflict" (Hayek 1973, p. 107).

I now wish to make some comments concerning Hayek's concept of nomos, the right of liberty:

1. For Hayek (and also for Steiner), property governs the relations between individuals with regard to certain objects.[33] This is compatible with the modern property-rights approach, which defines property rights as "the *sanctioned behavioral relations* among men that arise from the existence of goods and pertain to their use."[34] Thus property rights define protected domains. This means it is compatible when different persons are entitled to the right of use of one and the same object, as long as this does not result in these persons being able to perform incompatible actions. Thus, the rules concerning the use of public roads determine who may use a certain piece of ground for parking or driving in a certain period of time. However, they do not grant the right of excluding others from use, when the piece of ground is not occupied.

2. Compossibility of a set of rights is necessary, but not a sufficient condition for a regime of freedom. Compossibility is also possible in hot socialism, if the commands concerning the use of objects have been formulated with sufficient accuracy (cf. Kelley 1984, p. 112). But the criterion essential for Hayek's notion of liberty--that individuals can use their knowledge for pursuing their own goals--is missing.[35]

3. If one does not possess any rights to physical components he cannot pursue his own goals. His protected domain is empty, and his condition cannot be designated as freedom. (Think of a slave.) Thus it is questionable whether Hayek's statement--that individual freedom does not depend on the amount of property at an individual's disposal--will hold. Of course, the question that arises at the same time is to what extent infection with the concept of positive freedom can be avoided.[36]

To avoid misunderstanding, two levels should be distinguished: on Level I the capability of individuals and organizations to possess rights is settled. Furthermore, it is specified what we must not do with physical components. By contrast, Level II refers to the actual distribution of titles to physical components. Along with this, Level II determines the wealth structure in the society and therefore the scope of actions open to individuals and organizations.[37] Now a question arises: to which level does the concept of protected domain belong? If it is related to Level I, an individual (or organization) is said to possess a protected domain if it is generally capable of possessing rights, even if it does not possess any title. Thus, it would have to be regarded as free. If the concept of the protected domain is related to Level II, however, only persons (or organizations) who actually possess titles to physical components could be regarded as free.[38] On the contrary, to a free man a slave is not capable of possessing any rights (since he is not allowed to possess any). He does not possess any protected domain, whether defined on Level I or Level II. Thus, a slave committing suicide invades the protected domain of his master (possessor). It is possible, however, for a man who is free with respect to Level I (i.e., who is capable of possessing rights) to find himself in a position similar to that of a slave because his protected domain (on Level II) is nearly empty.

4. Universal rules of conduct (Hayek also often speaks of rules of just conduct[39]) determine the "domains of freedom." They make it possible for each individual "to ascertain where he is free to act" (Hayek 1973, p. 107). A precise definition of what freedom means can now be offered, as follows: "The statement that 'X is free to do A' entails that none of the physical components of doing A is possessed by an agent other than X."[40] But this condition needs to be met only if there should be a domain of freedom. As a further condition, we must claim that individuals can use their knowledge for pursuing their own goals.

5. Just as law and property are products of civilization, so also is freedom. Freedom does not exist except in a regime of rights.

6. Rules of just conduct, manifested in law, contain merely abstract guidelines for the demarcation of protected domains. However, they do not prescribe what the structure of the protected domains of various individuals (and thus the actual distribution of property) is to look like.[41]

7. Protected domains can be altered in many ways:

- transmutation of physical components,
- transfer of rights by way of exchange,
- transfer of rights by way of a present,
- new establishment of rights (e.g., if formerly free resources become scarce),
- attenuation of rights.

The rules of just conduct govern these alterations. The respective specification and the assignment of property rights in a Great Society result in an endogenous manner, being derived from what has preceded. They are the result of human actions, but not the result of human design.[42] Hayek's theory of law and of freedom is thoroughly evolutionary. It differs sharply from constructivist theories, from those which are intended for assigning rights in accordance with the maximization of wealth (when transaction costs are larger than zero).[43]

8. Coercion or the effective threat thereof is an action which is harmful for the coerced. As harmful actions can first be meaningfully discussed on the basis of Hayek's definition of a protected domain,[44] the definition of coercion is now based on a theory of law. Coercion means a violation of the protected domain of another. Coercion is an offense, an unlawful act.[45] The inherent element of coercion is to be found in the provoked alteration of the action space, for every offense alters the actual or potential disposal of physical components by the damaged. Coercion in this broader sense appears in theft, robbery, or enslavement. As a consequence, an alteration of the actual conduct of the coerced may occur, but not necessarily. When Hayek speaks about arbitrary coercion, he thinks of coercion in a narrow sense. By the offense, someone is compelled to act in a certain way, to tolerate an action or to abstain from an action. In other words: The offense does not alter the action space only, but provokes a change in individual behavior.[46]

The crucial factor in Hayek's concept of freedom is of course the principle of demarcation of protected domains. If a vicious circle is to be avoided, this cannot be "freedom," for freedom exists only within a protected domain and is first created by virtue of a protected domain. The same applies to "coercion" if an unlawful encroachment is meant. If, however, an attempt is made to define "coercion" without embodying it in a theory of law, then the conceptual muddles mentioned by Hamoway emerge.

By taking resource to the results of just conduct, Hayek at least found a logically satisfactory solution for this problem. Yet this is accompanied by an interesting shift of emphasis. Freedom is now based on the principle of justice: "(T)he rules of just conduct are essentially negative in that they aim only at preventing injustice, and that they will be developed by the consistent application to the inherited body of law of the equally negative test of compatibility; and that by the persistent application of this test we can hope to approach justice without ever finally realizing it."[47]

The test of compatibility consists of a test of internal consistency, within the framework of a given system of rules that do not constitute primarily logical consistency: "The consistency or compatibility of the different rules which make up a system is not primarily logical consistency. Consistency in this connection means that the rules serve the same abstract order of actions and prevent conflict between persons obeying these rules in the kind of circumstances to which they have been adapted" (Hayek 1976, p. 24). The criterion thus is the necessity which ensures that a spontaneous order may be preserved and further developed. The obvious implication is that the recourse to the inherited body of law serves exactly this purpose.[48] The test of compatibility poses a series of questions which cannot be dealt with in detail here. I will return to it later after I have presented a treatment of the concept of the Rule of Law.

THE RULE OF LAW

Under Hayek's Constitution of Liberty, the individual is to be protected not only against coercion on the part of other individuals, but also against arbitrary coercion on the part of the government. Hayek has therefore had to divide government actions into two groups: those actions which are compatible with a free society and those which are invasive or coercive. The threat and possibly the performance of coercion are compatible, if this is necessary for the establishment and preservation of a rule or a system of rules of just conduct. The threat or performance of an action by the government is coercive or invasive when it is <u>arbitrary</u>, that is, when the means that individuals may employ in pursuing their goals have been altered in an unexpected manner. Expectations are defeated, protected domains are lifted.[49] To prevent the latter, actions on the part of the state have to be contingent on the Rule of Law, according to Hayek: "Nothing distinguishes more clearly conditions in a free country from those in a country under arbitrary government than the observance in the former of the great principles known as the Rule of Law."[50]

The Rule of Law is a metalegal principle (a "higher order rule") that describes the properties which laws must have. A "law in its ideal form" which suffices the Rule of Law "might be described as a 'once-and-for-all' command that is directed to unknown people and that is abstracted from all particular circumstances of time and place and refers only to such conditions as may occur anywhere and at any time."[51] It is Hayek's considered opinion that any abstract rule[52] which is prospective, that is, "certain"[53] and is applied in an objective manner, that is, generally, is noncoercive. The discussion which has arisen concerning the Rule of Law, however, has shown that this view is incorrect. The observance of the Rule of Law is not a sufficient condition for the protection of individual liberty against a violation on the part of the government.[54] There is furthermore some evidence that Hayek is inclined to attenuate some elements of the Rule of Law as a necessary condition. Of course it would be an exaggeration to conclude that the Rule of Law is neither a sufficient nor a necessary condition for a regime of freedom.[55]

First of all, the criterion of a general applicability with regard to all members of a society is to be considered. It is designed to preclude the discrimination of persons or groups of persons and in particular to solve the problem of how to govern (control) those who govern. Now there are cases where general applicability is not possible because of the nature of the matter (e.g., a "prohibition of rape"). Hayek develops two subsidiary criteria for cases in which laws govern the behavior of specific groups: no names may be indicated in the law and the discriminating rule must be supported by a majority both inside and outside the group concerned (double-majority principle) (Hayek 1960, p. 154). But there is a problem associated with this: by making a skillful selection of abstract characteristics it can be assured that de facto only one person or one group of persons is affected (cf. Hamoway 1978, p. 292). When privileges (e.g., tariffs, subsidies, barriers to entry) that are of interest to a minority are at stake, then the majority will not object to the individual expecting to be affected by them only in an imperceptibly negative manner (cf. Hamoway 1978, p. 292). That holds true especially when protest is dispensed with as the price for the preservation of one's own privileges. It could be assumed that the double-majority principle is more effective in discriminating against a group. This, for example, would include racial discrimination. But does not a prohibition of marriage between members of different races that is supported by a majority of both groups infringe on the freedom of those who accept the interbreeding of races?[56]

There has been controversy concerning the validity of the criterion of abstractness for preventing arbitrary measures as well. It has been argued that with some sufficiently specific, yet abstractly defined inventiveness, there could be readily found characterizations that were directed toward specific situations (Hamoway 1978, p. 294). In order to circumvent the most-favored-nations clause, the German customs tariff, for example, contains a special rate of tariff "for brown or dappled cows reared at a level of at least 300 meters above the sea and passing at least one month in every summer at a height of at least 800 meters."[57]

The criticism leveled at the criterion of abstractness is justified when the expression abstract is used in the narrowly defined sense in which it is used in logic. Hayek actually did suggest this interpretation in his early writings, where he speaks of "certain abstractly defined conditions" (Hayek 1955, p. 35) or of "types of situations defined in general terms" (Hayek 1944, p. 74). Since this time he has recognized this loophole and has thus invalidated the objection for the most part, "what is meant by the term abstract is expressed in a classical juridical formula that states that the rule must apply to an unknown number of future instances."[58]

In Hayek's opinion, the most important requirement established by the Rule of Law, however, is that rules have to be certain.[59] What is meant by the expression "certainty" becomes particularly evident in the definition of the Rule of Law used in Road to Serfdom: "Stripped of all technicalities, this means that government in all its actions is bound by rules fixed and announced beforehand--rules which make it possible to foresee with fair certainty how the authority will use its coercive powers in given circumstances and to plan one's individual affairs on the basis of this knowledge" (Hayek 1944, p. 72). Under these rules everyone knows when he has violated a law and when he is to expect coercion on the part of the government; thus, he can avoid being coerced.[60] Coercion does not have to be reckoned with until an infringement of the rules occurs.

Although the criterion of certainty seems plausible at first sight, it proves to be friable on closer inspection. Does the general prohibition on producing alcohol, for example, not constitute coercion? What about the general prohibition on using one's car, without seatbelts being worn? Or a law prohibiting the wearing of green suits?[61] Hayek apparently sees the greatest threat to freedom in discriminating behavior on the part of the government. But are discriminating measures really more hateful than general prohibitions?

In his detailed discussion of The Constitution of Liberty Robbins pointed out that many of the prohibitions in communism are certain and generally applicable and that Hayek's criteria accordingly sufficed (Robbins 1963, p. 195). Was Solzhenitsyn free? He could have avoided government coercion by not writing any books.[62]

By now it should have become obvious: without additional restrictions (with regard to content) that go beyond prescribing formal characteristics of rules, generally applicable and certain law can become the instrument of a regime of arbitrariness (cf. Hamoway 1976, p. 296; Barry 1979, p. 102). This had already been recognized by Robbins, when he asked: "Cannot law in this sense be oppressive and restrictive?[63] Must we not distinguish between a liberal rule of law and others?" (Robbins 1963, p. 94).

As a matter of fact we must; the Hayek of the trilogy Law, Legislation, and Liberty did this, for he developed a material criterion here in connection with a substantial alteration of his theory of law,[64] which must be satisfied by the "rules of just conduct." This is the "test of compatibility" with the "inherited body of law."

Obviously, the formal criteria defined by the Rule of Law are not sufficient for the establishment and preservation of a free society.[65] Are they necessary? This can be answered affirmatively. But, nevertheless, it seems appropriate to point out a shift in Hayek's position.

In Law, Legislation, and Liberty Hayek attempts to show that one can also safely live in a common-law system in which laws are not fully formulated. Nomos: the law of liberty is a judge-made law. But is it not a property of judge-made law to be less certain than statutory law, or, to put it more carefully: Is it false to suppose that by judge-made law, rules satisfying the criterion of certainty may take longer to evolve?

In chapter 5 of "Rules and Order," which is central in many respects, Hayek shows that a judge does not derive decisions from prescribed principles like a subsumption machine, but first discovers and develops the principles which serve as guides in decision-making.[66] Many rules guiding our actions are not even expressed in words; in Hayek's opinion, a part of them cannot be expressed in words at all. Lucas expresses Hayek's intention precisely when he writes: "What we need is not that the rules should have been antecedently specified, but that the decisions of authority shall be reasonable, so that we can form a reasonable expectation of what they will be" (Lucas 1979, p. 161).

THE TEST OF COMPATIBILITY WITH THE INHERITED BODY OF LAW

Whoever wishes to avoid the road to serfdom must know what the road to freedom looks like. Hayek proffers a guide, albeit a very abstract one, when he suggests that all demarcations of protected domains be subjected to a test of compatibility with the inherited body of law. How far does this suggestion go?

If it is followed, then the probability of protected domains being arbitrarily demarcated is lessened, that is, in such a way that (legitimate) expectations, which may be entertained on the basis of society's accepted rules, are disappointed.

But does every inherited legal system guarantee a demarcation of boundaries that will promote freedom? If it consists of a (consistent) system of end-independent rules, the answer is affirmative. Obviously, then, it serves the preservation of a spontaneous order, which can only arise under a regime of individual freedom.

Whoever demarcates protected domains by defining or redefining the rules of just conduct merely guarantees "the conditions that a going mechanism require[s] for its proper functioning" (Hayek 1976, p. 128). The judge, and the legislator as well, become an "organ of that order," servants "endeavoring to maintain and improve the functioning of an "existing order."[67] All their decisions and measures must be oriented toward the "rationale of the existing order" (expressed in the inherited body of law). This is the principle of system conformity of measures, going back to W. Röpke.[68] Economic policy must be in accordance with it if it is to remain on the road to freedom.

To give an example, suppose a hitherto free resource, say, environmental resources, is going to become scarce. Then rivalry among users occurs, which must be managed. There are two ways:

1. A government agency obtains the property rights and plans the utilization of the scarce resource (central planning).
2. The allocation of the resource is entrusted to markets according to the "willingness-to-pay" principle.

Certainly, both may be in accordance with the criterion of compossibility. But what about system conformity? Suppose an analysis of the inherited body of law reveals that nearly all problems of scarcity are decided according to the "willingness-to-pay" principle. Then we can say that a policy creating the bases for the development of markets is "system conformity." With that, however, only a definition of the term "system conformity" is given. But what is the justification of this principle? Here a theory becomes necessary. For example: The mixture of different mechanisms of allocation may be in accordance with the principle of compossibility but could lead to waste of scarce resources because of relatively higher transaction costs. In any case, two questions must be distinguished: What is the meaning of the term "system conformity"?

(question of definition). Why should we propagate the principle of system conformity? (question of efficiency).

The road to freedom is abandoned when economic policy is not oriented toward the rules of just conduct but resorts instead to interference. In contrast to rules of just conduct that serve the "reconciliation of the different purposes of many individuals," an interference (or intervention) promotes the achievement of particular results.[69] Intervention constitutes coercion and is not compatible with the principle of system conformity (cf. Hayek 1976, p. 129). They destroy a liberal spontaneous order. This is a realization Hayek had already come to in Road to Serfdom.

An inherited body of law which guarantees freedom must provide for private property. This is in Hayek's opinion a scientific finding.[70] But private property is compatible with variously large protected domains, all of which, however, lead to spontaneous orders. How can they be distinguished? Freedom can be excluded as a criterion, as freedom first arises with the demarcation of protected domains. And then justice remains. Hayek has actually chosen this path. By investigating the Constitution of Liberty, he simultaneously laid the foundations for a (liberal) Constitution of Justice.

Thus Hayek added a further milestone to that of the Road to Serfdom and consolidated during the years which followed that classic which can be called the Road to Freedom. Certainly it holds that the last word in that respect has not been spoken.

NOTES

1. Road to Serfdom has been an extremely successful book. It has been translated into sixteen languages, there have been three different English language editions, and in 1944, the year it was first published, it was reprinted seventeen times. That is quite unusual for a book that the author himself says is "not intended for popular consumption" (Hayek 1967, p. 218). To be sure, Road to Serfdom has been at the center of acute controversy right from the beginning: "It aroused heated discussions, was lavishly praised and roundly panned by the critics according to their own political stance" (Machlup 1976, p. 39). After having read Road to Serfdom while en route to Bretton Woods, Keynes wrote Hayek, "In my opinion it is a grand book. We all have the greatest reason to be grateful to you for saying so well what needs so much to be said. You will not expect me to accept quite all the economic dicta in it. But morally and

philosophically I find myself in agreement with virtually the whole of it; and not only in agreement with it, but in a deeply moved agreement" (Keynes 1980, p. 385). Henry Hazlitt compared it to Mills's essay On Liberty: "It restates for our time the issue between liberty and authority with the power and rigor of reasoning with which John Stuart Mill stated the issue for his own generation in his great essay On Liberty." In the opinion of others it was an "abysmal distortion of history" (New Republic). Furthermore Road to Serfdom has been reviewed by respected economists in leading journals. Two reviews actually appeared in the American Economic Review in 1945.

2. This also partly applies to the collection of essays Hayek's 'Serfdom' Revisited 1984.

3. In Hayek's opinion, ch. 6, "Planning and the Rule of Law," is a "central chapter" (Hayek 1967, p. 222).

4. "Indeed, though I have in the interval learned much that I did not know when I wrote it, I was now often surprised by how much I did already see at the beginning of my efforts that later work has confirmed; and though my later efforts will, I hope, be more rewarding to the expert, I am now prepared unhesitating to recommend this early book to the general reader who wants a simple and nontechnical introduction to what I believe is still one of the most ominous questions which we have to solve" (Hayek 1944, p. xx). It must be added that Hayek "admits" here to not having reread the book until 1976.

5. Hayek 1944, p. xix. See also Hayek 1979, p. 152, n. 19 for the story behind Road to Serfdom. In Hayek's recent writings the search for an unequivocal agreement with the statement by Tocqueville that "democracy extends the sphere of individual freedom" would actually be in vain (Hayek 1944, p. 25; see also p. 70).

6. Machlup 1976, p. 40. "It was no more than the sketch or outline of a theory that was to be developed later" (Barry 1979, p. 185).

7. Hayek 1960, p. xx. In Machlup's opinion (p. 401) this is "a volume which some of Hayek's admirers regard as his chef-d'oeuvre."

8. In addition to admiration, there really has been criticism; this has been directed toward Hayek's concept of freedom on the one hand, and to the suitability and soundness of the concept of the Rule of Law on the other (cf. particularly Hamoway 1978 and Rothbard 1980 for the former; for the latter, cf. those two, as well as Baumgarth 1978, Cunningham 1979, and Robbins 1963). Hayek 1984, p. 237; cf. also Hayek 1944, p. xx: "The awareness that such a restatement [The Constitution of Liberty, D. S.] left certain important questions unanswered. . . ."

9. "(T)here are numerous points I should like to explain at greater length or to state more cautiously or to fortify by more illustration and proof" (Hayek 1967, p. 222).

10. Hayek 1967, p. 220. Hot socialism is defined more precisely in Road to Serfdom as "a central direction of all economic activity according to a single plan, laying down how the resources of society should be 'consciously directed' to serve particular ends in a definite way" (p. 35). Put even more succinctly: "central direction and organization of all our activities according to some consciously constructed 'blueprint'" (p. 35).

11. Hayek 1967, p. 220. With his characteristic modesty he adds (p. 220): "Nor was my general thesis, as such, original when it was published."

12. This vivid expression is used by Hayek in his lecture "Socialism and Science" (Hayek 1978, p. 300). However, a precise definition is lacking. What is meant here is a concept which basically provides for markets, but which considers interventions on the part of the government for correcting the results thereof necessary. This also applies to what Hayek refers to as the welfare state. Mises' concept of interventionism (hampered market economy) may well signify this best. Cf. Mises 1966, pp. 717-19 and Mises 1981, pp. 483-88.

13. Hayek 1967, pp. 221-22: "Only if we understand why and how certain kinds of economic controls tend to paralyse the driving forces of a free society, and which kinds of measures are particularly dangerous in this respect, can we hope that social experimentation will not lead us into situations none of us want. It is a contribution to this task that this book is intended" [my emphasis].

14. The central chapter in this respect is ch. 2, "The Great Utopia," in connection with ch. 7, "Economic Control and Totalitarianism."

15. "(M)erely another name for power or wealth" (Hayek 1944, p. 26).

16. Hayek 1944, pp. 26-27. This of course leads to the question of whether cold socialism results in hot socialism (full-fledged socialism). Hayek believes this (cf. Hayek 1944, p. xx; Hayek 1967, p. 221; Hayek 1978, p. 238; be sure to read the postscript). But this process is not analyzed in Road to Serfdom (cf. Hayek 1944, p. xxi and the preface to the German reprint, Salzburg, June, 1971). Hayek is apparently thinking of a type of self-enforcement effect, as was developed by Mises (cf. Hayek 1978, p. 301).

17. Hayek 1944, p. xxi. Elsewhere Hayek expresses this more drastically: "If you do not mend your principles you will go to the devil" (Hayek 1973, p. 58). Hot socialism served only as the object of demonstration here.

18. Road to Serfdom actually contains nothing other than the application of "public-choice" and "institutional-choice" thinking, which is referred to in the German-speaking community as "Ordnungstheorie" and "Ordnungspolitik." Cf. Schmidtchen 1984. For "public-choice" thinking, cf. particularly ch. 5, "Planning and Democracy," which deals with the

impossibility of establishing a coherent plan for the entire economy in a democratic manner. The central institutional-choice problem lies in analyzing the incentive structure, and therewith the economic and other consequences which can be expected to result from the centralization of planning power in the government.

19. Where he had to start had already been determined by Road to Serfdom. Cf. ch. 6, where the Rule of Law is designated not only as "safeguard" but also as "the legal embodiment of freedom" (Hayek 1944, p. 82).

20. Hayek 1960, p. 11. Thus Hayek supports what is called negative freedom. Cf. Berlin 1958. Freedom never requires that others act in a certain way, only that they do not act in a certain way. My freedom only serves to limit another in his actions, but the content need not be positive (positive commands) as a result.

21. Hayek 1960, p. 133: "It is not that the coerced does not choose at all; if that were the case, we should not speak of his 'acting' . . . Coercion implies, however, that I still choose but that my mind is made someone else's tool, because the alternatives before me have been so manipulated that the conduct that the coercer wants me to choose becomes for me the least painful one. Although coerced, it is still I who decides which is the least evil under the circumstances."

22. "The farcical implication is that if I am trussed up without the ability to move, I am, in Hayek's use of the term, still free" (Hamoway 1978, p. 288).

23. By referring to an example used by Hayek in this context, Hamoway (1978, p. 288) convincingly demonstrates that the dress code imposed by a host represents coercion and thus an intrusion upon the freedom of a potential guest who "must" accept the invitation in order to preserve his "social standing" and who values "social standing" most highly. For situations of this type Hayek denies the existence of coercion (Hayek 1960, pp. 135-36). Hamoway had already dealt with Hayek's concept of freedom in a critical manner (Hamoway 1961, pp. 28-31). At the time, Hayek reiterated and more precisely defined his position (Hayek 1967, pp. 348-50). It seems to me that the argument proffered by Hamoway meets Hayek's conditions, so that the conclusion he draws from this example is valid. Cf. Hamoway 1978, n. 9.

24. Berlin had already fallen prey to this type of fallacy (Berlin 1958, pp. 7-26), something which he himself recognized later (Berlin 1969, p. xxxviii). Such a pitfall is always effective when someone bases his argument on a negative definition of freedom, in which it is up to the individual to do what he wants, desires, or chooses.

25. Cf. Hamoway 1978, p. 289. The greatest danger of a concept which equates freedom with power or wealth is that it provides the justification for unlimited government intervention. Cf. Hayek 1960, p. 20.

26. Cf. also Hamoway 1978, p. 287.

27. Hamoway 1978, p. 287. That also has consequences for a competition policy. An attempt is often made here to measure market freedom in terms of the number of alternatives available.

28. Suppose the most highly valued goal of person X was to be painted by the famous painter Y. The latter demands a price which X cannot pay. Then X would not be subject to coercion if painter Y has the unlimited right to decide whom he will paint and under what conditions.

29. Cf. Steiner 1977, pp. 767-75. This idea is not alien to Hayek, as his reference to the "'compatibility' or the 'reconcilability' of the actions to which the laws refers" indicates (Hayek 1973, p. 106). Here he also quotes (p. 106, n. 17) Kempski's structural theory of law: "We ask which structural necessities actions must conform to, if they are to be compatible with one another; in other words, we observe a world in which actions do not collide with one another" (Kempski 1961, p. 90 [translation by me]). Here Kempski _inter alia_ also asks about the maximal set of actions which are compatible with one another.

30. Steiner 1977, p. 769. Although Steiner only speaks here of "possible," he really means "compossible" (cf. pp. 767-68).

31. "Thus 'in its beginnings law (in the lawyer's sense) had for its end, and its sole end, to keep the peace'" (Hayek 1973, p. 98). This is precisely what is at the center of a concept of negative freedom. "The historically important concept of negative liberty is that of non-interference with rights . . ." (McCloskey 1965, p. 489; quoted in Hamoway 1978).

32. Steiner 1977, pp. 769-70: "A rule or set of rules assigning the possession or exclusive use of each particular physical object to particular individuals will, if universally adhered to, exclude the possibility of any individual's actions interfering with those of another in any respect. Such property rules would thus assign, to individuals, ranges of permissible and inviolable actions--rights--composed of their uses of their allotted bundles of physical objects."

33. Steiner speaks of possession and means "a _triadic_ relation obtaining between an agent, an object, and all other agents" (Steiner 1974/75, p. 48).

34. Furubotn and Pejovich 1974, p. 3. The implication is that there is an interpersonal rivalry concerning the use of scarce goods and resources. Since we have to do with a problem of "reciprocal nature" (R. H. Coase) the management of this rivalry by means of the specification and assignment of property rights necessarily leads to interpersonal opportunity costs. So the property rights structure determines what person is allowed to legitimately pass opportunity costs on to other persons.

35. Things become difficult in a system with community property in which each individual has a share in the collective decision concerning the use and allocation of resources, in accordance with certain rules. This would be a sort of "democratic socialism." In Road to Serfdom Hayek deals with such participation problems in connection with the question of whether parliament can draw up a central plan free of contradictions. He doubts this on the one hand for practical reasons and on the other because of the incompatibility of individual preference orders.

36. But the danger is not as great as it seems at first. To be sure, it is the question here namely of the justification of a given assignment of rights. If it has arisen on the basis of the rules of just conduct, various large amounts of property are justified. Redistributions of rights would then constitute unjustified interference. This could not be justified by an increase or even a maximization of freedom, as then there would be losers (not to mention the question of whether freedom is even a metrical concept).

37. An interesting difference is noteworthy here. The general capability of possessing rights is a public good, without rivalry in consumption and without necessity of exclusion. Rivalry and necessity of exclusion are matters related to Level II only, and here they are essentials.

38. We should be aware of the fact that here we are concerned with matters of definition only. What we want to call freedom is a question of nominal definition and not a question of elaborating on what "real" freedom or the "essence" of freedom looks like. Striving to arrive at "objective" definitions of freedom leads to the pitfalls of essentialism, as Popper showed many years ago (Popper 1957, pp. 26-34). To be sure, clear-cut (nominal) definitions are not useless. But the real theoretical question is: What economic effects can be expected from different institutional arrangements on Levels I and II? Hayek has dealt with this question extensively. One is right to presume that for Hayek, equality on Level I and the guarantee of the actual property rights structure (Level II) will produce more wealth than any alternative institutional arrangement that is known. It can easily be shown that the principle of equal capability to possess rights is a necessary condition for maximizing national product. I would like to emphasize that we can analyze such questions without any recourse to the expression "freedom."

39. Hayek uses this expression to describe "end-independent rules which serve the formation of a spontaneous order, in contrast to the end-dependent rules of organization" (Hayek 1976, p. 31). They are multipurpose instruments because they make possible a peaceful collaboration of individuals who are pursuing completely divergent goals (pp. 3-4). This is precisely the typical characteristic of a Great Society. A division of labor cannot be made here on the basis of commonly pursued goals, as it can in a tribe, but rather only on the basis of end-independent rules that establish which means may be implemented for reaching a goal.

40. Steiner 1974/75, p. 48. "To be free to do A . . . entails that all of the physical components of doing A are (simultaneously) unoccupied and/or undisposed of by another" (Steiner 1974/75, p. 47).

41. "The classical formula that the aim of rules of just conduct is to assign to each his due (suum cuique tribuere) is often interpreted to mean that the law by itself assigns to particular individuals particular things. It does nothing of the kind, of course. It merely provides rules by which it is possible to ascertain from particular facts to whom particular things belong" (Hayek 1973, p. 108).

42. Chess is an informative parallel to this. There, the rules determine how to change protected domains and how they look at every stage of the game. The specification and personal assignment of "property rights" depend on the kind, number, and the spatial distribution of the chessmen. We should note that physical components in the sense of "material components" are not needed to play chess. Chessmen are only a bodily manifestation of bundles of rights. The interlocking of moves--the process of the game--is the result of human actions, but not the result of human design. The same holds for the state of the game in every moment.

43. Cf. Posner 1977. With zero transaction costs, the assignment of rights is "of no importance" anyway, as Coase has shown.

44. "It is only through thus defining the protected sphere of each that law determines what are those 'actions toward other' which it regulates, and that its general prohibition of actions 'harming others' is given a determinable meaning" (Hayek 1973, p. 108).

45. It may be difficult to identify coercion in a particular case, but that is not the point. The crucial factor is that coercion is to be viewed as an unlawful act and thus Hamoway's accusation of "conceptual muddles" is unfounded.

46. Possibly, Hayek, who studied jurisprudence, bears in mind the old section 240 German penal code which was valid until May 29, 1943, and circumscribed duress in the following manner: "1. Wer einen anderen widerrechtlich durch Gewalt oder Bedrohung mit einem Verbrechen oder Vergehen zu einer Handlung, Duldung oder Unterlassung nötigt, wird . . . bestraft. 2. Der Versuch ist strafbar." The national socialists altered it and added the following phrase: "Rechtswidrig ist die Tat, wenn die Anwendung der Gewalt oder die Zufügung des angedrohten Übels zu dem angestrebten Zweck dem gesunden Volksempfinden widerspricht." The implication of this was of course that duress could not be penalized, if it corresponded with the "sane feeling of the people" (gesundes Volksempfinden).

With that, the central critique Stigler made against Hayek's concept of freedom is without object. Stigler (1978) posed the question: " . . . can we distinguish coercion by other men from other limitations on our choice . . . ?" (p. 215). As a matter of fact we can, if we distinguish lawful (legitimate) and unlawful (illegitimate) limitations on our choice. The solution of the problems Stigler demonstrated with examples is self-evident. When Stigler asserts that "the distinction between wealth and liberty is not easily drawn, and in fact the task has not been undertaken in convincing explicitness" (pp. 215-16), he may be right with respect to the state of affairs in The Constitution of Liberty. But with Law, Legislation, and Liberty the problem is solved at least on the conceptual level.

47. Hayek 1973, p. 110. Cf. also Hayek 1979, p. 136, n. 4, where he quotes John Locke, who defines injustice as the invasion or violation of property.

48. "In our efforts to improve the principles of demarcation we cannot but build on an established system of rules which serves as the basis of the going order maintained by the institution of property" (Hayek 1973, p. 109).

49. This can happen by way of a redistribution of rights, by attenuation, and by the collectivization of formerly individual decision processes.

50. Hayek 1944, p. 72. "Under the Rule of Law the government is prevented from stultifying individual efforts by ad hoc action. Within the known rules of the game the individual is free to pursue his personal ends and desires, certain that the powers of government will not be used deliberately to frustrate his efforts" (p. 73).

51. Hayek 1960, pp. 149-50. This definition bundles the characteristics which Hayek deals with in ch. 6 of Road to Serfdom. For these characteristics of rules of just conduct ("law in its ideal form"), cf. also Hayek 1976, pp. 15-17, 35-38.

52. For this term cf. Hayek 1976, p. 35.

53. Hayek particularly emphasizes this point in Road to Serfdom, pp. 72, 83, 84.

54. In Hamoway's opinion (1978, p. 296), the Rule of Law guarantees a government such far-reaching power "that freedom as we commonly understand it rests on a foundation no more secure than governmental goodwill." Raz claims that even a despotic regime is compatible with the Rule of Law. Cf. Raz 1979, p. 4; also Rothbard 1980, p. 48.

55. See, however, Lucas 1979, pp. 160-61.

56. Cf. Hamoway 9178, p. 292. What about laws concerning "sexual assault"?

57. Quoted by Hayek 1960, p. 209, n. 19.

58. Hayek 1976, p. 35. The definition in the German customs tariff does not satisfy this condition. The same applies to a rule which only refers to persons "whose finger-prints show a particular pattern" (Hayek

1976, p. 35). Abstractness in the above-mentioned sense presupposes a minimum of constancy (permanence) of rules. This was already emphasized in Hayek 1944, p. 81. Cf. also Hayek 1976, pp. 29, 30.

59. "There is probably no single factor which has contributed more to the prosperity of the West than the relative certainty of the law which has prevailed here" (Hayek 1960, p. 208).

60. Provided that I know beforehand that I place myself in a particular position, I shall be coerced and provided that I can avoid putting myself in such a position, I need never be coerced" (Hayek 1960, p. 142). Cf. also Hayek 1944, p. 81.

61. Other examples are also offered by Rothbard 1980, p. 48. A solution might lie in additionally checking whether a general rule is necessary for reasons of the compossibility of the set of rights.

62. Coercion can also be avoided via arbitrary "ad hoc commands" that prescribe in a positive manner what is to be done. One need only obey to avoid being punished. In addition, I refer to Watkins's argument, which contains the conclusion that "all prohibitions contain less coercion than commands" cannot follow from the circumstance that "commands prescribe a certain course of action in a positive manner." Cf. Watkins 1961, p. 39. Of course Hayek saw the possibility of generally applicable and certain rules justifying "severe restrictions on liberty" (Hayek 1960, p. 154). But then he played down the importance of this circumstance by viewing religious reasons as the only cause. "But he goes on to minimize the difficulties" (Robbins 1963, p. 94).

63. This means: "Existence of known rules equally applicable to all."

64. Cf. also Lucas 1979, p. 160. Contrary to Hayek, in this respect not only is a supplement that fills gaps offered but also a substitution. This is due to the strong emphasis of justice as the basis of nomos and thesis.

65. Barry (1979, p. 102) is of the opinion that the legitimacy of laws is not dependent on form, but rather on whether they infringe on property rights. The first part of the sentence is correct, but the second part is of use only if it is imputed that liberal property rights are defined independently of laws, such as in the case of the rules of a game to which a referee must adhere. It is here that property rights are frequently first defined by laws (cf. Hayek's agenda of government). What does an invasion of property rights by a law mean?

66. For the advantages and peculiarities of the juridical process, cf. Hayek 1973, esp. pp. 100-101, 115-17.

67. Hayek 1973, p. 119. The judge is obligated "to [maintain] and [improve] a going order of action, and must take his standards from that

order" (Hayek 1973, p. 120). The entire section (pp. 118-22) is entitled "The Function of the Judge Is Confined to a Spontaneous Order."

68. The expression was originated by Röpke 1948, p. 259. Cf. Hayek 1976, p. 129, n. 21. It must be added that the principle of system (or order) conformity is at the center of the German "Ordnungspolitik." Cf. Schmidtchen 1984. Hayek's comprehensive agenda of government fits well here, when transaction costs are sufficiently high. It contains measures throughout that are designed to reduce transaction costs and thus increase the market's ability to function. Cf. Hayek 1944, p. 81; Hayek 1979, pp. 62-63. However, coercion for preventing free-rider behavior with regard to collective goods would have to be derived from the rules of just conduct. Isn't being allowed to play the role of a free rider part of the protected domain?

69. Hayek 1976, pp. 128-29. One essential property of a game under end-independent rules (spontaneous order) is the openness of its outcomes. Ex ante, the "true," "right" values of the economic variables (prices, outputs, allocation, size of the firms, market shares, etc.) are unknown in principle. It is the "purpose" of the game to find them out (discovery procedure). Whoever tries to fix the values exogenously either violates the rules of the game or commits a pretense of knowledge. (But what about prisoners' dilemmas?) O'Driscoll and Rizzo (1985, p. 141) paraphrase Robertson: "Market interventions generate islands of calculational chaos in a sea of markets." Every market intervention disappoints expectations that individuals and organizations could reasonably have because of their protected domains.

70. Whether private property is found depends on the tradition or opinion of a society. By tradition Hayek means "manifestations of rules governing both the actions and the perceptions of the people" (Hayek 1976, p. 12). The concept of "opinion" (cf. ibid., pp. 13-14) has been derived from this and means "the view about the desirability or undesirability of different forms of actions, or actions of certain kinds."

REFERENCES

Barry, N. P. 1979. Hayek's social and economic philosophy. London and Basingstoke.

Baumgarth, W. P. 1978. Hayek and political order: The Rule of Law. Journal of Libertarian Studies 2(1):11-28.

Berlin, I. 1958. Two concepts of liberty. Oxford.

------. 1969. Four essays on liberty. New York.

Cunningham, R. L., ed. 1979. Liberty and the Rule of Law. College Station and London.

Furubotn, E., and S. Pejovich. 1974. The economics of property rights. Cambridge, Mass.

Hamoway, R. 1978. "Law and the liberal society: F. A. Hayek's Constitution of Liberty. Journal of Libertarian Studies 2(1):287-97.

Hayek, F. A. 1944. The road to serfdom. 2nd rev. ed., with preface. The University of Chicago Press, 1976.

------. 1955. The political ideal of the Rule of Law. Cairo.

------. 1960. The Constitution of Liberty. London.

------. 1967. Studies in philosophy, politics and economics. London and Henley.

------. 1973. Law, legislation, and liberty. Vol. 1, Rules and order. University of Chicago Press.

------. 1976. Law, legislation, and liberty. Vol. 2, The mirage of social justice. University of Chicago Press.

------. 1978. New studies in philosophy, politics, economics and the history of ideas. London and Henley.

------. 1979. Law, legislation, and liberty. Vol. 3, The political order of a free people. University of Chicago Press.

------. 1984. Reflections on constitutional economics. Pp. 235-37 in R. B. McKenzie, ed., Constitutional economics. Lexington Books.

Hayek's 'serfdom' revisited. 1984. Essays by economists, philosophers and political scientists on The road to serfdom after 40 years. The Institute of Economic Affairs.

Kelley, D. 1984. Life, liberty, and property. Pp. 108-18 in E. Frankel Paul, J. Paul, F. D. Miller, eds., Human rights. Oxford: Basil Blackwell.

Kempski, J. v. 1961. Grundlagen zu einer Strukturtheorie des Rechts. In Abhandlungen der Geistes und Sozialwissenschaftlichen Klasse der Akademie der Wissenschaften und Literatur in Mainz, No. 2.

Keynes, J. M. 1980. Collected writings. Vol. XXVII, ed. D. Moggridge. Cambridge.

Lucas, J. R. 1979. Liberty, morality, and justice. See Cunningham 1979, pp. 146-66.

Machlup, F. 1967. Hayek's contribution to economics. Pp. 13-59 in F. Machlup, ed., Essays on Hayek. Hillsdale, Mich.

McCloskey, H. J. 1965. A critique of the ideals of liberty. Mind 74.

Mises, L. 1966. Human action. New Haven, Conn.: Yale University Press.

------. 1981. Socialism. Indianapolis, Ind.: Liberty Classics.

O'Driscoll, G., and M. Rizzo. 1985. The economics of time and ignorance. Oxford: Basil Blackwell.

Popper, K. R. 1957. The poverty of historicism. London.

Posner, R. A. 1977. Economic analysis of law. Boston, Mass.

Raz, J. 1979. The rule of law and its virtue. See Cunningham 1979, pp. 3-21.

Robbins, L. 1963. Politics and economics. London.

Röpke, W. 1948. Die Gesellschaftskrise der Gegenwart. 5th ed. Erlenbach-Zürich.

Rothbard, M. 1980. F. A. Hayek and the concept of coercion. ORDO 31:43-50.

Schmidtchen, D. 1984. German "Ordnungspolitik" as institutional choice. Pp. 54-70 in E. Furubotn and R. Richter, eds., The new institutional economics, a symposium. Zeitschrift für die gesamte Staatswissenschaft (ZgS)/Journal of Institutional and Theoretical Economics (JITE), 140.

Steiner, H. 1974/75. Individual liberty. Proceedings of the Aristotelian Society 75:33-50.

------. 1977. The structure of a set of compossible rights. Journal of Philosophy 74:767-75.

Stigler, J. 1978. Wealth, and possibly liberty. Journal of Legal Studies 7:213-17.

Watkins, J. W. N. 1961. Philosophy. In A. Seldon, ed., Agenda for a free society: Essays on Hayek's "The constitution of liberty." London: IEA.

PART THREE

SOCIALISM: ECONOMIC ISSUES

Chapter 7

INFORMATION, MOTIVATION, AND THE PROBLEM OF RATIONAL ECONOMIC CALCULATION IN SOCIALISM

By

Peter Bernholz*

INTRODUCTION

The fundamental problem of rational calculation in a socialist economy was stated as early as 1874 by the German economist Albert Schäffle in his _The Quintessence of Socialism_:

> Without the introduction of use value into social accounting, i.e., without analogous imitation of all value-determining processes of the present market, it would be unthinkable that some supreme board of the integrated production system could keep the demand for labor and goods quantitatively and in kind in agreement with the stocks of labor and goods; i.e., could maintain the economic equilibrium of labor and use which is nowadays brought about from day to day . . . under the influence of market prices responding also to changing use values (demands).
>
> It thus realized that three things depend on the determination of a theory of a social exchange value: (1) the possibility to steer and to keep in equilibrium such a vast body of labor, production, and need; (2) the granting of the necessary individual freedom to work and to consume; finally (3) the

*P. Bernholz is professor of economics at the University of Basel.

> all-embracing arousal in everybody of an economic application of labor and goods (Schæffle 1891, pp. 51-52).

Apart from a certain clumsiness owing to the absence of marginal utility theory, this seems to be a clear early statement of the problem. Schæffle notes that "the question has scarcely been discussed at all until now and is thus not ripe for discussion. But without any condition we venture the assertion that to take into account the use value in determining the exchange (social) value of labor and goods amounts to the first and most decisive preliminary question" (Schæffle 1891 p. 52).

Writing in 1920, Ludwig von Mises, who has the merit of calling attention to the problem, seems to have no doubts about the answer to Schæffle's question: "Socialism is the abolition of rational economy" (Mises 1935, p. 110). And in 1922 in his Die Gemeinwirtschaft he stresses that "economic calculation can only take place by means of money prices established in the market for production goods in a society resting on private property in the means of production" (Mises 1981, p. 123).

Other economists, however, seem to object strongly to this opinion, as shown by this quotation from Paul A. Samuelson:

> Around 1900 Pareto showed that an ideal socialism would have to solve the same equations as competitive capitalism. Around 1920, Ludwig von Mises, perhaps unaware of Pareto's proof, set forth the challenging view that rational economic organization was *logically* impossible in the absence of free markets. Fred Taylor of Michigan, A. P. Lerner of England and California, and Oskar Lange of Poland answered Mises with the view that socialism could conceptually solve the problems of economic organization by a decentralized process of bureaucratic trial and error (Samuelson 1976, p. 92).

The task of this chapter is to discuss the present state of the debate concerning rational calculation in socialism. This task is beset with a number of problems and pitfalls. First there is the problem of what constitutes a socialist economy. Does the term refer only to a centrally planned system (where and at which time?) with public ownership of production? Or can a socialist market economy, like that of Yugoslavia, with some property rights of workers in their firms, also be considered to be a socialist order? What of the many possibilities in between if one rejects one of these extremes as nonsocialist?

A second problem arises from the question whether one should discuss the topic for some existing socialist economies (which?) or some ideal socialist systems or both.

Third, there is the problem that real socialist economies as well as proposed ideal socialist systems have changed or been reinvented over time, presumably at least partly because of problems encountered with rational calculation and because of proposals made by economists.

Finally, rational calculation is dependent on the capabilities of gathering, retrieving, storing, processing, and passing on information, as well as on the costs of doing so. But these capabilities and costs change over time. As a consequence, what seemed impossible a hundred or fifty years ago with the old means of calculation and communication, could be possible today because of the computer. And calculations considered beyond our capabilities today may be possible in the future, when further technological and organizational innovations have taken place.

These problems will not be addressed directly but will be kept in mind in the following sections. Instead, it seems convenient to concentrate on a centrally planned economy and to considered more market-type or otherwise decentralized socialist economies only in the end, considering them to be at least partly an outflow of the problems occurring in the former system.

THE PROBLEM OF SHEER COMPLEXITY

Game theory tells us that chess is a "trivial" game. Let us assign 1, -1, and 0 to winning, losing, and stalemate. Then we realize that chess is a two-person zero-sum game. But such a game always has a definite solution, that is, a best strategy with a definite sequence of moves leading to the best outcome attainable by the respective player. If the two players knew only these best strategies chess would indeed by "trivial." It is not even surprising that chess should be trivial. For both players know the rules of the game, the initial positions, and the possible moves of all figures. They have perfect information; the solution to the problem faced by them is one of pure logic. It is tautological.

But unfortunately or fortunately game theory has not been able, until now, to find the best strategies. Thus we still observe chess players spending days and days, or even lifetimes, straining their wits with a trivial game. This seeming contradiction is a consequence of the sheer complexity of the problem, or put more humbly, of the utter limitations of the mind.

Similarly, everybody could have known, at least since Enrico Barone, that the same truth holds, at least in a stationary environment, for optimal planning by a central planning board (CPB) in a centrally planned economy. If it had perfect knowledge about preferences, available resources, and technology, then the solution of the problem would be an exercise in logic, in mathematics. Central planning would be trivial in the same sense as chess. Summing up his arguments in 1908 Barone concluded: "If, for a moment, we assume that the variability of the technical coefficients may be neglected and we take account of their technical variability only, it is not impossible to solve on paper the equations of the equilibrium. It would be tremendous--a gigantic work (work therefore taken from the productive services): but it is not an _impossibility_" (Barone 1935, p. 287).

Barone has proved that a solution to the problem of rational calculation in a centrally planned economy is logically possible if the CPB has perfect information. More, he even believes that it could have this information (though at a cost) and solve the problem in empirical reality in a stationary environment. It is doubtful whether this latter belief is true even today, and we will return to the related problems shortly. But let us point out here that Hayek and even Mises seem to agree that rational calculation is logically possible under these conditions. As Hayek states: ". . . it must be admitted that this is not an impossibility in the sense that it is logically contradictory" (Hayek 1935, p. 207). Mises' position is not as clear: "It is clear that under stationary conditions the problem of economic calculation does not really arise. When we think of the stationary society, we think of an economy in which all the factors of production are already used in such a way as, under the given conditions, to provide the maximum of the things which are demanded by consumers" (Mises 1981, p. 120). This is a curious way of thinking.

The solution for chess has not been found, even though the rules have remained stationary for centuries. But it is certain, on the other hand, that for Mises "the problem of economic calculation is of economic dynamics" (p. 121). Moreover, he chides Pareto and Barone for not penetrating "to the core of the problem" (p. 117).

Let us return to the problem of complexity. We know by now that it is not a problem of logic and that it stems from the mind's woefully limited capacity to process information. But contrary to chess, with its simple rules and initial conditions that can be easily retried and memorized, the vast quantity of information relevant for centrally planning a whole economy cannot be retrieved, stored, and passed on by the individual mind. A second problem of complexity exists. The question to be asked is whether the degree of complexity is such that no computers or means of communication could, together with a group of human beings, solve the problem at hand, given that information were costless and would be readily provided in an undistorted way by its holders.

Oskar Lange (in 1967), seemed to believe that the problem could be solved then but not forty years before:

> Not quite thirty years ago I published an essay "On the Economic Theory of Socialism." Pareto and Barone had shown that the conditions of economic equilibrium in a socialist economy could be expressed by a system of simultaneous equations. The prices resulting from these equations furnish a basis for rational economic accounting under socialism (only the static equilibrium aspect of the accounting problem was under consideration at that time). At a later date Hayek and Robbins maintained that the Pareto-Barone equations were of no practical consequence. The solution of a system of thousands or more simultaneous equations was, in practice, impossible, and consequently the practical problem of economic accounting under socialism remained unsolvable.
>
> In my essay I refuted the Hayek-Robbins argument by showing how a market mechanism could be established in a socialist economy which would lead to the solution of the simultaneous equations by means of an empirical procedure of trial and error. . . .
>
> [Today] my answer to Hayek and Robbins would be: so what's the trouble? Let us put the simultaneous equations in an electronic computer and we shall obtain the solution in less than a second. The market process . . . may be considered as a computing device of the pre-electronic age" (Lange 1972, pp. 401-402).

THE PROBLEM OF COMPLEXITY UNDER NONSTATIONARY CONDITIONS

We have already seen that Barone and probably Mises would agree with Lange that not only the logical but also the practical problem of rational calculation in a centrally planned economy could be solved in a stationary environment. Hayek, however, would not agree (see Hayek 1935, pp. 207-14; Vaughn 1980), since he believes that kinds of knowledge exist that are not readily available and/or are not transferable to the CPB. A discussion of these important problems must be postponed until later. Apart from this it is quite clear that Barone (1935, pp. 287-90), Mises (see Murrel 1983), and Hayek (see Vaughn 1980), in contrast to Lange, all considered the computational solution impossible because the environment is constantly changing.

Since the problem is a very difficult one, let us approach it in a stepwise fashion by first assuming that only the coefficients of the preference and production functions, but not the type of functions, change. The problem would then only become unsolvable if the capacity of the CPB were not sufficient to receive and to send each period the necessary number of messages.

The situation would become more difficult if the types of preference and production functions would change and differ for different households and firms. This would first require that the type of function applicable be transmitted to the CPB before information about its parameter values would be given. This would not merely increase the number of messages necessary; since most households would not be able to specify the type of function even if such a function existed, it would become impossible to send adequate information in any other form than a graphical or a numerical description containing a great set of numbers. The latter would be also true if no function existed. All this would either make it impossible to send the required messages or would only allow the transmission of inaccurate and incomplete information.

The possibility of introducing new kinds of goods complicates the situation even more. In this case firms do not know anything about the production function, but have only some vague ideas until they have actually experimented with producing the goods. Moreover, consumers do not know how to evaluate the new product before they have really used or consumed it. Most information is thus only available after the introduction of the new product, especially information concerning the inputs needed for production and the wants of consumers.

New kinds of goods--and not only consumer goods--pose another problem. Since they are not invented by the CPB, a complete and detailed description of the characteristics has to be given to the CPB, a requirement which is often beyond the capabilities of the language. The same is true for new kinds of labor skills developed. How could the capabilities of a new type of cellular biological engineer and of his possible uses in several lines of production be transmitted to CPB and its computers? Moreover, the members of the CPB would probably not understand the microbiological terminology that would be used to transmit the message.

There are other reasons why the parameters of production functions may not be known in advance. Their dependence, for example, in agriculture on weather conditions, is obvious and cannot be predicted. Thus only probable results could be calculated by CPB. The same is true if the quality and available quantity of inputs, especially of labor, are variable. Moreover, these variations may be consequences of the economy's administrative organization and of the nature of its plans (see next section).

It is obvious that these were some of the problems envisioned by Mises and Hayek. But if they are present, the real question becomes: How can and how does the CPB adapt its economic calculation to ever-changing circumstances? Can its efficiency ever attain that of the markets, which themselves, admittedly, are in many respects a rather crude instrument of calculation?

Let us give one more example. Mises points out that it is nearly impossible for the CPB to decide which firms and industries should produce what amounts of goods, which firms and industries should be created, and which should be closed. He denies that these problems can be solved without capitalists and a capital market (1981, pp. 119-23). This problem would not arise at all in a stationary environment. It is a well-known theorem of economic theory that with externalities absent and the kind of linear production function assumed, it does not make any difference how many firms produce what amounts of each product. As a consequence, the structure of industries does not matter either. Moreover, no firms or industries have to be created or expanded if no new goods, new production functions, or changes in preferences arise.

With different and changing production functions, the size of firms and the structure of industry become a problem. The same is true if externalities are no longer neglected. New goods and changing preferences also pose the problem of which firms or industries to expand, to contract, to abolish, or to create. But we have already seen that under these conditions the CPB will not be able to get the information necessary for reliable ex ante planning because of the nature and complexity of the situation. Rational calculation does break down if central planning is used.

MOTIVATION AND STRATEGIC INFORMATIONAL BEHAVIOR

Up to this point we have assumed that each household and firm is prepared to transmit willingly, truthfully, and without costs or delay all information which is available and which can be formulated. This meant, given the assumptions of complexity in a stationary environment, that we place the CPB in the same position of partial omniscience as a chessplayer observing the board and knowing the rules of the game. Since perfect knowledge concerning all relevant data does not imply the knowledge of the logical consequences which can be inferred from this information, we speak only of partial omniscience. The chessplayer or the CPB under the conditions stated could know everything, be totally omniscient, if only the capacities to process the given knowledge were not so limited, or, put another way, the situation too complex.

Now there is no doubt that the assumption of partial omniscience for the CPB is quite unrealistic even in a stationary environment. Information is not costless; it is often, as we have seen in the previous section, not available ex ante or cannot be formulated in a simple way at all. Perhaps, more importantly, individuals may not be prepared to provide the correct information given the ruling property rights and the exigencies of the planning bureaucracy. Concerning this question the theory of property rights has helped to make big advances during the last three decades.

Let us begin with the problem of public goods, which has not been adequately solved even in market economies until today (see, however, the proposals for the demand-revealing process in Tideman 1977, and for an insurance scheme in Thompson 1966). It is well known that households can benefit by understating the intensity of their preferences for public goods if the CPB wants to reach an optimal solution. By such an understatement a household would have to "pay" less in terms of private goods forgone if the CPB believed it. It follows that households are motivated to give false information to the CPB, which could thus not succeed with optimal planning even if the problem of complexity could be overcome.

One could, of course, argue that market systems are facing similar problems with public goods. But the problem may be more far-reaching in planned economies, since it may include all private goods. This can be seen if we assume that all goods are private goods and the CPB tries to maximize a social welfare function. For then individuals could misstate their utilities to get more of the private goods.

Let us now turn to the motivational situation of firms relative to their informational behavior in a planned economy with public ownership of the means of production. We can only give a short sketch of the problems involved (but see Bernholz 1975, ch. 7-8; Furubotn and Pejovich 1972; Wagener 1982; and Leipold 1983). It has been shown in the previous section that it is impossible for the CPB to get reliable information on all aspects of available technologies and resources. It follows that the plans worked out on the basis of such incomplete and partly distorted (see above) information are not fully corresponding to reality. As a consequence firms may often find themselves either unable to fulfill the plan or able to easily overshoot its targets. Knowing this situation, how will the managers take these possibilities into account? This depends, of course, on how the CPB or the leading politicians sanction or reward deviations of individual firms from planned targets. Now it is obvious that the CPB finds itself in a certain dilemma, too. Since it knows well that its own plans are inadequate, it cannot always discern without a perfect independent monitoring system whether the fact that a firm did not meet its targets has been caused by mismanagement, bad work, laziness, a lack of available inputs, or to its own unrealistic plan. But an extensive monitoring system is too expense to cover all firms adequately and develops, moreover, its own distortions. Thus the information acquired by independent monitoring remains inadequate, too.

Given this situation, the CPB would know to act arbitrarily if it punished or rewarded each small downward or upward deviation from the planned targets, since it could not be sure whether its own unrealistic plans or the behavior of the firms were responsible. A graduated response by the CPB would thus seem a most plausible reaction to such a situation: premiums increasing with the degree of overfulfillment of the plan. No premiums if the plan targets have not been reached, but degradation, removal, or imprisonment of managers only if the targets have been missed by substantial degrees.

How do managers and workers react to this reward structure with their informational behavior taking into account that they have no property rights in the results of their work except the premiums? In answering this question we have to recall that even able and willing managers and well-trained and industrious workers may sometimes not be able to reach the plan targets because of their somewhat unrealistic nature. It is obvious that a first aim must be to reach plan targets under all conditions and a second aim to overfulfill them to a certain degree to get some premiums and thus to make employees satisfied and reliable and to increase the chances for a promotion of managers.

To accomplish this goal several informational strategies are available. First, it is appropriate to understate production capabilities and available capacities. Second, it is advisable to ask for more current inputs than probably needed. Third, investment requirements may be somewhat overstated to extend existing capacities and to possibly become able to produce part of the needed inputs within the firm itself. Concerning this latter point, however, the management has to be rather careful. Demands for new investments that are too high may be taken by the CPB as a signal to increase targets in the next plan. It follows that the somewhat unrealistic nature of the plan and the property rights given in the centrally planned economy lead firm managers to transmit false information to the CPB, thus worsening the quality of the plans.

It should not be overlooked, moreover, that firms have to take a long-term perspective. Too big an overfulfillment of plans would probably mean higher plan targets and consequently the greater likelihood of not reaching the targets in the next period. It follows that it is not advisable to transmit too great an overfulfillment of plans (see Weitzman 1980, for the elaboration of an optimal policy of this kind). Rather, it is better to understate the rate of production reached and/or not to produce too much. The latter would, moreover, make for quieter work. The former would make it possible to set aside part of the production for getting required inputs in exchange if the requested inputs are not granted or are not sufficient.

It is true, of course, that the CPB learns about the informational biases mentioned and tries to take them into account. For example, the CPB eventually learns that managers understate the capacities of their firms and may not produce as much as they could because they fear higher targets in future plans, and so the CPB will try to take these facts into account. But this reaction can never be perfect, since the CPB does not know the degree of understatement. Of course, in time, some policies might be worked out to reward managers who seem to be more reliable concerning the information given, with more generous allocations of inputs, thus encouraging further reliable information and saving control costs. But it cannot be expected that this system will be optimal or even work all the time.

Let us conclude by mentioning that intermediate bureaucracies like industry ministries and regional agencies face similar incentives to provide false or distorted information to the CPB, though their position and thus the direction of distortions is somewhat different. Even the CPB may face similar problems vis-à-vis the supreme political authorities. Lack of space prevents discussing their peculiar incentives, but it is clear that additional sources of false and distorted information exist even on these levels of the hierarchy.

THE SEARCH FOR KNOWLEDGE, INVENTION, AND INNOVATION IN CENTRALLY PLANNED ECONOMIES

Until now, we have mostly assumed that the information relevant for central planning existed somewhere in the economic system and was already known or at least readily and cheaply available. This is, however, very often not the case. For knowledge is not only dispersed among members of the system; in many cases it must be searched for even if it is somewhere available. And how well and how efficiently this search is undertaken may depend on the kind of economic system. This fact has been stressed by Hayek several times, especially in his "Competition as a Discovery Process" (1969).

It may, for example, not be known to anybody that a kind of cheap synthetic material can be used for certain purposes instead of cotton or wool, but it may be rewarding to look for a cheaper substitute of these materials if one can make a profit by doing so. But to profit from such a search presupposes private property rights according to which one can keep the rewards gained by the new application found and introduced. "The use of widely dispersed knowledge in a society cannot be based on the knowledge of single individuals of all concrete ways of possible uses which can be made from things of their environments. Their attention is guided by prices, which the market offers for the different goods and services. . . . The knowledge of which I am speaking is based mainly on the capability to detect special circumstances, a skill which can only be effectively used by individuals if they are told by the market which kind of things and services are demanded with which intensity" (Hayek 1969, pp. 253-54).

It should be clear, however, that it is not only the market and competition, though their role is not at all negligible, which is providing the incentive to search for information. It is the profit to be gained from a successful search for and use of knowledge and the losses to be endured if only competitors find and apply such information, which drive individuals to undertake these activities. And profit or loss is highly dependent on the kind of ruling property system. If no private property exists, if the property rights of individuals consist only in a premium for overfulfilling or a penalty for not fulfilling the central plan, then the search for knowledge will be restricted to finding ways to reach the planned targets better and more easily.

The same factors are at work concerning the invention and use of new knowledge (innovation) which has not been available in a given economic system before. One may argue that for basic scientific research, the difference of incentives is not very big between market economies with private property and centrally planned economies with public property, as long as research is free, not too strongly regulated, and sufficiently funded. The competition of scientists for fame and international prestige may be a sufficient incentive.

The situation is, however, quite different for applied research and its application (innovation). It is obviously impossible to plan centrally the introduction of unknown production processes or goods. Of course, resources can be directed into certain lines of research. But nobody knows in advance which line of research may be most useful. Bureaucrats have even less understanding, since they are too far removed from the possible needs and potentialities of production. Similarly, it is generally not possible to provide wage premiums and inputs for the production of yet unknown goods and the development of superior production processes to all firms.

These facts should have several consequences. Individual firms and individuals or groups have scarcely any incentive to develop and introduce radically new production processes or goods, since the inputs needed would have to be taken away from the production of the goods assigned by the plan, thus threatening its underfulfillment. As a consequence, there will be motivation only for small-scale innovation in the traditional lines of production. We have already seen that the CPB is inclined to increase targets each time plans are overfulfilled. To get premiums in the future, managers and workers are therefore interested in increasing productivity as long as this is not revealed at once to CPB and does not lead to an immediate increase of production quotas. There exists thus a rather strong incentive to invent and innovate, but only in a very limited and traditional range of production.

These incentives are not present for fundamentally new goods and production processes. Not only are the traditional production targets threatened by the necessary diversion of inputs, but the plans themselves becomes less reliable because of unforeseen innovations. This would increase the risk to bureaucratic planners, and so they are often motivated against such changes. Managers would have to fight for additional resources for research and development vis-à-vis badly informed and risk-averse bureaucrats and must themselves bear the risk of sanctions for possible failure without being able to keep a substantial part of the benefits in case of success. Moreover, even if a firm should be successful in developing pathbreaking new products or production processes, there is no guarantee at all that the CPB or the production ministry will entrust the firm with the task of producing the new product. Finally, competition among firms is lacking, so the danger is very small that other firms could threaten the existence of a firm by pushing ahead with innovations, if the firm does not follow these new developments as soon as possible.

The CPB will, of course, try to compensate for these disadvantages by allocating research and development resources to different research institutes and perhaps to certain firms. But the latter have no strong incentives to develop absolutely new goods and production processes that are urgently needed. And the former are scarcely aware of the problems and potential possibilities faced by firms. Moreover, the bureaucrats of CPB are inclined to ask for specific results to keep the situation more amenable to planning. Finally, such selection of research institutes, firms, lines of research, and of innovation by the CPB precludes all other firms and individuals from getting resources to search for and to apply new information.

We conclude that the creation and especially the application of new information is severely hindered in centrally planned economies. It is thus not surprising that the Hungarian economist Kornai finds that most revolutionary new products have been developed in capitalist and not in socialist countries. "It should be noted that with the exception of a few initiatives no socialist country figures among those introducing the product in question for the first time" (Kornai 1971, p. 288).

ESCAPE ROUTES: DECENTRALIZATION, IMITATION OF MARKETS, AND MARKET SOCIALISM

Chessplayers are playing chess in spite of the fact or rather because they do not know the optimal strategy. Socialist and more or less centrally planned economies have existed and grown for more than sixty years in spite of the impossibility of optimal planning. Is it impossible that some functionaries benefit from the fact that planning is so inadequate? But another question is more relevant here. Some chessplayers play better than others and some socialist economies seem to work more efficiently than others. What are the reasons?

We know very little to help us answer this question. But it would seem, from the earlier discussion, that the kind of economic organization allowing some decentralization of processing information and of decision-making should be responsible for a more or less rational economic calculation and thus the more or less efficient use of resources. It is thus interesting to note that practical experimentation in socialist countries as well as theoretical design of somewhat decentralized systems have been strong responses to the practical and theoretical problems faced by the centrally planned economy. Several reorganizations have taken place in different socialist economies at different times and to different degrees, because of not only economic but also political and perhaps ideological reasons. The Hungarian economic reform with, for example, two-level planning (Kornai and Liptak 1965) and the introduction of a socialist market economy in Yugoslavia (Horvat 1969) have moved these systems far away from the centrally planned system of the Soviet Union in the 1930s or 1950s, for example. It is not even obvious that these systems should still be described as "socialist."

Similar far-reaching (and sometimes related) developments have been taking place in the responses of economists to the problem of information in socialist economies. Hayek pointed out in his review article of 1940 that the proposals of a "competitive solution" put forward by Dickinson (1939) and by Lange and Taylor (1938) were a response to the presumed impossibility of solving the problem by centralizing and mathematically processing the necessary information through a CPB: "It seems then, that on the point, the criticisms of the earlier socialist schemes have been so successful that the defenders, with few exceptions, have felt compelled to appropriate the argument of their critics and have been forced to construct entirely new schemes of which nobody thought before" (Hayek 1949, p. 183).

These developments have been going on since then, and it is not only socialist economists that have concerned themselves with the development of new proposals supposed to allow economic calculation in socialism. Moreover, many works have looked critically at the information and incentive problems in capitalist market economies and thus put forward the very general question of the more or less rational use of resources and information in big economies depending on the kind of organizational setting.

Indeed, we have already pointed out that given the limited mental capabilities of human beings, an institution- and organization-free economic theory cannot help us understand the nature of the problems. To overcome the problems of sheer complexity, of strategic information behavior, and of incentives, man has been helped by the developments not only in logic, mathematics, and computers but also in institutions and organizations like markets, money, and firms. Without the often unplanned emergence of these human artifacts, these crutches of our mental faculties, the development of modern society would have been impossible.

Lack of space prevents a survey of the practical and theoretical developments in this field. After a short sketch of developments following Seidl (1982) (for reviews see Brandt 1976, ch. 5; Seidl 1978; Wagener 1982), I will thus have only some short comments on problems of the simulated markets proposed by Lange and others and on the socialist market economy.

The development of decomposition algorithms provided a first step out of the problems of pure complexity, since a drastic reduction of computer capacity and of calculation time required can be reached under certain conditions. The use of these algorithms can be economically interpreted as a dialogue between the CPB and subordinated units. The well-known two-level planning process proposed by Kornai and Liptak (1965) can be considered to belong to the decomposition algorithms. It is characteristic that these algorithms imply centralized decision-making but reduce the complexity problem by decentralizing the processing of information. The problems of strategic information behavior and of an incentive structure to motivate correct and complete information are not, however, solved by these systems. The same is true for the dynamic problems, especially concerning the creation and application of new information.

A next step in the development of mathematical models is reached with the theory of allocation mechanisms, in which the concepts of environment, information phase and allocation were explicitly introduced. Hurwicz (1960), who pioneered this work, constructed artificial mechanisms of economic allocation that are not abstractions of empirical systems. By doing so the mechanisms themselves, that is, the artificial economic systems, could be considered as a variable. It is impossible to discuss these theories here (see Seidl 1978; Brandt 1976, ch. 5 for a sketch). We note, however, that they, too, assume that the information is initially dispersed among individuals and will be correctly transmitted by them.

The most recent development of modeling allocation mechanisms takes the possibility of false, incomplete, or misleading information into account. Hurwicz (1972) has coined the term "incentive-compatible allocation mechanisms" for mechanisms that are constructed in such a way that individuals, or coalitions of them, reap no advantage by providing false information. My knowledge of this literature, as well as of that formerly mentioned, is rather limited. It seems, however, that first, these allocation mechanisms do not take into account the dynamics of the system, that is, they do not even consider the fact that individuals react in their information behavior to the decisions taken by the planners (CPB) in the preceding period. The models are still limited to one period; they are static (but see Myerson 1981). Second, "with the postulates of decentralization of information (in the sense of Hurwicz), Pareto-satisfactoriness and incentive-compatibility allocation mechanisms are obviously overstressed. Apart from the competition process with infinitely many participants, no allocation mechanism could be found until now which satisfies all these attributes, such that Hurwicz suspects the existence of a general impossibility theorem" (Seidl 1978, p. 142; concepts defined pp. 131-42). Finally, I am under the impression that the property rights corresponding to the different allocation mechanisms have not been adequately specified.

Let us next turn to socialist systems imitating markets, as proposed by Lange (1938), Dickinson (1939), and Lerner (1937). Lange assumes that the CPB announces the prices of all goods and services. (In his main version he allows the prices of consumer goods and of labor services to be determined in markets, but since this is not important for his system, it is neglected here.) In cases of excess supply prices are lowered; in cases of excess demand they are increased until an equilibrium is reached for all goods.

Consumers behave as in a capitalist economy, that is, they maximize their utilities at given prices and incomes. The latter are composed of a labor income and a social dividend stemming from the surpluses of revenues over costs of the publicly owned firms. The managers of firms and industries are obliged to follow two rules: (1) Factors of production have to be combined in a way to minimize the average cost of production, and (2) output has to be such that marginal cost is equal to the price of the product. Together these rules determine not only output and supply but also the use of and demand for means of production by existing firms. Moreover, managers of whole industries (like the National Coal Trust) have to apply the second rule to guide them in deciding whether the whole industry ought to be expanded by building new or extending old plants, or whether the industry ought to be contracted by attrition of aging plants.

Lange prefers that the rate of capital accumulation be determined by the CPB and not by the savings of consumers. The rate of accumulation together with the demand for capital determines the long-term rate of interest.

There can be no doubt that Lange's scheme strongly reduces the complexity of the information problem. The CPB has only to know the amounts of excess supply or demand in each market and to announce the prices of goods. This problem can be handled in this social system by a central bureaucracy using artificial prices to steer the economy. A critique of Lange's and of similar solutions was anticipated by Mises in 1922 (1981; see Murrel 1983, for a discussion) and was explicitly stated by Hayek in 1940 (Hayek 1949, ch. 9). I shall thus confine my critical remarks to the following short comments.

First, Lange never discusses the problem of how to motivate managers and workers to follow the rules postulated above. Perhaps this defect could be mended by letting them participate in the profits made by their firms. Second, the two rules imply that demand and supply of firms are determined only by current prices and (marginal) costs. As a consequence, the adaptations of prices reflecting excess demand and supply are also not oriented to the future. Of course, no speculators are present. The system is static in its conception. Expectations about the future are not a determining factor for demand, supply, and prices. This is especially disturbing concerning investment, expansion and contraction of firms, and the building and closing of plants.

Third, the latter problem is aggravated by the fact that firm and industry managers are not motivated or punished by profits and losses caused at least partly by their decisions. Since they do not get a share of the profits but will probably be punished or have their careers stalled if their investment decisions should turn out wrong, it is to be expected that they will take a rather risk-averse attitude. The orientation about the success or failure given by developments in stock markets is clearly missing. No selection process by capital owners detecting good and removing bad managers is available.

Finally, Lange does not say anything about the incentives to create new information, that is, to find and to apply new production processes and to introduce pathbreaking new goods. The remarks made in the last section thus remain fully valid for the simulation of the competitive solution proposed.

Lange would, however, also object to the critical remarks about missing future-oriented information in his system by stating that no future markets exist for most goods in capitalist economies. In his 1967 article he turns to the problem and states, "An important limitation of the market is that it treats the accounting problem only in static terms. . . It does not provide a sufficient foundation for the solution of growth and development problems. . . For planning economic development, long-term investments have to be taken out of the market mechanism and based on judgment of developmental economic policy. . . Mathematical programming turns out to be an essential instrument of optimal long-term economic planning. . . Here, the electronic computer does not replace the market. It fulfills a function which the market was never able to perform" (Lange 1972, pp. 404-405).

Here, Lange admits that the market simulation proposed in 1938 would not solve the problems of long-term investment and economic growth. Lange, however, overlooks two facts in his comparison of planning and capitalist markets. First, optimal investment planning with the computer would not be possible since the CPB cannot know in advance the kind and nature of new products and production processes. This is in fact one of the reasons why no futures markets exist for many goods in market economies. Second, whereas in capitalist societies the search for new information and the selection of able future-oriented managers and capitalists is guided by capital markets, competition among managers, and profits or losses made by capitalists, no such selection process exists for the public managers or bureaucrats and functionaries on which "judgment of developmental policies" long-term investment decisions have to be based in the socialist economy.

Let us finally turn to market socialism. This system has been widely discussed (Ward 1967; Furubotn and Pejovich 1974; Nutzinger 1979; Schlict and Weizsäcker 1977; Bernholz 1979, ch. 1-2). Thus, no description and only a short sketch of the information problem is necessary. First, there is no doubt that the information problem posed by a CPB directing economic activities has been abolished in this system. But stock markets and labor markets for managers do not exist. Thus, decisions to create or to close firms and industries face about the same problems as the Lange system. Because of labor participation in firms and limited property rights of workers, there are no adequate signals in the labor market as to the scarcity of the different types of labor. The nature of property rights will probably lead to a decreasing supply function for goods, higher unemployment, and a tendency to finance new investments by taking bank credit and to strongly restrict self-financing. Taken together, the socialist market economy seems to provide market signals which are less complete and less adequate to allow rational economic calculation than those given in a capitalist market economy. It must be doubted, moreover, whether there are sufficient incentives to motivate the search for and use of new information.

Let me conclude this section by stating that the critical remarks concerning the different proposed or actual, more or less decentralized socialist systems should not be taken to imply that such systems may not solve the information problem better than a totally centralized economy. In fact, they often do. For example, systems with simulated markets, even if they are not future-oriented and do not take into account how to get individuals to provide correct information, may be superior in allowing economic calculation since they strongly reduce the problems of complexity. The same may be true for systems using two-stage planning. And a socialist market economy may fare even better since it not only further reduces complexity but also motivates individuals to provide correct signals in many markets.

DEGREE OF CENTRALIZATION, FIRMS AND MARKETS, AND THE INFORMATION PROBLEM

The information problems encountered by more or less centrally steered systems do not prove that markets are always and in every respect informationally superior to centralized organizations. The existence of private organizations, especially of the corporate firm within capitalist market systems, seems to be a strong indication for this statement. For firms do struggle in the absence of internal markets within their boundaries with all the internal disadvantages we have discussed. But they are still used to organize economic activity. "[F]irms and markets are properly regarded as alternative governance structures to which . . . transactions are to be organized into discriminating (mainly transaction cost economizing) ways . . ." (Williamson 1981, p. 159).

We have thus to ask ourselves which factors are responsible for the boundary between markets and firms in a society in which property rights are such that this boundary can, more or less, be freely determined by individuals. For this is obviously a relevant question for an economy with, in a sense, only one firm, the centrally planned economy. We will thus ask ourselves whether it could be true that firms show not only informational disadvantages but also informational (and other) advantages compared to market coordination. And is it possible that not only technological innovations, such as the computer, but also organizational innovations, such as the introduction of the divisional structure of the firm, could enlarge the sphere of centrally guided organizations (e.g., firms) and reduce the domain of markets?

In analyzing these problems we first have to discuss the informational characteristics of market systems. Prices obviously aggregate information about the present and expected scarcity of goods and services, inform everybody about rational use or saving of resources and about unused opportunities, and guide in search of new, valuable information (Hayek 1945). But as Meckling and Jensen have stressed (1984), it is not just the existence of a price system but above all a system of strong private property rights that secures the full informational advantages of markets. Such property rights allow individuals or groups not only to destroy and use goods in production and consumption, to let, to buy, to sell, and to transfer them to others, but also to capture the full value of the goods when alienating these rights.

The possibility of alienating (selling, bequeathing, transferring) property rights and enjoying the full market value of sold goods has important bearing on the problem of information. More often than not, knowledge that could be applied together with a certain combination of resources (e.g., factors of production) to produce new goods or to offer new combinations of goods and services that could be sold at a profit is not available to the owners of the respective resources. Whenever this happens, there are two possible ways to bring knowledge and resources together: either transfer the knowledge to the people who own the rights to use the resources or vice versa. Obviously in centrally planned economies only, or mainly, the first possibility is used, a tendency reinforced by the legal nature of publicly owned property. A private property system with markets, on the contrary, has both alternatives available, since the means of production, which can be used together with the respective knowledge, are alienable, that is, they can be bought by the holder of the information. Moreover, this holder is able to compensate the owner of the resources, since he is assured by his knowledge that he can make a more profitable use of the resources than the present proprietor.

There is no doubt that knowledge is also transferred to owners of resources. But such transfers are sometimes very costly (they may also reveal all or part of the information to outsiders and so decrease its value), difficult, or even impossible. Hayek mentions the knowledge of particular circumstances (of time and place). Moreover, particular skills acquired by individuals often cannot easily be transferred (taught) to others. Finally, one would expect that new inventions are generally very difficult to transmit, since new concepts and descriptions must be used, since only a few persons (e.g., specialized engineers or scientists) may be able to understand the new messages, and since a general mistrust of unknown new developments exists. But in all these cases in which it is either impossible or too costly to transfer knowledge, it may well be possible to acquire the rights to the complementary resources at low transfer costs. This fact thus constitutes an obvious informational advantage of a market system with strong property rights.

This system implies at the same time a rather efficient control of the use made of property rights and of information. Since property owners get the full value of their goods in the market, a value that reflects the discounted expected stream of values stemming from possible future uses, they receive the profits or losses caused at least partly by the good or bad use of their resources and of the knowledge they can apply. This system of rewards and punishments is, moreover, strongly information-saving and selective according to actual performance.

Let us return to the firms as more or less centralized organizations using no markets for their internal transactions. Why do they exist? It is well known from modern property rights and organization theories that economies of scale, specialization (asset specificity), opportunism (shirking), and negative externalities are mainly responsible for the advantages enjoyed by organizations like firms (Williamson 1984). The better solution of these problems, which can be reached under certain conditions by firms (compared to markets), explains that firms can, up to a certain point, overcompensate with such benefits for the disadvantages concerning information and efficient control. It is, however, important to realize that the limitations of informational human capacities are also necessary to make organizations important to deal with the last three of the four factors mentioned above, namely specialization, opportunism, and negative externalities. "But for the simultaneous existence of bounded rationality and opportunism, all economic contracting problems are trivial and the study of economic institutions is unimportant. Thus, but for bounded rationality, all economic exchange could be effectively organized by contract" (Williamson 1981, p. 1545).

It seems puzzling that the limitation of human information capacities--bounded rationality--not only leads to informational difficulties for organizations like firms and whole planned economies, but also limits the usefulness of markets. What are the reasons? First, very specific kinds of knowledge owned by different persons that are hardly transferable, often have to be brought together, especially in production (think of the production of houses or automobiles). In principle, it is true that an entrepreneur could assemble the relevant

> pieces of knowledge by buying them piecemeal from those who have them. In other words, the knowledge could be assembled on the basis of individual exchanges. . . . But the evidence suggests that quid pro quo knowledge transfers are dominated by employment contracts. . . . Such contracts tend to be general in nature--the contents of the exchange are not precisely specified. . . . Single proprietors who contract on a case by case basis for production and application of all the knowledge it takes to operate on any but the smallest scale would soon find themselves swamped by transaction costs.
>
> The value of certain kinds of knowledge to competitors or potential competitors is another reason for long-term employment relationships. . . . Finally, longer run relationships encourage individual participants to invest in firm specific knowledge--knowledge which has little or no value except within the particular organization (Meckling and Jensen 1984, pp. 10-11).

The above factors, apart from preventing the flow of information to competitors, relate to human asset specificity. It is possible to economize on transaction costs by substituting a small number of employment contracts for a large number of contracts and obtaining knowledge piecemeal whenever it is needed. A further reason is problems of control, which would not arise if all information about the behavior of others were available at no cost. This is true, for example, for negative externalities caused by some people since, with complete property rights and perfectly informed damaged persons and judges, compensation payments would easily prevent the problem, if it is not of a public "bad" character. The same is true for opportunism. For example, there are defects in the market system if a retailer injures the reputation of a product by poor services in installation or repair, since it is difficult and costly for the producer to get information about the retailer's behavior and to control it. It is obvious that such information problems, which can arise in the market, may be solved better by integrating the people responsible for negative externalities and the people damaged, or the producer and the retailers, into one firm. And this occurs in spite of the information and control problems which are typical for the firm, with its weak internal property rights, no possibility of alienating them and capturing their value, and with no internal markets.

But what is the relevance of all this to the problem of rational calculation and information in socialism? The answer should be obvious. Karl Marx himself stressed the fact that the introduction of the joint stock company was moving society toward socialism. What would he say to the giant modern corporation, the conglomerate, the multinational firm? It is obvious that the boundary between an efficient organization of economic activity, including an efficient search for and use of information with the help of either markets or firms and other more or less centralized organizations, is shifting over time, depending on technological innovations like telephones and computers and on organizational innovations like the introduction of new types of markets, the joint stock company, or the divisional organization of the firm. To mention one more example, this divisional structure has been used by the conglomerate to manage diversified assets and thus to partly supplant capital markets (Williamson 1981).

If nobody is able--as we have to assume--to determine theoretically and/or by political decree the efficient boundary between markets and more or less centralized organizations like firms, then the greatest disadvantage of socialist systems concerning information problems stemming from bounded human rationality may well be that they *impose* organizational structures on the whole economy that can be changed only if politicians, functionaries, and bureaucrats deem it necessary. By forgoing the free small-scale and medium-scale experimentation with the unexpected consequences that are possible in markets with private property rights, they prevent the emergence of more efficient combined production, allocation, and information systems for the whole economy.

REFERENCES

Barone, Enrico. 1935. The ministry of production in the collectivist state. Pp. 245-90 in F. A. Hayek, ed., Collectivist economic planning. London: George Routledge & Sons. Originally published in Italian in Il Giornale degli Economisti, 1908.

Bernholz, Peter. 1975. Grundlagen der Politischen Oekonomie. Vols. 2 and 3. Tübingen: J.C.B. Mohr.

Brandt, Arno. 1976. Grundlagen und Anwendungen einer allokationsorientierten ökonomischen Nachrichtentheorie. Institut für Sozialwissenschaften, doctoral thesis, Goepfert and Dürr AG, Basel.

Dickinson, H. D. 1939. Economics of socialism. Oxford.

Furubotn, Eirik, and Svetozar Pejovich. 1972. The Soviet manager and innovation. A behavioral model of the Soviet firm. Revue de l'Est 3:29-45.

------. 1974. The economics of property rights. Cambridge, Mass.

Hayek, Friedrich A. von. 1945. The use of knowledge in society. American Economic Review 35(4): 519-30.

------. 1949. Individualism and economic order. London: Routledge & Kegan Paul.

------. 1969. Der Wettbewerb als Entdeckungsverfahren. Pp. 249-63 in F. A. Hayek, Gesammelt Ansätze. Tübingen: J. C. B. Mohr. First published in E. Schneider, ed., Kieler Vorträge, Neue Folge 56, Kiel, 1968.

------, ed. 1935. Collectivist economic planning. London: George Routledge & Sons.

Horvat, Branco. 1969. An essay on Yugoslav economy. White Plains, N.Y.

Hurwicz, Leonid. 1960. Optimality and informational efficiency in resource allocation processes. Pp. 27-48 in K. J. Arrow, P. Suppes, and S. Karlin, eds., Mathematical methods in the social sciences. Stanford.

------. 1972. On informationally decentralized systems. Pp. 297-336 in C. B. McGuire and R. Radner, eds., Decision and Organization. Amsterdam and London: North Holland Publ. Co.

Kornai, Janos, and T. Liptak. 1965. Two level planning. Econometrica 33:141-69.

Lange, Oskar. 1936. On the economic theory of socialism. Review of economic studies, vol. 3. Reprinted in Oskar Lange and Fred M. Taylor, On the economic theory of socialism, ed. B. E. Lippincoff, Minneapolis: University of Minnesota Press, 1938.

------. 1972. The computer and the market. Pp. 401-405 in Alec Nove and D. M. Nuti, eds., Socialist economics. Harmondsworth, Middlesex: Penguin Books. Originally published in C. Feinstein, ed., Capitalism, socialism and economic growth, pp. 158-61.

Lange, Oskar, and Fred M. Taylor. 1938. See Lange 1936.

Leipold, Helmut. 1983. Der Einfluss von Property Rights auf hierarchische und marktliche Transaktionen in sozialistischen Wirtschaftssystemen. Pp. 185-217 in Alfred Schüller, ed., Property Rights und ökonomische Theorie. Munich: Vahlen.

Lerner, Abba P. 1937. Statics and dynamics in socialist economics. Economic Journal 47: 263-67.

Meckling, William H., and Michael C. Jensen. Knowledge, control and organizational structure. Presented at the Seminar on Analysis and Ideology, Interlaken, Switzerland, June, 1984.

Mises, Ludwig von. 1935. Economic calculation in the socialist commonwealth. In Friedrich A. von Hayek, ed., Collectivist economic planning. London: George Routledge & Sons. First published as: Die Wirtschaftsrechnung im sozialistischen Gemeinwesen. Archiv für Sozialwissenschaften, vol. 47, 1920.

------. 1981. Socialism. Trans. J. Kahan. Indianapolis: Liberty Classics. First English edition London: Jonathan Cape, 1936. First published as: Die Gemeinwirtschaft, Jena, 1922.

Murrel, Peter. 1983. Did the theory of market socialism answer the challenge of Ludwig von Mises? A reinterpretation of the socialist controversy. History of Political Economy 15(1): 92-105.

Myerson, R. B. 1981. Mechanism design by an informed principal. Discussion paper No. 481, Northwestern University, June, 1981.

Nutzinger, Hans G. 1975. Investment and financing in a labor-managed firm and its social implications. Pp. 181-201 in Economic analysis and workers' management, vol. 9(3-4).

Samuelson, Paul A. 1976. Economics. 10th ed. New York.

Schäffle, Albert. 1891. Die Quintessenz des Sozialismus. 13th ed. Gotha: F. A. Perthes. First published in Deutsche Blätter, 1874.

Schlict, Ekkehart, and Carl von Weizsäcker. Risk financing in labour managed economies: The commitment problem. Zeitschrift für die gesamte Staatswissenschaft, Special Issue on Profit-Sharing, ed. H. Sauermann and R. Richter. vol. 133.

Schüller, Alfred, Helmut Leipold, and Hannelore Hamel. 1983. Innovationsprobleme in Ost und West. Stuttgart and New York: Gustav Fischer.

Seidl, Christian. 1978. Allokationsmechanismen. Pp. 123-205 in K.-E. Schenk, ed., Oekonomische Verfügungsrechte und Allokationsmechanismen in Wirtschaftssystemen. Schriften des Vereins für Sozialpolitik, vol. 97 N.S. Berlin: Duncker and Humblot.

------. 1982. Allokationsmechanismus, asymmetrische Information und Wirtschaftssystem. Jahrbücher für Nationalökonomie und Statistik 197(3): 193-220.

Taylor, Fred M. 1929. The guidance of production in a socialist state. American Economic Review 19:1-8. Reprinted in Lange and Taylor 1938.

Thompson, Earl A. 1966. A Pareto optimal group decision process. Papers on Non-Market Decision Making (now Public Choice), vol. 1, pp. 133-59. Charlottesville.

Tideman, T. Nicolaus, ed. 1977. Public Choice vol. 29(2). Special Supplement on Demand Revealing Process.

Vaughn, Karen I. 1980. Economic calculation under socialism. The Austrian contribution. Economic Enquiry 18(4): 535-54.

Wagener, H.-J. 1980. Economische Systemen. Alphen a.d. Rijn.

------. 1982. The economics of socialism as economics of shortage. A critical review. De Economist 130(4): 514-35.

Ward, Benjamin. 1967. The socialist economy. New York.

Weitzmann, Martin L. 1980. The "Ratchet Principle" and performance incentives. Bell Journal of Economics 11(1): 302-308.

Williamson, Oliver E. 1981. The modern corporation: Origins, evolution, attributes. Journal of Economic Literature 19: 1537-68.

Chapter 8

RATIONAL EXPECTATIONS IN CENTRALLY PLANNED ECONOMIES

By

Jan S. Kowalski*

INTRODUCTION

The rational expectations approach (RE) has been the major development (alongside the theory of market disequilibrium) in Western economic theory in the 1970s and early 1980s. It continues to stimulate research in almost every branch of economics.

In this chapter I present first a brief summary of the RE doctrine and its implications for theory and policy in the industrialized market economy countries. Next, a description of the salient features of the functioning of centrally planned economies (CPEs) is provided, with reference to the writings of Professor Janos Kornai of Hungary. This description includes an explicit consideration of the political framework of the decision-making mechanisms existing in the CPEs. It is postulated that Kornai's analysis of the shortage economy, referring mainly to the

---

*J. Kowalski is associated with the Economics Department at the University of Karlsruhe.

microscale of the enterprise and the political decision-making underlying macro-policy together provide an instructive model of the real functioning of the CPEs.

Following an evaluation of the CPE-relevant aspects of the RE approach, it is shown that at least some propositions derived from the RE approach, if properly reformulated to fit the CPE context, seem to be highly relevant and instructive regarding some of the problems facing economic policy-makers in communist countries.

The analysis will be limited to the model of the functioning of the CPEs as presented in this chapter, although the RE approach is of interest for the traditional normative models of the planned economy. As those models are far removed from the realities of the CPEs, we shall disregard them.

THE RATIONAL EXPECTATIONS DOCTRINE: ITS CREATION AND IMPLICATIONS

The birth of the RE doctrine is historically associated with the pathbreaking paper by John Muth (1961). In a discussion concerning the way people, acting as economic agents, form expectations about future levels of some relevant economic variables, Muth took the position that these actors form their expectations using the same economic model that actually shapes the behavior of these variables.

This implies that the economic actors "know" the real behavior of the economic system and that they use--gather, process, and consider--all the relevant information related to their expectations, as long as the economic costs of obtaining and using this information do not exceed the benefits.

Put more formally, this statement means that

$$\text{Subjective expectations of economic agents} = {}_{t-1}X_t^{\varepsilon} = E[X_t/I_{t-1}] = \text{Conditional expectations} \qquad (1)$$

$$\text{with} \qquad E[X_t/I_{t-1}] = \int_a^b X_t f(X_t/I_{t-1})dX_t$$

where $f(X_t/I_{t-1})$ is the conditional probability density for a variable X_t given the information available at time t-1, and ${}_{t-1}X_t^{\varepsilon}$ stands for subjective expectations of economic agents at t-1 based on their personal set of information at t-1 concerning the level of X at time t (Scheffrin 1983).

Equation (1) means that the subjective probability distributions in the minds of economic actors equal the true mathematical probability distribution in the real-world system.

This should not be confused with the case of perfect information or perfect insight. Economic agents may make mistakes; they use only some subset of the total information. But their mistakes will be caused by random, unpredictable shocks to and changes in the economic system. If some additional relevant information becomes available at some point in time, it will be processed and included in the process of expectations formation, so that again the error in the expectations may be due only to random factors.

For about a decade the rational expectations concept remained dormant, until R. Lucas, Jr. and some other writers "rediscovered" it using this approach as a focal point in their efforts to reinvigorate classical economic theory (see, e.g., Lucas 1972, 1973; Sargent and Wallace 1975, 1976). What has been their starting point and what were the implications of adopting the RE hypothesis?

The main research interest lay in explaining the apparent breakdown of Keynesian interventionist economic theory and policy. Since the late 1960s the standard Phillips curve implying an inverse relation between unemployment levels and wage and price inflation no longer seemed sound. Rising levels of unemployment have been accompanied by steadily rising inflation rates, and none of the traditional demand-steering instruments were solving this problem.

In 1968 Milton Friedman in his presidential address to the American Economic Association put forward the concept of a "natural" rate of unemployment that can be maintained without changing the rate of inflation (Friedman 1968). Given the microeconomic structure of the economy, the behavior of economic agents in the private sector (business people, workers, consumers), based on correct expectations about the rate of inflation, results in unique levels of aggregate output, employment, and unemployment--"natural" levels. Friedman maintained that there is no involuntary unemployment: given the expectations of inflation the unemployed workers are unwilling to work at the prevailing market wage rate. The workers suffer under the "money illusion" and misjudge often the changes in their nominal wage rate to be changes in the real wage rate. Friedman's conclusion was that only the unanticipated levels of inflation--below or above the inflation rate that has come to be generally expected--can move the levels of output and employment below or above their natural levels.

It is important to notice that in Friedman's concept it is still possible to influence the real level of economic variables in the economy. He maintained that because the expectations about inflation are slow to adapt to the changes, the government, through its monetary and fiscal policy, will probably cause discrepancies between the expectations and the real levels of inflation, thus bringing about the changes in real value of economic variables.

People adopting the RE approach go one step further than Friedman. They maintain that as the public wants to maximize its benefits and utilizes all economically available relevant information, it will include information about the intended monetary and fiscal policies. This means that only the unanticipated changes in the money supply, not caused by government's systematic economic policy, can make the expected inflation rate diverge from the actual inflation rate. Any anticipated monetary or fiscal policy will be incorporated into people's expectations of inflation level. Because unemployment may diverge from its natural rate only if people make mistakes about the inflation rate, this means that the systematic, publicly known economic policy has no effect on output and employment. It changes only inflation levels.

This is essence the "neutrality" of economic policy proposition, which has been the most spectacular and most hotly debated result of the application of the RE hypothesis in macroeconomic theory. It states that all systematic moves of the economic authorities will rapidly be learned and anticipated, so that only nominal but no real adjustments result. (Of course if the systematic government policy changes the underlying microstructure of the economy, it will affect the economic aggregates in a way that will result in some new "natural" levels of these aggregates.)

A simple figure may illustrate this argument (see Figure 1). Let us assume that in period t=0 the economic actors expect the authorities to increase the money supply in period t=1. This will shift the demand curve from D^0 to D^1. Assuming that the economic agents form rational expectations, they will expect prices to rise as a result of the increased money supply. Correct expectations lead them to anticipate a price increase from p_0 to p_1. Accordingly, the suppliers will shift their supply curve from Y_0^S to Y_1^S, and the only result of the increased stock of money in the economy will be the change in the price level at the "old" real production and consumption levels.

Formally stated: Output will deviate from its normal level (i.e., level corresponding to the natural unemployment rate, which is then denoted as the full employment level of output) only if actual prices differ from the expected prices (Maddock and Carter 1982) (in logs):[1]

$$Y_t = Y_p + \beta(P_t - {}_{t-1}P_t^{\varepsilon}) \qquad (2)$$

where

$${}_{t-1}P_t^{\varepsilon} = Ep_t/I_{t-1}$$

and where expected forecast error:

$$E(P_t - {}_{t-1}P_t^{\varepsilon}/I_{t-1}) = 0$$

Y_t = output in period t, Y_p = "full employment" output level, p_t = actual inflation rate, ${}_{t-1}p_t^e$ = inflation rate at time t expected at time t-1.

This implies that a mistake in the forecast can be caused only by unsystematic, random, impossible-to-anticipate factors.

One significant result of these considerations is that in order to achieve real quantity effects, the government must somehow try to "fool" the public, must try to generate incorrect expectations of price trends. Only then will it succeed in bringing about real effects.

In countries with a record of stable, regular monetary and fiscal policy that normally follows certain rules, it is easy to make the public believe that changes in the economy are real and not merely nominal (Lucas 1973). This helps to explain why the Keynesian fine-tuning of the economy through variable demand policy has increasingly led to changes in inflation levels, influencing to a decreasing degree the real economic

FIGURE 1

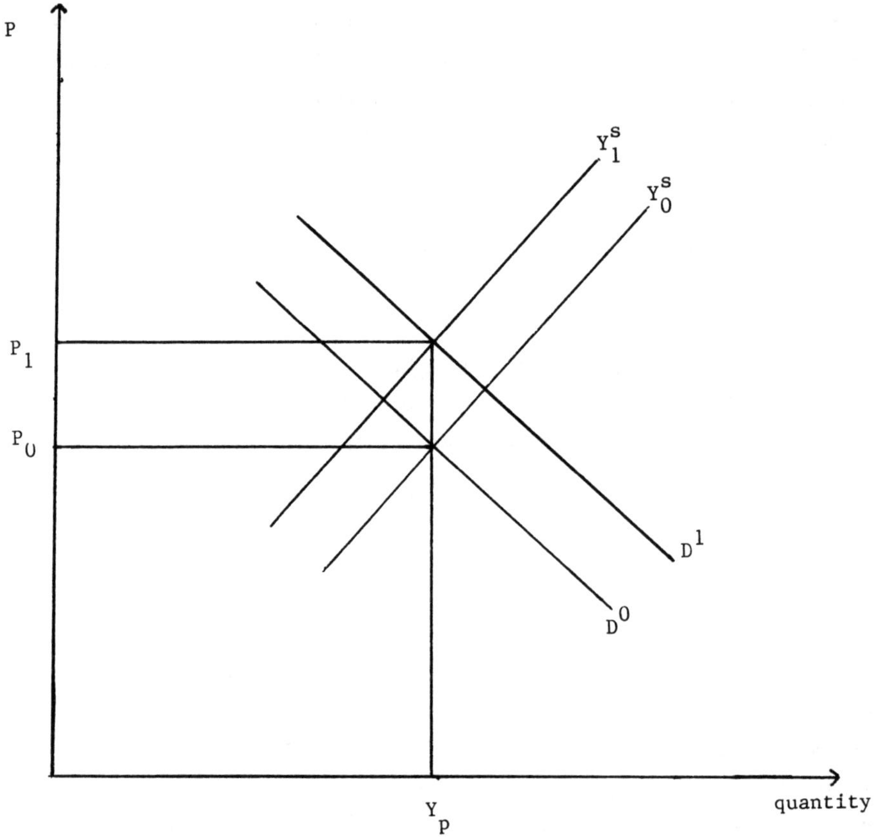

Source: Scheffrin 1983, p. 28.

aggregates. W. Fellner's (1979) suggestion concerning the importance of the credibility of the government monetary and fiscal policies is relevant here. He assumes that those who set wage and price levels take into account the response of the authorities to their decisions. If the economic actors believe that the government's policy is weak-willed and accommodating, they will push forward with their demands for higher wages and prices. If they perceive this policy as credible and consequential in its proclaimed money stock targets, they will refrain from it, recognizing that recession and unemployment will follow.

There is no unique body of complete, coherent theory based on the RE approach, as there may be with other recognized theoretical viewpoints, such as the economics of market disequilibrium. There is also no consensus about the empirical validity of the statements based on RE and neutrality of economic policy. But the RE approach and the neutrality hypothesis have changed the way most people think and theorize in economic science. Before I proceed to the discussion of the relevance of the RE approach to the centrally planned economies, I must devote some time to an outline of the ways in which these economies function.

THE FUNCTIONING OF CENTRALLY PLANNED ECONOMIES: "SHORTAGE AND POLITICAL VOLUNTARISM"

The description here of the way CPEs function is based on Kornai's studies (1980, 1982), extended by the author (Kowalski 1983, 1984a,b). The primary point is that CPEs are in fact not planned economies at all in the usual sense given to this term. It is true that a large and complex planning apparatus exists in these countries, that a large number of plans are produced and proclaimed legally binding, but as I shall try to show, they have rather limited influence on the real course of events in the economy.[2]

I shall start with the economic behavior in the micro-scale, namely, the behavior of enterprises, and then I shall describe the macro-level, the behavior of enterprises, and then I shall describe the macro-level, that is, decision-making at the central level. Following Professor Kornai, the main thesis is that the socialist countries (i.e., those with

CPEs) are best described as shortage economies, with all the resulting psychological behavioral rules of the actors in the system. Why is this so?

We take first the situation of the socialist firm in the short-term, that is, when production capacities are given and no expansion is possible. This means that such a firm can adjust only the composition of its inputs and the quantity and to some extent quality of its output. The firm faces several constraints in its functioning.

The most important point here is the softness of the budget constraint. When this constraint is hard, it means that a firm cannot spend more than it earns or takes in credits which have to be repaid. In the history of Eastern European CPEs no case is known of a firm going bankrupt because of a lack of funds. (In 1983 some firms were liquidated in Hungary because of their low earnings. There are also laws calling for bankruptcy of insolvent firms in Poland. It remains to be seen if this means a real change or not.) Even if the regulations state otherwise, in real life it is always possible to get more money if necessary from the state or ministerial budgets.

Now, bearing in mind that the budget constraint is soft, we must take into consideration the fact that in most cases people identify themselves with their firms, even if the earnings do not directly depend on their work efforts. This is true especially in the case of management, which always wants production of its firm to grow, mainly for the simple reason that the persons involved grow in importance together with the growth of their firm. Apart from that the management strives always to get good "grades" from superiors. The best and easiest way to obtain this favorable opinion from above is to overfulfill the plan and produce as much as possible from the given production capacities, bearing in mind that no demand constraint exists.

It seems paradoxical, but in the planned economy no firm wants just to fulfill the plan. It tries to produce more. At the same time, because the budget constraint is soft, it is natural on the part of the management to hoard as much of the inputs used in the production process as possible, or, we should way, as is possible to buy on the materials market. Experience teaches these managers that shortages of most inputs are the rule.

The fact that a firm has too much inventory in its warehouse never leads to serious trouble even when occasional controls are imposed by the superior authority. If, however, the lack of certain materials results in difficulties in the fulfillment of the plan, no explanation about "objective" problems can save the skin of the director of such a firm.

The soft budget constraint is also the main reason for the creation of the seller's market in the socialist countries. The existence of the seller's market reinforces the tendency toward the accumulation of shortages.

Now we turn to a larger time frame, in which the expansion of capacities is possible. The same psychological mechanisms lead to general shortages. The management of a firm (or of the ministry) never contemplates renouncing any investment project, on the grounds that it may prove unprofitable or that the output will not be bought. Management wants to grow with the firm. It wants to produce more. The budget constraint is soft. The demand constraint is assumed to be nonexistent. Thus, the best way to achieve the aims of the management is to expand production capacities to the maximum.

Even if some formal rationing schemes are introduced for some kinds of inputs or consumer goods, the tendency to hoard will reinstate itself through manipulability and overbidding in the rationing system. The first concept of "manipulability" says that the upper bounds of deliveries set by the rationing authority are perceived as soft or at least not very hard by the ration-wielding economic agents. Figure 2 illustrates this clearly: $\tilde{d}_j$ stands for purchase demands of the agents, and d_j^* denotes actual performed transactions. The upper part of the figure shows the nonmanipulable case of rationing, and the lower part, the manipulable scheme. It will be shown in the following paragraph that the economic agents in the CPEs will probably consider rationing schemes to be manipulable, and as a rule they will be right. This phenomenon will be accompanied by overbidding, that is, the agents will express higher demands for rations than their real desired transaction levels. This happens because the rationing agents perceive the rationing scheme as manipulable and because they realize that they face numerous other claimants for the rationed resources. This situation is shown in Figure 3, where the target

FIGURE 2

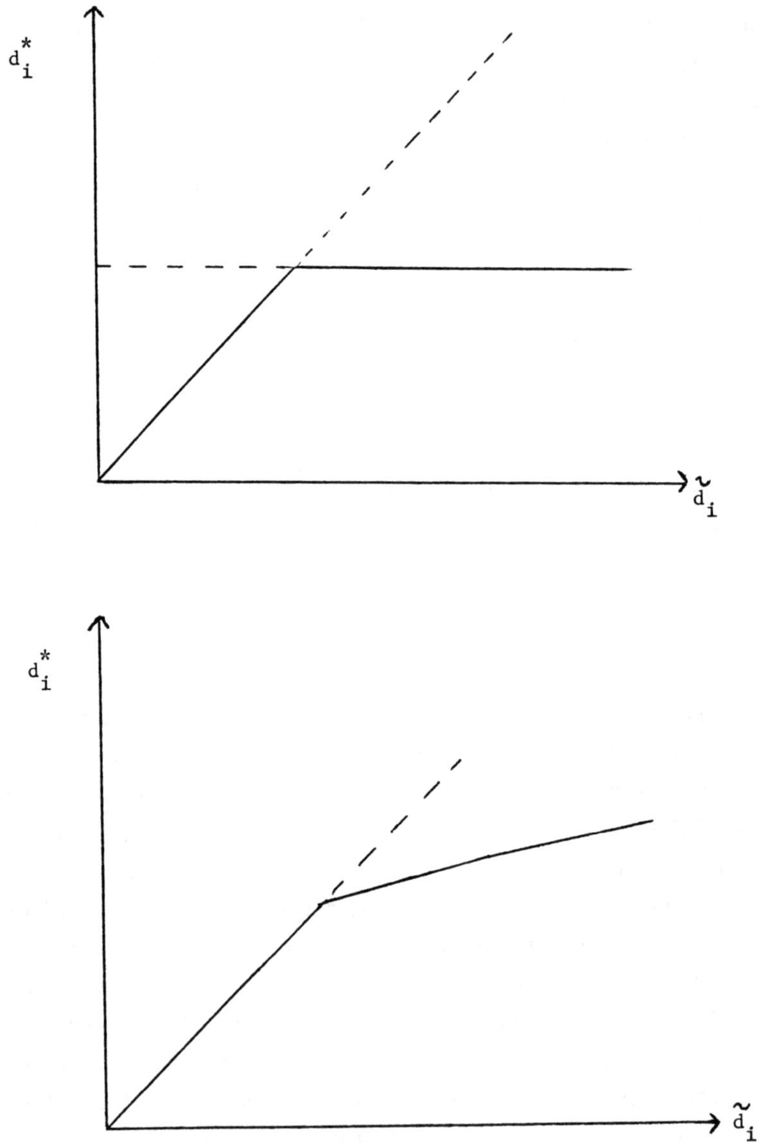

Source: Benassy 1982, p. 32.

transaction is denoted by $\hat{d}_j$. Moreover, the competition of different claimants will lead to the displacement of the perceived rationing scheme. Agents will notice that the same levels of expressed demands result in decreasing actual transaction levels, which will induce them to express ever-increasing demands in the hope of achieving the same transaction level ex post. Figure 4 shows this phenomenon.

On the whole it seems that the key point at which the economic system starts to evolve toward a shortage economy is the softness of budget constraints. The mechanisms outlined above are found in all CPEs, Hungary being to some extent an exception, although Kornai himself maintains that the effects of the economic reforms pursued in his country are not very strong.

The processes described above show already that a large gap can occur between the way the planned economy is supposed to function in the CPEs and its actual behavior. This is the case in the CPEs because some features of the economic system (like the soft budget constraints) provide for deviations from these norms. In a "planned" system every enterprise gets prescribed amounts of inputs and and it provides in turn the quantities of output that were planned. Everything is or rather should be coordinated.[3] In life, however, even if the enterprise has certain quantities of inputs assigned to it in the plan, it must fight to get them--it must resort to devious schemes to "win" the seller of the inputs. A complex network of information exchange channels and decision-making procedures develop, which form the underlying structure of the system.

Central Decision-Making

The way central decision-making takes place stems from the organization of the political system that not only concentrates power in one party but also assigns to it a very limited number of people at the top of the hierarchy of nomenklatura. These top decision-makers are able to act effectively beyond the rules and laws applying to people lower on the social pyramid in socialist countries. This makes any sort of planning completely impossible. To put it in another way, planning means making decisions concerning what should be produced in what quantity, in what

FIGURE 3

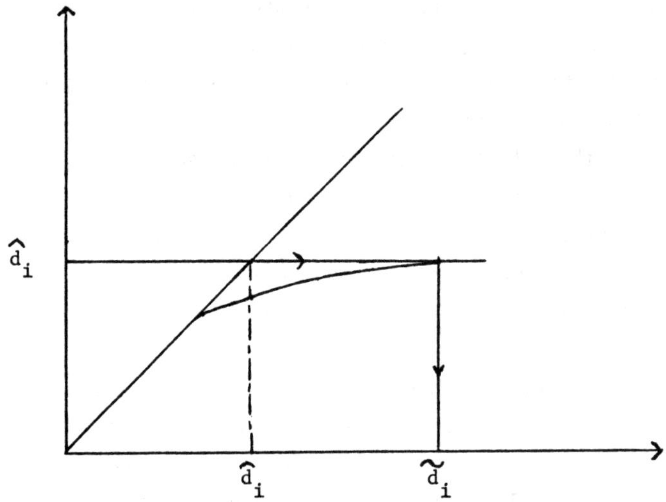

Source: Benassy 1982, p. 34

FIGURE 4

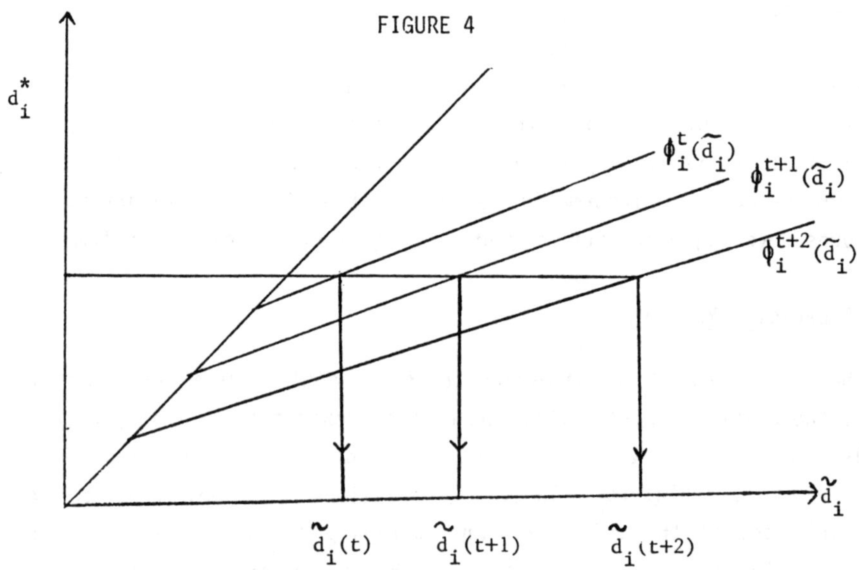

Source: Benassy 1982, p. 35.

place, at what time, and in what way. Once those decisions are made, they should be legally binding and stable for a specific period of time, allowing of course some deviation if some extraordinary event occurs. The crux of the matter is that in the so-called "planned economies," plans prepared by all those different organizations mentioned above, passed through parliaments and considered binding, remain pieces of paper whose content can and often actually is changed without notice.

The organization of power in the countries with CPEs results in a situation where the important consideration is not whether a given economic, locational, or investment decision is lawful, or consistent with the obligatory plans, but <u>who</u> has made this decision.

Bargaining for limited funds between ministries does not necessarily follow planning guidelines, institutional framework, or organizational structure as foreseen by the designers of the system It is to a much larger extent influenced by the actual personal configuration of the "nomenklatura." This has immense economic and logistical consequences. In the case of Poland in the 1970s several "courts" around the leading members of the political bureau were formed, with the members of the courts--the vassals--scattered throughout the economy.[4] Information exchange and decision-making usually followed channels inside those courts, circumventing the official institutional organization of the public life, creating inexplicable decision networks.

This also resulted in a large degree of impotence in the execution of orders from the proper decision-makers. This may seem paradoxical that we are now talking about a very centralized, directed system of economic management. In practice, however, many examples could be given of directives from certain command centers, theoretically responsible for a given field, having been ignored by their institutionally subordinated units when people to whom these orders had been addressed belonged to another group within the power structure.

The prime minister or some top politburo members can give an order without feeling constrained by laws or plans. Whether their orders will actually be executed remains questionable. One good example is provided by the attempts to reduce investment spending in Poland in 1977. One day in a speech by the first party secretary E. Gierek an economic "maneuver" was proclaimed and orders were given, without any reference to the legally binding five-year plan, to halt numerous investment projects. These orders were largely ignored, however. Regional and sectoral officials used all their available channels to various politburo members to defend "their" investment projects as absolutely indispensable for the future growth of the national economy. In the end of course the aggregate resource constraint of that period diminished the overall level of investments. But instead of a planned, orderly "maneuver" a "survival of the fittest" mechanism governed the investment cuts. This mechanism was based not on economic considerations but on the political bargaining of the involved members of the various power groups. The projects that were stopped were not the least promising in terms of future production and efficiency but those which had not been protected by some powerful politicians.

Let me give one more example of what I have in mind when I say that lawlessness makes planned functioning of the economy impossible (lawlessness in the sense that it is possible to disregard legal norms. This does not mean that the economy does not follow certain rules in its functioning. Some of these rules are precisely the subject matter of this chapter).

From 1973 on a partial reform of the system of management of the national economy was introduced in Poland. In a selected and growing number of the large industrial enterprises, the wage fund for the employees was supposed to be formed as a part of the value added created in a given enterprise within a year. The part of the value added earmarked for wages was to be determined by a certain parameter R expressing growth of value added in the whole industrial complex or sector from year to year. This parameter R was determined by the respective ministry. Up till that time the wage fund for an enterprise was fixed by the ministry for the coming year and could vary only negligibly in response to different results achieved by the enterprise. The point is, however, that after the introduction of the new "parametric" way of creating the wage fund, if a given enterprise worked inefficiently and the wage fund computed according to the agreed formulas was considered to be unsatisfactory by the management of the enterprise, all that was needed was to have proper access to the minister, or still better, to the prime minister, in order to obtain some additional wage funds assigned to the enterprise. Such examples are plentiful; some very interesting cases are to be found in state agricultural enterprise management and in location decisions. I have devoted more space to these problems elsewhere (Kowalski 1983, 1984b); in my 1983 paper I describe the case of the steel mill Katowice, which may be one of the main reasons for the disorganization of the Polish economy in the latter half of the 1970s.

What is of importance is that the whole notion of planning disappears when it is possible for the decision-makers to disregard previous decisions that are supposed to be the law. The resulting chaos tends to produce self-perpetuation through all the interindustry input-output linkages. It also reinforces the mechanisms leading to overall shortages, which were analyzed in the preceding pages.

I should like to point out that I do not reflect here on the merits or demerits of the planned economic system as such. What I imply is that without some degree of lawfulness, no system can function according to the rules that should in theory guide its motion. The political system makes it impossible to determine whether the planned system in the socialist countries can or cannot function efficiently.

Let me conclude this section with a five-point summary of the salient features of the CPEs, which will serve as building blocks in the next step, that is, the inclusion of the RE approach into the analysis.

1. The CPE is a shortage economy. Widespread shortages in consumer as well as on interindustry markets are a normal phenomenon influencing long- and short-term behavior of the economic agents.

2. Firms have soft budget constraints, which, together with the experiences concerning shortages, lead to hoarding, siphoning of all possible inputs from the markets, and to the expansion drive of the firms, sectors, regions. Households or individual consumers are the only actors in the system facing hard budget constraints.

3. Money and prices play no role in the decision-making of firms, sectors, and regional authorities, in either the short or the long term.

4. Soft budget constraints are accompanied by "voluntaristic," lawless, unplanned decision-making. This stems from the political system, which excludes top decision-makers from legal control.

5. "Normal" values of some variables play a key role in the functioning of the system. The word "normal" is used to denote levels of variables which at a certain point in time in a given place (country, region, etc.) are considered by the people to be normal (e.g., three-year wait for a car, three months for the execution of an input-purchase order, etc.). When the levels of variables remain at those "normal" levels, the economic system is in equilibrium, with some socially accepted levels of shortage, investment, production, and consumption. Deviations from the "normal" levels bring about adjustment mechanisms.

RATIONAL EXPECTATIONS AND THE BEHAVIOR OF ECONOMIC AGENTS IN THE CPE

Against the background of the two preceding sections we can now regard the key issue here: to what extent and in what way are the RE, natural rate, and the neutrality statements relevant for the CPEs?

Let me start with the RE hypothesis. There is no reason not to assume that in the CPEs the economic agents form their expectations in a rational manner, taking into account all relevant, available information about the way the economy functions and the way in which various government and nongovernment bodies behave concerning the economy. The actors facing soft budget constraints will be limited in their information gathering not by the costs but by the required efforts.

The possible objection to the above assertion, quoting ideological, noneconomic factors in the expectations and decision-making of at least some actors in the system, is invalid insofar as I consider the awareness of the ideological framework, the drive to achieve some unmeasurable ideological goals, or the wish to maximize power to form a part of the relevant information about the system. Some actors will simply have in their utility functions ideological elements which they try to maximize. This does not change the main idea that the actors try to get, process, and utilize all available information on the functioning of the system while forming their expectations of future levels of various economic variables.

I have mentioned earlier that the formation of rational expectations is influenced by (1) the speed of changes in the structure and in the rules of behavior of the economic agents and by (2) the availability of information about it.

In the case of the CPEs there is reason to assume that the RE hypothesis cannot be renounced either because the changes in the system are too fast or that there is no information about it. The CPEs, at least after the first post-World War II period of industrialization and social upheavals, are experiencing, as a rule, slower and less profound structural and institutional changes than the developed market economies. Again as a rule, in normal times economic agents have enough time to learn to recognize the rules of the system. On the other hand, concerning the information on government economic policy actions, it is often less readily available and disseminated than in most industrialized market economies. Of course there are some policy moves which are officially and noisily proclaimed, but in practice many important decisions happen without the public learning about them. This stems also from the informal decision-making mechanism described in the second section of this chapter.

So, at least in part, one can expect that the information reaching the economic agents is less complete than in the case of the industrialized market economies (but this is not true in the case of the actors who belong to the broadly defined government). This means that we certainly can expect that the rational expectations about economic variables formed by the agents will often deviate from the real levels of these variables. This will, however, occur with varying force and bring different consequences in the case of various types of economic agents with the system. But before we proceed to the discussion of those different kinds of actors and their expectations, we must devote some more attention to the general problems of the relevance of the RE approach in the context of the CPE.

There are some fundamental differences between the market economies and the CPEs with respect to the RE approach. First of all, the subject matter of expectations relevant to economic developments is different. In the context of the American economy, for which Lucas and the others developed the new approach, it has been the expectations concerning inflation rate, wage rate, and profits and their changes which were analyzed and which through deviations of the expected from the actual levels were postulated to bring about changes in output and employment.

It is obvious from the preceding section that such expectations concerned with <u>money</u> can have only a very limited importance in the CPEs. The only actors in the system who face hard budget constraints, that is, for whom money plays an active and not a passive role, at least in decision-making, are households. For other agents money and money-related economic variables play only a marginal role. Even in the case of households, if we assume the persistence of widespread shortages not only on the input but also on consumer goods markets, wages and prices will play a subordinate role in decision-making of households acting as producers and consumers.

Secondly, it follows that if expectations concern not money variables (i.e., we may disregard problems of "money illusion") but the real quantity variables, then the expectations themselves <u>and</u> their deviations from the actual levels will <u>both</u> affect real levels of some economic variables.

From my earlier description here of the functioning of the CPEs, it is clear that we consider the shortages of materials and consumer goods to be the most important features of these "resources constrained economies." It follows that the expectations concerning the general shortage level and shortages on specific partial markets should be taken as a focus for the RE approach to the CPEs.

There is a certain "normal" level of shortages (in Kornai's terminology) that corresponds to the "natural" inflation rate and unemployment levels from the Friedman and Lucas approach. This level is perceived by all concerned actors as acceptable and usual. The economic system will find itself in a situation comparable to an equilibrium with non-cleared markets from the "Western" theory (cf. Benassy 1982 on non-Walrasian equilibrium).

In contrast to the market economy, a change in shortage levels and a change in expectations about them (and not just deviations from the actual levels) bring about adjustments in quantities of output and employment

(employment will be defined below). This is so because, as mentioned above, there is no "money illusion"; changed expectations about shortages already consider things belonging to the real sphere. In the long run, however, people may accept new levels of shortages as normal and the adjustments may stop, bringing the economy to the new equilibrium position (meaning, of course, non-Walrasian equilibrium). One can observe here a certain similarity to the market economy, when the changed microstructure of the economy results in new "natural" levels of inflation and unemployment (see the first section in this chapter. In the CPE the new equilibrium will be characterized by new normal levels of shortages). But deviations from the expected levels of shortages from their real levels also will produce real effects.

The effects of changes in actual levels of shortages and their deviations ex post from normal levels are the subject of Kornai's research (especially his 1982 book). Here we focus attention on the changes of expectations about the future and their divergences from the levels of economic variables achieved in the future. This supplements the analysis of Kornai, who, in my opinion, did not devote enough attention in his books to the problems of expectations ex ante.

One could extend the subject of the relevant expectations to cover not only shortage levels but (similarly to Kornai's set of quantity signals in the economy) also expectations, and their divergence from the real levels of output and input stocks, investment commitment, investment vintage, and so on. These other signals employed by Kornai are, however, all very strongly related to the shortage level and are really only proxy variables because it is so difficult to define and measure shortages operationally. As long as my analysis remains on "safe," purely theoretical ground, we shall disregard these other shortage-related signals, and concentrate on shortage levels only.

I have written above that real, quantity adjustments result from expectations.[5] But as _quantities_ are fixed in various plans, which are very often, as we have learned in the previous section, formulated without taking into account economic factors, the most important quantity adjustment concerns the actual quantity of work performed by workers and managers in the socialist enterprises. It is through the changes in the quantity of work actually performed that the changes in output levels are brought about ex post (expectations will also affect plan formulation; see below).

Of course, there are other factors influencing the quantity of work actually performed, such as organizational structure of the enterprise, input supplies (shortages), to some extent ideological motivation, and in the longer term also advances in technology. Most of these factors are, however, very much subject to the tough resource constraints in the shortage economy, and everybody familiar with the situation in the socialist countries is well aware of the limitations of ideological incentives.

One should also not misunderstand the expression "changes in quantity of work actually performed" to mean the changes in the employment levels measured by the number of employed persons. We assume, in conformity with the observed reality of labor shortages in the socialist countries (labor is hoarded just like the other inputs), that the number of employed persons remains relatively stable in the CPEs, being limited by the supply of people willing to take a job. What can change, however, is the psychological propensity of people to work well, intensively, and efficiently in their work positions, or to do nothing, to pretend, and the like.

This is one of the major elements in my interpretation of the relevance of the RE approach to the CPEs, and how this propensity to work depends on rational expectations will be expounded on below in discussing the expectations and reactions of various kinds of economic agents.

What are those different kinds of economic agents whose expectations shape the course of the economy in the CPEs? Roughly they may be enumerated as follows:

1. <u>Authorities</u>
   (a) top party and government nomenklatura in the country's capital
   (b) central planning commission
   (c) sectoral ministries
   (d) regional party and government bodies
   (e) managers of enterprises.

There are of course some personal overlappings in the classification of actors belonging to the category of "authorities." The enumerated sub-actors have, as will be shown, different expectations, aims, and reactions.

2. Workers, in the enterprises acting as producers.
3. All people acting as consumers (i.e., without the "nomenklatura" officials supplied with everything according to their needs).

The question is, what happens? What are the reactions of these different actors if the expected shortage levels deviate from the real ones? First of all, let us notice that there are basically two types of reactions. Some actors in certain roles want to increase the levels of certain economic variables, while other actors intend to decrease levels of certain economic variables. Let me illustrate this enigmatic statement with examples. We assume that the actors expect the shortage level to rise. Then all the above-listed actors will want output to grow. Regional and sectoral authorities as well as the managers of the enterprises will want to increase their investment expenditures. All actors with the exception of the central decision-makers (1a and 1b in the classification above) will want to increase their purchases of inputs and of consumer goods. On the other hand, central planners and other top political decision-makers will want to diminish investment outlays.[6] Workers will want to diminish the supply of work actually performed. We should also observe that in all those different reactions (which are initially intentions but are then followed by actions) two subsets may be distinguished. One concerns a short- and long-term bargaining game between the various actors belonging to the sphere of authorities at all levels. The second may be understood as a game between all authorities and the workers acting as producers.

Let us turn to the first game. The actors of this game are the central decision-makers (planning commission and top nomenklatura), sectoral and regional authorities, and managers. Expectations of the increased shortages lead the central decision-makers to try to diminish investment outlays. All other actors, facing soft budget constraints, and expecting higher shortages, will try to squeeze more investments from the central level. This can be done by changing plans or rationing schemes in the future. This change of plans as a result of rational expectations about shortages amounts to the shifting of the supply and demand functions, in "Western" economic terminology. The actors belonging to the lower echelons of the "authorities" may also revert to the outright informal bargaining for immediate deliveries of investment goods and inputs, following the "survival of the fittest" principle. If the political decision-making mechanisms described in the second section of this chapter are plausible, a clear case of manipulability and lack of credibility of government policy seems very probable. In practice then, the claims of various lower-echelon authorities very often will compensate or even overcompensate for the intended decrease in investments, leading to increases in nominal expenditures. With hard resource constraints and sticky prices, this must result in increased shortages. Examples of such "self-defeating" policies are easy to find (they are mentioned in the second section of this chapter).

Regarding the process described above, I would like to emphasize a very interesting similarity to the neutrality proposition from Lucas's studies. As the mechanisms of decision-making that lay at the base of this "intra-authorities" game are inherent in the CPEs' socio-political systems, it seems that changing this situation is an almost impossible task. Really credible central government policy would call for such an upheaval in the political configurations and ways of doing things that, with the exception of some extraordinary periods of time (like the Solidarity interlude in Poland), it does not seem plausible. Another point is that because of the dense interrelations, contacts, allegiances, and lobbies, the idea that the central authorities may try to "fool" the other actors belonging to the authorities category is not feasible.

The situation is more complex in the second game, the one between all the actors named "authorities" and the people acting as producers. Again, as before, we assume that expectations of increased shortage levels cause all "authorities" actors to want to increase output. On the other hand, however, the reaction of the workers, expecting worse shortages, is to lower their supply of work actually performed. To elaborate on why this is so: I mentioned before that households are the only actors in the economy who face hard budget constraints. People can in the long run spend only as much as they earn, and this means that their wages are important to them. But the widespread shortages on the consumer goods markets may make it difficult to spend money. Getting access to certain things, tapping the right channel of rationing is often more important than having the money. So, if the expected shortage level is higher, people lose motivation to provide more intensive work effort. Of course, in the CPEs there is no direct, clear-cut relation between the work effort and the wage. This is one of the issues discussed and lamented upon in the economic literature of socialist countries. This separation is not absolute, however. There are legal ways of earning more money for more work within the enterprise; there are even <u>more</u> ways to earn money for work effort quasi-legally or illegally within and outside the enterprise (cf. the discussion on the role of the shadow economy in the CPEs in Wiles 1984). If the shortage of consumer goods is already acute and is expected to worsen, this extra effort, these attempts to do something to earn more, will fail to materialize. There is no sense in earning more money if it is impossible to get things for it. In the opposite case, if the employees expect the shortages to decrease, their work effort is apt to increase.

This sort of reaction is fully concomitant with the assumption of the rational formation of expectations. In this case however there will be no "neutrality" tendency as there was in the preceding situation, when we analyzed expectations and reactions of the "authorities" actors only. On the contrary, the expectations of the employees concerning the future levels of shortages will tend to have the character of the self-fulfilling prophecy. By affecting real quantities, they will reinforce the trends that are expected and remove the system from the non-Walrasian equilibrium. Let me explain this with the help of some equations and figures.

The situation described in the second game may be expressed by the two equations below. The first shows the reaction of all kinds of authorities:

$$y_{s,t+1} = y_p + \beta({}_tZ^{\varepsilon}_{t+1} - Z_t). \tag{3}$$

The second describes the reaction of the workers:

$$L_{s,t+1} = L_{sp} - \beta({}_tZ^{\varepsilon}_{t+1} - Z_t). \tag{4}$$

In the first equation the intention of the authorities to achieve output (planned supply) $y_{s,t+1}$ in period t+1 equals a certain normal level of output, which has up to now customarily been achieved from the employed fixed assets and labor y_p, plus the influence exerted on the intentions of the authorities by the difference between the expected shortage level in t+1 and the real shortage level in t. (If we take divergence of ${}_tZ^{\varepsilon}_{t+1}$ from real Z_{t+1}, we obtain the same results.) I do not want to go into detail on how we can actually measure y_p or Z_t (see Kornai 1982). Suffice it to say that the simplest way is to assume that $y_p = pN$, where p is the "normal" productivity of labor and N is the number of employeed persons. Z_t may for example be measured by observing the length of queues in the shops, by questionnaires determining the share of households' time budgets devoted to shopping and future expectations about it, and so on. In the first equation the expectations of increased shortage levels lead to an increase in the output level, which the authorities want to achieve. In the second equation the intention of the workers to supply work actually performed $L_{s,t+1}$ in the period t+1 equals their normal supply of this work L_{sp} minus the influence of the difference between the expected shortage level in t+1 compared with the present shortage level in t.

What is immediately apparent here is the fact that these two equations seem to suggest an inherent contradiction in the direction of reactions of the economic actors on their expectations in the second game. The authorities' desire to increase the output comes up against the opposite reaction of the workers to decrease their work effort. Of course, the individual workers, when asked, would say that they are well aware that theoretically they can achieve the decrease in the future shortage level only by an intensified work effort. But the moment they see themselves in their concrete, specific context within the CPEs, with their accumulated information and experiences from the past, and with their awareness of the lack of a link between their individual effort and the overall output levels, they react rationally: they diminish their supply of labor. They have learned the system and have reason to be pessimistic.

The contradictory reactions of the authorities and the workers help to explain why it is so difficult to improve the performance of the CPEs once they become shortage economies. These reactions tend to reinforce the mechanisms (discussed in the second section of this chapter) that make the economy move away from the equilibrium; they activate cumulative processes, which are extremely difficult to reverse. To make it clear how the contradictory reactions of the actors influence the developments of the whole economy, let us now use some figures.

Kornai (1982) has postulated the following relationship between the shortage levels and the actual levels of output and consumption (Figure 5). His idea was that up to a certain level of shortages, rising shortages lead, _ceteris paribus_, to increased output and decreased consumption. (After the shortage level exceeds a critical level, it exerts such a negative impact on the efficiency of the economy as a whole through bottlenecks, slacks, etc., so that these relationships no longer hold.) So a kind of Marshallian cross results with one equilibrium point at a normal state of a certain shortage level.

I postulate that the course of events will also be influenced by the intentions of the actors in the economy, reacting to rationally formed expectations. This is shown in Figure 6, where Y_s denotes the intentions of the authorities with respect to output and L_s the intentions of the workers with respect to work actually performed. Further, let us assume that the authorities' intentions to increase output mean that the authorities' demand for work actual performed increases. As we mentioned before, the intentions of the authorities to increase output will probably be followed by some input allocation, perhaps some organizational moves. But, as we argued above, in the resources-constrained economy it is safe to assume that the potential to achieve much in this sphere is rather limited. This means that Figure 6 can be replaced by Figure 7, where L_d denotes demand for work actually performed.

Figure 8 shows what happens if the expected shortage rises from time t=0 to t=1.[7] The demand of the authorities for work actually performed rises then from q_0 to q_{1d}. In the same period, however, the intended supply of real work will diminish from q_0 to q_{1s}. A disequilibrium situation occurs, and adjustments in real quantities will follow.

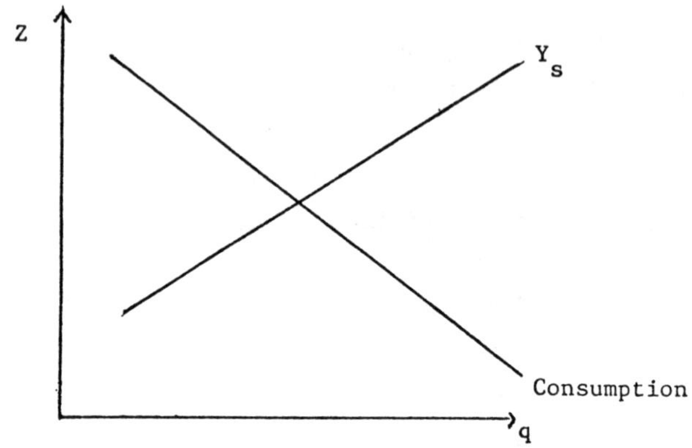

FIGURE 5

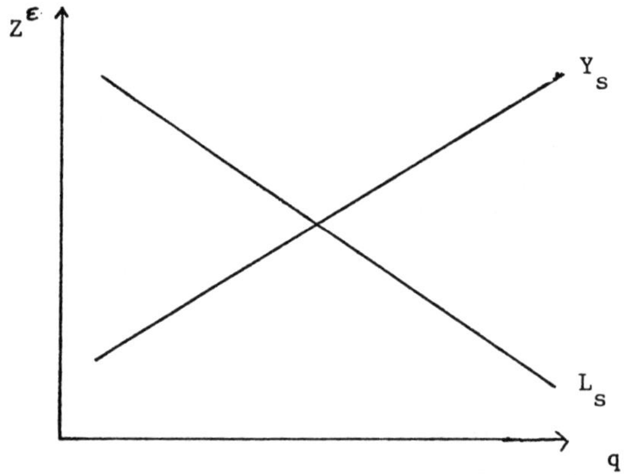

FIGURE 6

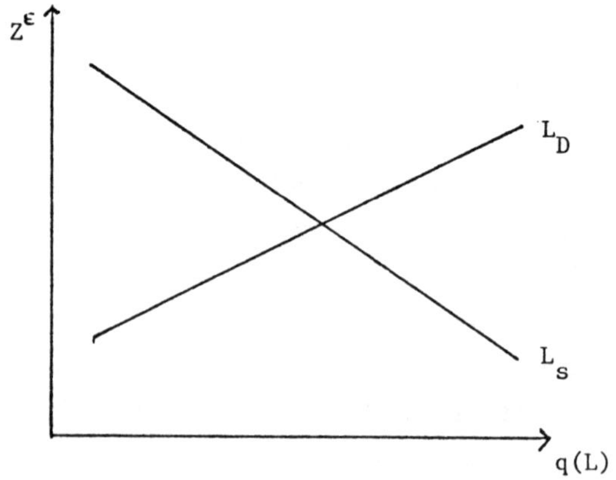

FIGURE 7

Source: Kornai 1982, p. 32.

FIGURE 8

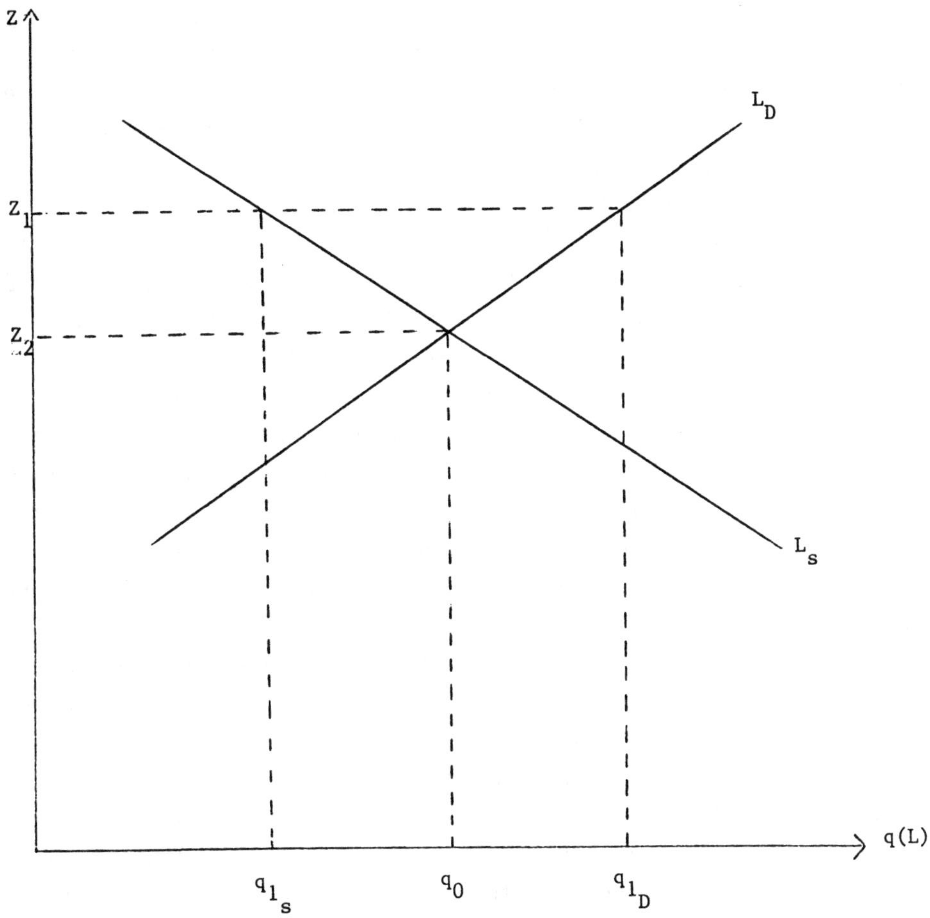

Finally, Figure 9 shows how this initial disequilibrium situation caused by expected shortages may give way to a cumulative process of moving away from the initial equilibrium position. Let us commence the explanation at the lower right part of Figure 9. It contains the already familiar relationship between the expected shortage and the intended demand for and supply of work actually performed. In time t=0, shortage level Z_0 equals the normal level. This corresponds to an equilibrium between the demand and supply of labor. Moving upward in the figure we project the relationship between the quantity of labor and the production level (a classical production function is assumed). In the next step to the left we show that there exists simultaneously a negative relationship between the production level and the shortage intensity (because of bottlenecks, etc.). Moving again to the left in the upper part of Figure 9, the product achieved in the economy is expressed as produced national income Y_s, which in the absence of foreign trade equals the distributed national income Y_d. In the lower left part of the figure this distributed income is "compared" with the ideal national income Y^W, which denotes income level when all the purchase demands in production and consumption spheres are realized (Y^W means thus a Walrasian equilibrium). The difference between Y^W and Y_d determines then the shortage intensity and together with additional information about the future, this leads to expectations concerning shortage levels (this is a move from the lower left to the lower right part of the figure). You may notice that on the level of shortage Z_0 we achieve, <u>ceteris paribus</u>, again the non-Walrasian equilibrium position. Now let us assume that the expected shortage rises from time t=0 to t=1, because of some external shocks or some new information. One can observe that after going through Figure 9 we achieve not point Z_1 again, but a new and even higher level of expectation concerning shortage levels, namely Z_2. The system as shown here does not return to the equilibrium position; it goes spiraling down to ever lower levels of production and higher levels of shortage. In other words, because the workers expect higher shortages they work less, and indeed they realize their expectations. I must emphasize here that I do not imply in any way that the workers are guilty of bringing the economy to this miserable state. They react to their rational expectations, formed on the basis of

FIGURE 9

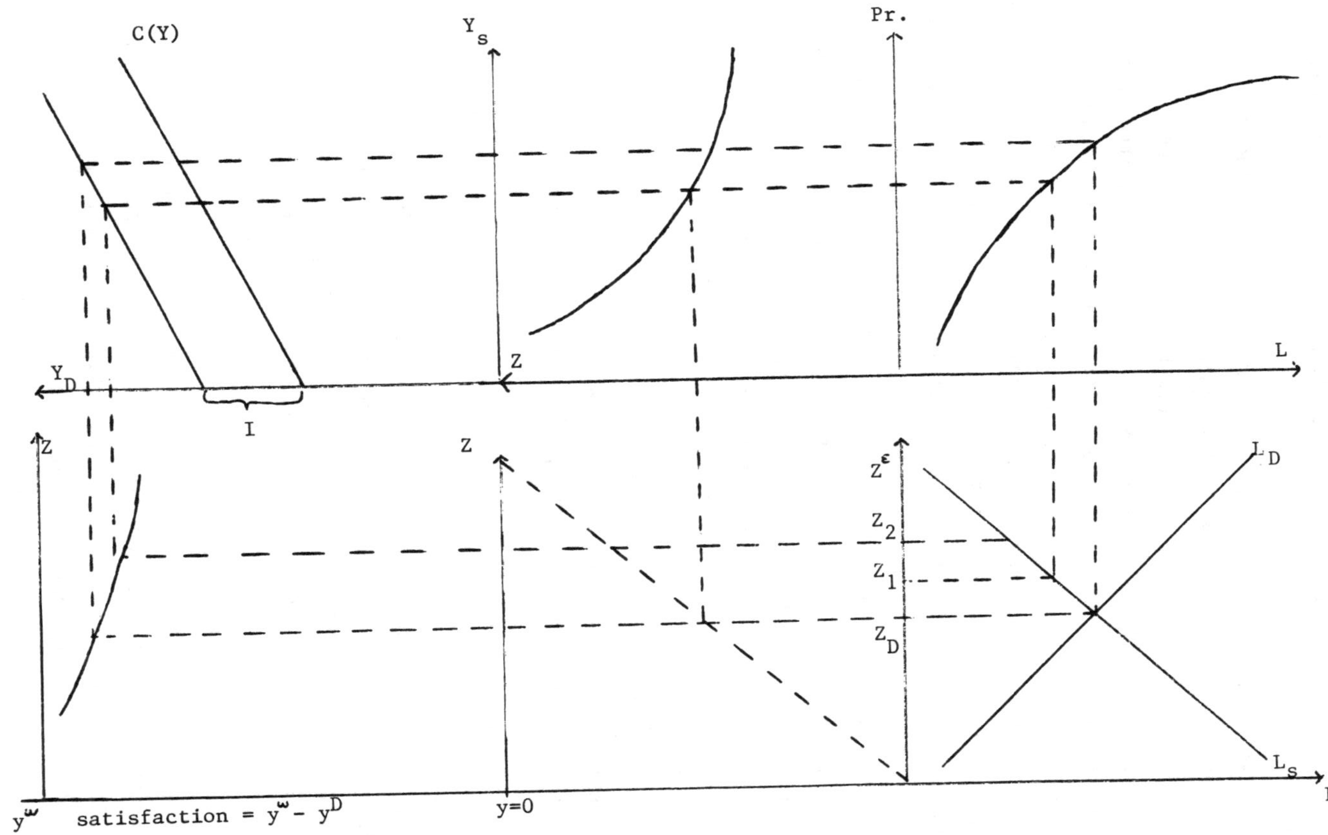

all available information on the past, present, and future developments in the economy.

We know that there are some ways of countering these tendencies through organizational and technological changes that increase productivity of labor. I have also indicated that within the existing CPEs there are clear limitations to this plan of action. But we know that in reality the economic systems in the socialist countries do not diverge too much from the "normal" shortage levels. (Poland in the last couple of years remains in a way beyond economic theory because of the extraordinary character of political events there.) The explanation of the fact that there are limits to the deviation of the CPEs from the normal course of development lies in the fact that after certain critical levels of shortage intensities have been achieved, people may change their expectations. This may happen either because they refuse to believe that things can get even worse or because of some new development on the political scene. Thus, the same cumulative mechanisms that brought about the worsening of the situation may result in its amelioration. The improvement will also have its limits because of the inherent problems of the functioning of the CPEs. After some time people's moods change again; they notice that the economy does not develop as they would wish. A good example of these phenomena are upswings in the public mood that often follow a new political administration's rise to power, promising improvements in the economy, and the downturns which follow a couple of years later, when it becomes clear that the promised economic and political reforms will not materialize (as in the case of Gomulka and Gierek in 1956 and 1970 in Poland). Together with the explanation of the accumulation of the false investment decisions coming in waves, these changing expectations of the populace help explain the nature of the cyclical development of the CPEs.

One perhaps surprising conclusion of this analysis is that there is in fact a place for and some sense in trying to "fool" the public in the CPEs. If the authorities could succeed in persuading the workers to expect the future shortage levels to decline, it would activate mechanisms which would help fulfill these expectations. But as we know, it is very seldom possible to persuade people to that effect. Historical experiences and repeated lessons make it actually a more and more formidable task (with the possible exception of Hungary, where the positive cumulative mechanism seems to be already working). People form expectations rationally, and to fool them is not easy. Credibility of government economic policy is not one of the strong merits of the policies in the CPEs, and because of the decision-making mechanisms inherent in the sociopolitical systems obtaining there, it seems doubtful whether it is really possible to conduct a credible policy or to fool the public into expecting improvement in the economic situation, without the far-reaching changes in the superstructure of those systems.

CONCLUSIONS

The RE hypothesis is not bound to any socioeconomic system. It is a behavioral postulate concerning all human beings. There are differences in the subject matter of the economically relevant expectations because of the different role of money and money-related variables in the functioning of different kinds of economic systems. In the CPEs shortage-related variables take the place of monetary variables as the subject of expectations.

There are differences in the implications of the RE hypothesis. Specifically, neutral economic policy statements in the CPEs may be considered plausible only with respect to the decision-making within the sub-system of economic agents belonging to the broadly defined authorities. The expression of the neutrality hypothesis is the impotence of the central economic decision-maker to implement its policy in the face of the countervailing claims of other authorities.

The expectations of the actors not belonging to the authorities category produce disequilibrium effects through the cumulative processes of decreasing the supply of labor actually performed, leading to lower levels of output.

Stabilization policy through influencing of expectations seem, as a rule, rather difficult to implement because of the historical experiences and inherent features of the sociopolitical system. Expectations of economic agents must be taken into account in analysis of the CPEs, as they influence real economic developments there.

NOTES

1. Equation (2) is known as the Lucas supply equation because it was first suggested in Lucas's 1972 paper. We shall need it in the next section for a discussion of rational expectations in the CPEs.

2. I will however continue to use the term "CPE" because of the widespread use of it in the literature on Eastern Europe.

3. This is valid in the case of the so-called directive central planning model. As in practice, these systems prevail in the CPEs. I feel justified in disregarding other theoretical models of CPEs.

4. Similar mechanisms influence the functioning of economies in other socialist countries. It occurs every time new leaders come to power. They organize their support groups, putting their adherents in various ministerial and subministerial positions.

5. Apart from the already mentioned fact that expectations deal with real variables, one should also bear in mind that as a rule wages and prices are very sticky in the CPEs, being fixed by central authorities. They are relatively sticky even after the economic reforms pursued in some socialist countries.

6. In the short run, that is. In the long run the central decision-makers want also to increase investments.

7. The reasons for this may be knowledge that the country has to repay foreign debt or supply something in large quantities to "Big Brother," for example.

REFERENCES

Barro, R., and H. Grossman. 1976. Money, employment, inflation. Cambridge: Cambridge University Press.

Benassy, J. P. 1982. Economics of market disequilibrium. Academic Press.

Fellner, W. 1979. The credibility effect and rational expectations: Implications of the Gramlich study. Brookings Paper on Economic Activity 1:167-78.

Friedman, M. 1968. The role of monetary policy. American Economic Review 58:1-17.

Grossman, H. 1980. Rational expectations, business cycle and government behavior. In Rational expectations and economic policy, ed. S. Fischer. Chicago: National Bureau of Economic Research.

Kornai, J. 1980. Economics of shortages. North Holland.

------. 1982. Growth, efficiency, shortages. Berkeley: University of California Press.

Kowalski, J. S. 1983. On the relevance of the concept of the Centrally Planned Economies. Jahrbuch für Sozialwiss 2 (1983):255-66.

Kowalski, J. S., and U. Blum. 1984a. Efficiency and inefficiency in regional perspective: An econometric study of the economic performance of the Polish regions. Discussion Paper 1/1984. Inst. f. Wirtschaftspol. u. Wirtschaftsforsch. Univ. Karlsruhe.

Kowalski, J. S. 1984. Conflicts between regions and spatial polarization in centrally planned economies. Paper presented at the 6th Advanced Inst. in Reg. Scien. August 17-25, 1984, Bamberg, West Germany, forthcoming.

Lucas, R. E., Jr. 1972. Expectations and the neutrality of money. Journal of Economic Theory 4:103-24.

------. 1973. Some international evidence on output-inflation tradeoffs. American Econ. Rev. 63:326-34.

Maddock, R., and M. Carter. 1983. A child's guide to rational expectations. Journal of Economic Literature 20, No. 1 (March, 1983).

Muth, J. 1961. Rational expectations and the theory of price movements. Econometrica 29:315-35.

Okun, A. M. 1981. Prices and quantities. The Brookings Institution.

Sargent, T., and N. Wallace. 1975. Rational expectations: The optimal monetary instrument and the optimal money money supply rule. Journal of Polit. Econ. 83:241-54.

------. 1976. Rational expectations and the theory of economic policy. Journal of Monetary Economics 2:169-84.

Scheffrin, S. 1983. Rational expectations. Cambridge: Cambridge University Press.

Wiles, P. 1984. Schattenwirtschaft in Kommunistischen Ländern. Paper presented at "Tägliches Leben in der kommunistischen Ländern," H. M. Schleyer Stiftgung, February, 1984, Munich.

Chapter 9

THE CASE OF CENTRAL PLANNING IN THE USSR

By

Andrzej Brzeski*

> There is no such thing as 'economic growth in general'--as growth in all-purpose economic capacity. We cannot avoid the question: capacity for what?
>
> - G. Warren Nutter (1975)

Lenin is reported to have said in October, 1917: "Either death or we must overtake and surpass the advanced capitalist countries." It was this Bolshevik obsession with the tempo that ushered in the age of growthmanship, and however indirectly, led to the present volume. A discussion of

---

*Originally presented at the 19th International Seminar of CESES (Florence, 1983), this chapter appeared as "Lo sviluppo economico sovietico" in Rivista di politica economica (1984):VII. Comments by the participants in the seminar, especially Murray Feshbach, John H. Moore, and Svetozar Pejovich, are gratefully acknowledged, but are not reflected here. Only a short postscript has been added; otherwise the text is unchanged.

A. Brzeski is professor of economics at the University of California (Davis).

economic growth here, leaving out the Soviet case, would therefore be rather like a performance of *Hamlet* without the Prince of Denmark. In lieu of those better qualified, I shall try to prevent such a gaping omission.

Thanks to Western scholarship, there is now a rich store of pertinent data.[1] A recently released study, *USSR: Measures of Economic Growth and Development, 1950-80*, is of special importance--a veritable *summa* of research on the subject. I shall simply draw on the findings of this study, supplementing my second-hand account with points from other sources, including an occasional *spravochnik* (reference book) or *yezhegodnik* (annual; yearbook; annual report).

My approach to data is admittedly casual. I shall gloss over index number subtleties: combine time series, compare internationally, and so forth. Moreover, territorial changes and resulting discontinuities will be disregarded.

My purpose is limited: to provide a rough assessment of the dimensions and an overview of the main characteristics of an economic process that started with the First Five-Year Plan. Yet figures, even when complete and accurate (and mine are flawed on both counts) are not enough. The already quoted essay by Nutter, a prodigious quantitative researcher, reminds us that "the basic issues involved in the subject of economic . . . growth cannot be put in such a way that any single number--or any set of numbers--will resolve them" (Nutter 1965). In economics, as in other social sciences, numbers acquire meaning only when we understand the system to which they pertain. A qualitative, causal, and, given the role of central direction, teleological interpretation is thus necessary if one is to make sense of the Soviet experience of economic growth.

DIMENSIONS

Long-term Indices

An index of overall growth since 1928 can be compiled by splicing the estimates in *USSR: Measures* with those of Bergson. Probably because of the Gerschenkron effect,[2] there is a significant divergence between the indices for 1950-55 in the two sources; according to *Measures* the gross national product (GNP) rose by 30.6 percent, while Bergson's estimate is 44.1 percent.[3] As a compromise, 37.2 percent--the geometric mean of the two indices--is incorporated in the spliced series in Table 1.

Table 1. Soviet (real) GNP, 1928-80.

Year	1928=100	1940=100	1950=100	1960=100	1970=100
1928	100				
1937	275				
1940	332	100			
1950	398	120	100		
1955	546	164	137		
1960	671	202	168	100	
1965	857	258	215	128	
1970	1,107	333	278	165	100
1975	1,390	419	349	207	125
1980	1,517	457	381	226	137

Sources: Bergson 1961, p. 210, and USSR: Measures, pp. 52-54. All figures rounded.

There are approximations, but nevertheless they probably reflect the order of the magnitudes: (1) a fifteenfold increase in output between 1928 (hence, presumably also 1913!) and 1980; (2) a less than fourfold increase since 1950 (the year that marked the end of postwar reconstruction); and, (3) a more than twofold increase since 1960 (roughly, the end of "extensive growth"). The long-term indices need to be put in perspective.

First, let me point out that official Soviet statistics present a much more dramatic growth record (see Table 2).

Instead of the fifteenfold increase in output, the Central Statistical Administration of the USSR claims for the 1928-82 period a fantastic seventy-fivefold increase! To be sure, product concepts differ: the Soviet figures refer to the so-called (Marxist) produced national income, that is, net material product, rather than to the more comprehensive GNP. In addition, there is the issue of valuation, that is, of weights, all very familiar to the student of Soviet growth (see, e.g., Wiles 1964, ch. 12). Still, technicalities alone do not explain the disparity. Rather, they themselves require explanation. Let me offer a simple conjecture: ever since the purge of Gosplan minimalists, Soviet statisticians, as well as planners, have labored to make the *tempo* look spectacular.[4] Concepts and methods with a built-in "growth-augmenting" bias were just a means of coping with the cognitive dissonance from which the embellishers of statistics must have suffered.

Table 2. Comparison of Soviet NMP and GNP indices, 1928-80.

Year	Official Soviet (A)	Western Estimate (B)	Ratio (A):(B)
1928	100	100	---
1980	7,556	1,517	4.98

Sources: *Narodnoie khoziaistvo SSSR, 1922-1982* (Finansy i statistika: 1982), p. 52, and *Strana sovietov za 50 let* (Statistika: 1967), p. 29; and Table 1 above. Soviet data refer to net material product, Western estimates to GNP.

In this connection, it is interesting to note in Table 3 the temporal pattern of the differences.

Table 3. Comparison of Soviet NMP and GNP indices by decade, 1928-80.

Period	Official Soviet (A)	Western Estimate (B)	Ratio (A):(B)
1928-40	513	332	1.54
1941-50	160	120	1.33
1951-60	275	168	1.64
1961-70	198	165	1.20
1971-80	162	137	1.18

Sources: *Narodnoie khoziaistvo SSSR, 1922-1982* (Finansy i statistika: 1982), p. 52, and *Strana sovietov za 50 let* (Statistika: 1967), p. 29; and Table 1 above. Soviet data refer to net material product, Western estimates to GNP.

For whatever reason, the disparities seem to be less extreme in the last twenty years. Accounting, statistics, valuation, and, of course, shifts in the use of resources may have been the main cause of the narrowing of differences. But most likely a letup in the pressures to fabricate impressive numbers was important, too; compared with Stalin, Brezhnev was a moderate. At any rate, in the all-important matter of the tempo, the reality principle is apparently taking an upper hand over ideology and agitprop. But even now, Soviet statistics, presumably mirroring ambitions, continue to exceed actual accomplishments.

Second, Soviet long-term growth can be compared with the parallel performance of, say, the United States--another country both very large and abundantly endowed in varied resources. For the 1928-80 period as a whole, Soviet growth was considerably faster: the fifteenfold increase in the Soviet GNP compares with a fivefold U.S. increase.[5] For the time period 1940-80, however, the indices nearly converge (see Table 4).

Table 4. Soviet and U.S. GNP growth, 1940-80.

	1940	1980
Soviet	100	457
U.S.	100	430

Sources: See Table 1 above and Gordon 1981, Appendix B, pp. XVI-XVII as updated in "Annual Data (Revised) 1930-1930" (mimeographed). U.S. GNP calculations are at 1972 prices.

There is a prima facie comparison, its validity no doubt impaired by Soviet war-time population and capital losses. But then again, there were some offsetting postwar Soviet gains: annexations, massive reparations, as well as the notorious unequal trade with bloc countries until at least 1956. Be that as it may, the last four decades lend little support to the notion that the Soviet system is exceptionally good at fostering growth. Had the comparison been with one of the really fast-growing countries, for instance Japan, the Soviet performance would have seemed even less impressive. The long-term Soviet growth, though creditable, has been far from overwhelming by international standards. Hence, to paraphrase an expression of Peter Wiles's: They may still be eyeing our efficiency, but we have hardly a reason to eye their growth.

Per Capita Growth

Another more illuminating gauge of long-term economic growth is per capita output. Table 5 shows its dynamics.

Table 5. Soviet per capita GNP, 1928-80.

Year	1928=100	1940=100	1950=100	1960=100	1970=100
1928	100				
1940	257	100			
1950	334	130	100		
1960	476	185	142	100	
1970	692	268	206	145	100
1980	862	336	258	182	125

Sources: GNP indices from Table 1 above; population figures (as of January 1) from Soviet Economy in the 1980's: Problems and Prospects, part 2 (Government Printing Office: 1983), p. 267 and (for 1928) from Mickiewicz 1973, p. 53; for 1940, Narodnoie khoziaistvo SSSR, 1922-82, p. 9.

Again, the long-term gains seem substantial when measured against the low (close to the 1913 level) base of 1928: an increase of eight and a half. With other years as benchmarks, Soviet per capita growth appears more modest. A comparison with U.S. figures (in Table 6) is instructive in this respect.

Table 6. Soviet and U.S. per capita growth, 1940-80.

	1940	1980
Soviet	100	336
U.S.	100	257

Sources: Table 1; Gordon 1981, and Statistical Abstract of the United States 1980, p. 6.

Assessing relative Soviet gains--the increase of per capita GNP by a factor of three and one-third vis-à-vis the two and one-half times increase in the United States, one needs to keep in mind the disparate economic levels of the two countries. Questionable as any precise estimate must be in this case, dollar calculations rank Soviet per capita GNP at 37 to 44 percent of the corresponding U.S. figure (see, e.g., World Bank Atlas; 1977 World Population Data Sheet; World Military Expenditures), say, somewhere between one-third and one-half. Owing to "advantages of backwardness"--technology backlog, extensive resource margins, and so on--one would naturally expect the Soviet economy to grow faster. It may actually be deemed strange that the catching up, which was announced with fanfare more than half a century ago at the 16th Party Congress (Stalin, Political report, passim), if not earlier, has not been more successful. Stalin's heirs at the Kremlin had surely counted on greater success. The party program adopted by the 22nd Congress confidently promised that "in the current decade (1961-70) the Soviet Union . . . will surpass the strongest and richest capitalist country--the USA--in production per head." Furthermore, "by the end of the second decade (1971-80) . . . Soviet society will come close to a stage where it can introduce the principle of distribution according to needs" (Program of the Communist Party, p. 70). These high hopes have obviously been disappointed. Decades of comprehensive planning, forced saving, and severe regimentation have not brought the first socialist country closer to U.S. productivity levels. Indeed, in absolute terms, the lag in per capital GNP seems to have more than doubled since 1940.[6]

The Slowdown

When Bergson's Real National Income came out more than two decades ago, the New York Times reported: "It Says the Soviet Economy May Overtake U.S."[7] This was an apt capsule summary, but, as I already indicated, the possibility has so far remained theoretical. In reality, Soviet chances of catching up in this century appear nil. A loss of vigor, clearly reflected in the declining tempo, warrants the skepticism (see Table 7).

Table 7.. Average annual percentage growth in Soviet GNP, 1928-80.

Five-Year Period	Per Year GNP growth (%)
1928-40	10.5
1941-50	1.8
1951-55	5.5
1956-60	5.9
1961-65	5.0
1966-70	5.2
1971-75	3.7
1976-80	2.7

Sources: Table 1 above for 1928-50; other figures from USSR: Measures, p. 15.

Soviet growth rates are placed in a broader international context in Table 8.

The assessment of those figures by their original compilers (in USSR: Measures) merits quotation:

> For the entire 1951-79 period, the figure for the Soviet Union is roughly in the middle of the OECD range. Japan, West Germany, Spain, and Turkey clearly achieved faster growth than the Soviet Union, and several other nations achieved rates close to the Soviet figure. In comparison with the United States, the Soviet Union consistently enjoyed a higher growth rate until the late 1970s. The average annual growth rate of Soviet GNP is a full percentage point higher than that of the United States for the entire 1951-79 period. Since 1970, however, the growth rate of Soviet GNP has declined steadily, while the U.S. growth rate has continued at roughly an unchanged tempo. As a result, the U.S. and Soviet economies grew by almost the same average rates in the 1970s (p. 19).

These judicious conclusions fully support the view that unless present trends are reversed, the Soviet goal of "catching up" and "surpassing" the United States, and other Western countries, will remain unattainable in the foreseeable future. This issue we will return to.

Allocation Patterns

Lest GNP, total or per capita, be taken as the only or even the most important indicator of economic growth, it is necessary to pose the

Table 8. Annual percentage growth[a] for selected OECD countries and the Soviet Union, 1951-79.

	1951-55[b]	1956-60	1961-65	1966-70	1971-75	1976-79	1951-79[b]
Total OECD	•	•	5.2	4.8	3.1	4.0	•
Canada	5.2	4.0	5.7	4.8	5.0	3.7	4.8
United States	4.2	2.3	4.6	3.1	2.3	4.4	3.4
Japan	7.2	8.6	10.0	12.2	5.0	5.9	8.3
Australia	3.8	4.0	4.8	6.0	3.5	2.4	4.2
New Zealand	3.8	4.0	4.9	2.7	4.0	0.3	3.3
Finland	5.0	4.1	4.8	4.8	3.9	2.5	4.2
France	3.7	5.0	5.8	5.4	4.0	3.7	4.6
West Germany	9.2	6.5	5.0	4.4	2.1	4.0	5.1
Italy	5.6	5.5	5.2	6.2	2.4	3.8	4.8
Netherlands	5.9	4.0	4.8	5.5	3.2	3.1	4.4
Norway	3.8	3.3	4.8	3.7	4.6	4.2	4.1
Spain	5.2	3.2	8.5	6.2	5.5	2.5	5.3
Sweden	3.4	3.4	5.2	3.9	2.7	1.1	3.4
Switzerland	4.9	4.3	5.2	4.2	0.8	0.9	3.5
Turkey	8.1	4.6	4.8	6.6	7.5	4.1	6.0
United Kingdom	3.9	2.6	3.1	2.5	2.0	2.4	2.7
USSR	5.5	5.9	5.0	5.2	3.7	3.0	4.8

Sources: USSR: Measures, p. 20.

[a]Gross Domestic Product for OECD countries, GNP for the Soviet Union.

[b]Data in column 1 for Japan and the United Kingdom are for 1953-55; for Finland, France, West Germany, Italy, and the Netherlands--1952-55; and for New Zealand and Spain--1955 only. The corresponding data in column 7 are for 1953-79, 1952-79, and 1955-79, respectively.

question: growth for what? Table 9 shows the relentless investment drive that has become the distinct mark of Soviet economic policies.

An ever-climbing share of gross investment and a decline of the consumption share in the GNP was understandably the outcome of such allocation priorities (see Table 10).

To broaden the perspective, Soviet allocation pattern, that is, output use, is compared with that of OECD countries in Table 11.

Table 9. Consumption and gross investment indices, 1928-80.

Year	Consumption		Investment	
	1928=100	1950=100	1928=100	1950=100
1928	100		100	
1940	157		437	
1950	174	100	741	100
1960	321	184	2,009	271
1970	497	286	3,871	522
1980	675	388	6,201	836

Sources: Bergson 1961, p. 210 and USSR: Measures, pp. 79-81. Because of divergent indices for the 1950-55 period, geometric means were taken (as in Table 1). Indices obtained thus were spliced with the Measures series to obtain the values for 1960 and later years. Bergson's figures for 1928-1950 pertain to household consumption outlays and overstate the growth of total consumption (communal services grew at a slower rate).

Table 10. Consumption and investment percentage shares in the GNP, 1928-80.

	Consumption Share	Investment Share	
		Gross	New Fixed
1928	82.3	13.8	•
1940	60.5	20.6	•
1950	59.9	14.2	12.0
1960	57.7	24.2	20.0
1970	54.2	28.2	23.4
1980	53.6	33.0	26.0

Sources: Bergson 1961, p. 149 for 1928, 1940. The calculations are for household consumption outlays plus community services at 1950 factor cost. Other figures from USSR: Measures, pp. 76-78 at 1970 adjusted factor cost prices. Comparison of overlapping calculations for 1950 and 1955 indicates minor differences in the consumption share, but serious incomparability in the case of investment: according to Bergson, 27.9 and 29.2 percent of the GNP in 1950 and 1955, while the Measures estimate of the respective shares is only 14.2 and 19.5 percent.

Table 11. Percentage distribution of national product* by end use in selected OECD countries and in the Soviet Union, 1950-79.

	Consumption				Investment				All Other Expenditures			
	1950	1960	1970	1979	1950	1960	1970	1979	1950	1960	1970	1979
Total OECD	•	60.1	59.3	61.0	•	20.2	22.8	21.2	•	19.7	17.9	17.8
Canada	55.2	57.5	53.5	57.0	21.1	22.5	21.7	22.2	23.7	20.0	25.0	20.8
United States	62.1	60.9	52.2	64.6	19.5	18.2	18.4	17.4	18.4	20.9	19.4	18.0
Japan	63.2[a]	63.2	54.4	55.4	15.1[a]	23.1	34.9	33.2	21.7[a]	13.7	10.7	11.4
Australia	67.5	61.5	57.7	59.3	24.4	24.6	26.5	21.2	8.1	13.9	15.8	19.5
New Zealand	•	68.2	59.9	62.4	•	•	•	•	•	•	•	•
Finland	52.8[b]	54.4	55.1	54.1	25.5[b]	30.1	28.6	23.2	21.7[b]	15.5	16.3	22.7
France	60.0[b]	60.3	59.1	62.6	17.3[b]	19.3	23.8	21.5	22.7[b]	20.4	17.1	15.9
West Germany	52.5[b]	52.0	53.3	54.7	20.1[b]	24.0	24.1	22.2	27.4[b]	24.0	22.6	23.1
Italy	66.1[b]	59.4	63.6	62.4	15.6[b]	26.0	24.4	18.9	18.3[b]	14.6	12.0	18.7
Netherlands	56.9[b]	51.8	57.4	59.8	18.6[b]	21.6	25.3	20.8	24.5[b]	26.6	17.3	19.4
Norway	61.1	57.9	54.1	48.6	27.3	26.3	28.2	26.3	11.6	15.8	17.7	25.1
Spain	72.9[c]	69.9	67.4	68.8	15.6[c]	16.7	23.1	20.0	11.5[c]	13.4	9.5	11.2
Sweden	62.3	56.8	52.3	52.5	16.7	20.6	21.6	19.0	21.0	22.6	26.1	28.5
Switzerland	67.4	58.7	58.4	63.9	16.2	23.7	25.5	23.6	16.4	17.6	16.1	12.5
Turkey	77.3	79.7	73.9	72.9	16.8	15.5	19.4	16.6	5.9	4.8	6.7	10.5
United Kingdom	62.6[a]	63.7	61.0	61.4	12.7[a]	16.7	20.7	17.9	24.7[a]	18.6	18.3	20.7
USSR	59.9	57.7	54.2	53.2	14.2	24.2	28.2	32.5	25.8	18.1	17.6	14.3

Source: USSR: Measures, p. 21.

*Gross Domestic product for OECD, GNP for the Soviet Union.
[a]The data are for 1952.
[b]The data are for 1951.
[c]The data are for 1954.

In analyzing Table 11, one needs to remember that the shares "are not strictly comparable . . . because Soviet government expenditures for health, education, and physical culture are included in consumption. These expenditures were equal to 5.5 percent of Soviet GNP in 1970 and serve to inflate Soviet consumption data relative to OECD data" (USSR: Measures, p. 19). To put it differently, the Soviet consumers' reduced share in the GNP, by 7 percentage points, represents a relatively deeper cut than it appears to at first glance. As pointed out in USSR: Measures, "the only other country to have a similar change in output-use patterns is Japan, where investment has risen from 15 to 33 percent of GDP, while private consumption has fallen from 63 to 55 percent. Most of the other OECD countries show either stable patterns of distribution or shifts from private consumption to other (mostly government) expenditures" (USSR: Measures, p. 23).

Thus, whatever else one may say about its purpose, Soviet growth has certainly not been primarily "for the consumers." Although the latter's lot has improved with time, the backwardness vis-à-vis the industrial West has increased in absolute and possibly also relative terms. Soviet per capita consumption of goods and services is now perhaps one-fourth to one-third of the corresponding U.S. volume.[8] However one might stretch and manipulate index number formulae and value weights, the disparity (so clearly visible to anyone familiar with conditions in both countries) persists. The Soviet Union may be a superpower, but in providing for the needs of the people it has remained a laggard. This conclusion emerging from binary comparison with the United States is also otherwise confirmed. Table 12 shows Soviet relative standing in per capita consumption among a fairly representative group of developed countries.

Furthermore, as a comparing of the rates of growth in per capita consumption suggests (see Table 13), Soviet prospects for catching up with, not to mention surpassing, the advanced Western countries are dim.

Aggregate statistics, on which I must rely here, can conceal almost as much as they reveal. It is tempting, for instance, to explain lagging Soviet consumption as simply a matter of time preference of the politburo: sacrificing the present for the sake of the future. In some sense, arithmetically, this is true, but a look at the Japanese case, in which a

Table 12. Per capita consumption levels in seven countries, 1970, 1973, and 1976.

Country	Level Relative to U.S.		
	1970	1973	1975
United States	100.0	100.0	100.0
France	65.9	67.9	72.1
West Germany	64.7	63.9	66.0
United Kingdom	62.5	62.2	57.6
Japan	49.3	53.5	54.3
Italy	47.9	47.4	46.3
Hungary	41.3	42.0	43.8
Soviet Union	•	•	34.4

Sources: Consumption in the USSR: An International Comparison, p. 19.

Table 13. Average annual rate of growth of per capita consumption in selected OECD countries and the Soviet Union, 1950-79.

	1951-55[a]	1956-60	1961-65	1966-70	1971-75	1976-79	1951-79[b]
Total OECD	•	•	3.7	3.7	2.8	3.1	•
Canada	2.5	2.1	2.6	2.7	5.2	2.4	2.9
United States	1.5	1.0	2.8	2.7	2.0	3.4	2.2
Japan	7.0	6.8	7.9	8.6	4.8	3.9	6.6
Australia	0.4	0.9	2.5	2.9	2.5	1.1	1.7
New Zealand	•	•	1.5	0	1.2	0.1	0.7
Finland	3.7	2.0	5.0	4.1	3.6	1.5	3.4
France	3.7	3.2	4.5	4.0	4.1	3.6	3.9
West Germany	8.1	5.5	4.1	4.0	2.6	3.7	4.6
Italy	3.9	4.1	5.3	6.1	1.8	2.6	4.0
Netherlands	3.4	2.3	4.9	4.9	2.3	3.3	3.5
Norway	1.8	2.2	2.6	2.9	3.2	1.9	2.5
Spain	4.6	1.5	7.3	4.8	4.8	1.6	4.1
Sweden	1.8	1.8	3.6	2.3	2.3	0.9	2.2
Switzerland	1.4	2.3	3.1	3.0	1.4	2.1	2.2
Turkey	5.4	1.9	1.8	3.0	4.5	1.7	3.1
United Kingdom	3.9	2.2	2.0	1.6	2.0	2.4	2.2
USSR	3.1	3.8	2.1	4.3	2.6	1.7	3.0

Sources: USSR: Measures, p. 22.

[a]Data in column 1 for Japan and the United Kingdom are for 1953-55; for Finland, France, West Germany, Italy, and the Netherlands--1952-55; and for Spain--1955 only. The corresponding data in column 7 are for 1953-79, 1952-79, and 1955-79, respectively. The value in column 7 for New Zealand is for 1961-79.

steep climb of the investment share was accompanied by a rapid increase in per capita consumption, suggests other reasons as well.

An inordinate expansion of Soviet military spending is certainly a very important factor. Someone was quoted as having said, "the USA _has_ a military-industrial complex, the USSR _is_ a military industrial complex" (Becker 1982, p. 22). I think this epitomizes the situation. According to some estimates "defense expenditures amounted to 11 to 13 percent of GNP in 1970 and have increased at an annual rate of 4 to 5 percent per year since 1965" (_USSR: Measures_, p. 15). Consequently, the present share of military spending in the Soviet GNP should be at least 15 percent, that is, more than twice the corresponding U.S. proportion. Personally, I suspect that even this may be a gross underestimation of the relative burden of Soviet military outlays.[9]

From a different point of view, still other causes might have limited Soviet consumption gains, for example, the Soviet system's inefficiencies: inappropriate product mix, poor quality of goods, excessive use of resources, and so on--all as ubiquitous as they seem ineradicable. Consumption, though faring much better than in Stalin's time, has continued to serve as Soviet planning's "buffer sector"; military programs have always been sacrosanct, as have investment plans of higher priority. Therefore, any reduction of available output through misallocation, mismanagement, and outright waste must have affected mainly consumption levels (if not necessarily rates of growth).

CHARACTERISTICS

Having studied Soviet industrial growth in painstaking detail, Professor Nutter concluded that "the process of economic growth is mysteriously complex and cannot be summarized in . . . brief comments" (Nutter 1983, p. 173). And indeed, short of dealing, however sketchily, with Soviet economic history _in toto_, it is difficult to characterize the growth process in a satisfactory manner. Here I can but touch upon one or two topics. The importance attached to investment--"accumulation" in Soviet terminology--has already been mentioned and is crucial. Other germane characteristics fall under the headings of resource (especially labor) margins, of technology and organization, and of sectoral priorities.

Resource (Especially Labor) Margins

Abundance of labor was a constant in Soviet growth, except during the war. Precise estimates of labor "surpluses" are questionable, if at all possible, but demographic data do shed some light on the problem. For instance, the percentage of rural population (see Table 14) is of great interest, inasmuch as the main reservoir of unemployed and underemployed labor in an industrializing country is to be usually found in the countryside.

Table 14. Proportion of rural population, 1928-80.

Year	Percentage
1928	81.6
1940	68.4
1950	61.6
1960	51.2
1970	44.0
1980	37.0

Sources: 1928-60 from Eason 1963, pp. 72-73; 1970 and 1980 from Narodnoie khoziaistvo SSSR 1922-1982, p. 9.

The downward trend in the proportion of rural population was (indirectly indicative of a gradual exhaustion of Soviet labor surpluses. A comparison of changes in the size of labor force and of nonagricultural employment also points to such a conclusion (see Table 15).

With the exception of the last decade, increments in nonagricultural employment exceeded, both absolutely and relatively, the additions to labor force. This had to drain the reserves of labor. Respective magnitudes may be in question; however, the gradual disappearance of labor surpluses is not. It is a fact which ultimately accounts for both the slowdown of Soviet growth and the climbing investment rate.

Table 15. Increments (Δ) in labor force* and nonagricultural employment, 1928-80.

Period	Δ Labor Force Absolute (mln)	Δ Labor Force Relative (%%)	Δ Nonagricultural Employment Absolute (mln)	Δ Nonagricultural Employment Relative (%%)
1928-40	14.7	17.1	19.1	192.2
1940-50	-3.8	-3.8	6.8	23.4
1951-60	11.7	12.0	19.0	53.1
1961-70	11.1	9.3	26.0	47.4
1971-80	24.2	18.5	20.1	24.9

Sources: For labor force (working age and able-bodied population): Eason 1963, p. 77 (1928-60); L'emploi en URSS. 1959-1984 (Direction de la Documentation: 1971), p. 18 (1961-70), and Soviet Economy in the 1980's: Problems and Prospects, part 2 (Government Printing Office: 1983), p. 292. Figure for 1960 estimated.

For nonagricultural employment: Eason 1963, p. 86 (1928-60); Narodnoie khoziaistvo SSSR 1922-82, p. 399 (1970-80). There is a difference in the two series, rendering the estimate for 1961-70 doubtful, probably too low.

*For 1961-70 "working age population;" for 1971-80 "able-bodied population."

A massive infusion of labor was at the very heart of Stalin's prescription for rapid growth: millions of peasants driven to construction sites of the piatiletka (Five-Year Plan). As the employment expansion began falling off, marginal labor/capital and output/capital ratios declined. Consequently, the rate of growth started slowing down, in spite of Soviet planners' ruthless investment drive. Doubling the share of investment did not prevent a slowdown, since as a result of labor scarcity, the incremental output/capital ratio dropped by more than one-half.

Some tentative calculations bring about these consequences of a gradual exhaustion of extensive margins of growth. Most important of all are the changing incremental labor/capital and output/capital ratios, shown in Table 16.

The indices in Table 16 were obtained from decadal data.[10] To verify the decreasing tendency in the Soviet output/capital ratios, the latter were also calculated, by a different method, from year-to-year data.[11] The results (in Table 17) are reassuringly close, confirming the scale of the phenomenon--a decline in the marginal output/capital ratio by two-thirds over a period of thirty years.

Table 16. Incremental labor/capital and output/capital ratios, 1951-80.

Period	Incremental Ratios, 1951-60=100	
	Labor[a]/Capital[b]	Output[c]/Capital[b]
1951-60	100	100
1961-70	45	73
1971-80	55	39

Sources: Labor from Table 15 above; output and capital from <u>USSR: Measures</u>, pp. 52-54, 65-67.

[a] Because <u>kolkhoz</u> (collective farm) employment data are not available, labor force (working age, able-bodied population) figures were used as proxy.
[b] Capital figures represent a sum of "new fixed investment," at 1970 adjusted factor cost rubles, again only a proxy for the net increase in fixed capital stock.
[c] GNP at 1970 adjusted factor cost rubles.

Table 17. Incremental output/capital ratios, 1951-80.

Period	Ratio 1951-60=100
1951-60	100
1961-70	76
1971-80	32

Sources: <u>USSR: Measures</u>, pp. 56-58, 76-78.

It is because of this downward trend that Soviet planners, trying to maintain the pace of growth no matter what the cost, have steeply increased the share of investment in the GNP. Observers of the Soviet economy keep stressing that as of late, the Kremlin has been sacrificing capital formal goals (see Levine 1983, esp. pp. 161-62). Even though investment targets were at times reduced, I consider this emphasis misleading. To quote once again Nutter's apposite remark, "the experience of a five-year period, plucked from history, carries no permanent message with it" (Nutter 1983, p. 177). The consistent feature of Soviet policies has been to push up the rate of investment as high as is humanly, and often inhumanly, possible. Some time ago, Polish economists introduced the concept of an "investment ceiling," that is, the maximum level of investment beyond which additional capital projects can be neither completed nor fully utilized due to technical and socioeconomic conditions.[12] Personally, I am convinced that the Soviet economy has been operating close to some such "ceiling" for quite a long time: BAM (railway), the pipelines, new oil and gas fields, power generation, chemicals, heavy and light manufacturing, shipping, in addition to agriculture, housing, and so forth. The reported rise in the proportion of investment from 14.2 percent in 1950 to 33 percent in 1980 only partly expresses the resultant strains: shortages of construction materials and of skilled labor, transportation bottlenecks, prolonged project gestation, imbalances in productive capacity and so on. Even with outside assistance--the much-publicized pipeline case is just one example of Western contributions to Soviet growth--it would be hard to undertake much more.

The dwindling of extensive labor margins is amenable to quantification, however imperfect. The disappearance of other resource margins--land, in the traditional terminology of economics--is more elusive. Yet, undoubtedly, the phenomenon is symptomatic of Soviet growth. The shifting geographical focus of investment, especially in raw material and fuel extraction, toward the less accessible territories beyond the Urals, is certainly a case in point. And so is, in retrospect, the by now half abandoned Virgin Land program. Just as labor scarcity did, these and similar developments must have contributed to the higher capital requirements of growth.

Soviet (and other East European) economists refer to all that as "intensification" of growth, a rather popular if confused notion in the socialist world, it would seem (see Brzeski 1971, vol. 2, pt. 2). Yet, as the Soviets must have already found out, there are definite limits to this way of maintaining the _tempo_. Not even a Stalin could continue to raise the rate of investment indefinitely. Therefore, unless other sources of growth (mainly technology and organization) can be tapped with more success than in the past, further loss of economic momentum appears inevitable.

Technology and Organization

Without estimating an aggregate production function--a procedure that strikes me as extremely tenuous given the quantity and the quality of data--one cannot properly identify the contribution of "technical and organizational progress" to Soviet growth. It is possible, however, to form an idea about the role of technology and organization from surrogate figures. Statistics on labor productivity are of particular value in assessing the tendency of the so-called residual, usually taken as a measure of "progress." Regardless of type--"embodied," "disembodied," or what not--the progress shows up in labor productivity.[13] Table 18 suggests an ever-diminishing role (relative share) of "technology and organization" in Soviet growth; the labor productivity gains have been on a downward slide at least since 1960.

Table 18. Soviet labor productivity, 1960-80.[a]

Period	Annual Rate of Growth in Percent
1960-65	3.4
1965-70	3.2
1970-75	2.0
1975-80	1.3

Source: Levine 1983, p. 154.

[a]GNP per man hour.

According to one study "Soviet productivity trends compare unfavorable with those of most Western countries. From 1960 to 1973 Soviet labor productivity (output per worker) grew at an average annual rate of less than 2 percent--the lowest of any of the industrialized countries. Since 1973, its growth has been below France, Germany, and Japan" (Cohn, pt. 1,

p. 173). Coupled with the already discussed falling output/capital ratio (i.e., capital productivity), this lackluster labor productivity growth demonstrates Soviet inability to generate and diffuse the kind of technological and organizational innovations that sustain high growth rates in spite of the exhaustion of extensive resource margins. Belying Marxist theories, and Soviet pretensions, the system of central planning and management has so far proved itself inferior to advanced capitalist economies in exploiting the opportunities of technology and organization. To maintain high rates of growth, Soviet planners have consequently had to rely on socially costly increases in the volume of inputs.

Sectoral Priorities

I have already mentioned the salient features of the Soviet allocation pattern: a preponderance of military spending and investment. Notwithstanding the increased role of trade (Treml 1983), which modifies the input-output-end use nexus, these allocational objectives have been rather directly translated into a specific production pattern. By disaggregating the mythical GNP, we abandon the purely abstract "economic growth in general" for a more concrete approach, thus gaining additional insights into the answer to Nutter's initial question: "capacity for what?" Table 19, which shows the growth by the sectors of origin of the GNP, further illuminates Soviet priorities.

Despite ambiguous pronouncements, the familiar "primacy of Group A industries" seems to have prevailed over the long haul: heavy industries expanded faster than those producing for consumers. Sectors of special importance to the military--transport and communications--were among the growth leaders too. This is not to imply that there were no changes in relative sectoral priorities. Table 20 shows the differential annual growth rates by quinquennia.

Soviet sectoral priorities are also manifested by the distribution of investment (see Table 21).

Again some shifts of emphasis are noticeable, but the larger picture appears stable. With some important exceptions (fuels, power generation and machine building), a further breakdown confirms this impression (Table 22).

Table 19. Growth indices of GNP by sector of origin, 1950-80.

Sector	1950	1960	1970	1980
Industry	100	241	451	711
Ferrous metals	100	240	440	565
Nonferrous metals	100	255	533	811
Fuel	100	241	417	624
Electric power	100	330	830	1,460
Machinery	100	232	464	882
Chemicals	100	290	780	1,401
Wood, pulp, paper	100	225	247	279
Construction materials	100	427	727	1,036
Light industry	100	226	363	470
Food industry	100	242	446	561
Other industry	100	237	450	700
Construction	100	289	491	726
Agriculture	100	145	198	179
Transportation	100	302	642	1,044
Communications	100	214	471	886
Trade	100	236	418	607
Services	100	121	183	245
Housing	100	147	208	265
Utilities	100	183	367	600
Repair and personal care	100	123	209	382
Recreation	100	177	238	285
Education	100	132	210	265
Health	100	156	223	273
Science	100	264	557	871
Credit and insurance	100	91	127	209
Government administration (incl. military personnel)	100	73	191	129
Other sectors	100	150	275	350

Source: USSR: Measures, pp. 52-54.

Table 20. Average annual rates of growth (in percent) of GNP by sector of origin, 1951-80.

Sector	1951-55	1956-60	1961-65	1966-70	1971-75	1976-80
Industry	10.2	8.3	6.6	6.3	5.9	3.4
Ferrous metals	11.1	7.6	7.2	5.1	4.0	1.1
Nonferrous metals	12.8	6.9	7.6	7.4	5.9	2.6
Fuel	9.4	8.9	6.3	5.0	5.0	3.3
Electric power	13.1	11.4	11.5	7.9	7.0	4.5
Machinery	9.6	7.9	7.4	6.9	7.9	5.3
Chemicals	11.6	10.5	12.0	8.9	8.6	3.8
Wood, pulp, paper	7.4	5.8	2.6	2.9	2.6	-0.1
Construction materials	15.7	14.7	5.4	5.7	5.4	1.8
Light industry	10.4	6.4	2.6	7.2	2.7	2.6
Food industry	10.2	8.4	6.8	5.9	3.9	0.7
Other industry	10.2	8.3	6.6	6.3	5.9	3.4
Construction	11.8	10.5	5.0	5.8	5.6	2.4
Agriculture	3.5	4.2	2.8	3.5	-2.3	0.3
Transportation	12.3	11.3	9.0	6.7	6.5	3.5
Communications	8.1	7.0	7.1	8.9	7.3	5.8
Trade	9.9	8.2	4.8	7.0	4.6	3.0
Services	1.9	3.5	4.4	4.2	3.4	2.8
Housing	2.9	5.0	4.0	3.1	2.7	2.2
Utilities	5.4	9.1	8.1	5.5	5.1	5.0
Repair and personal care	1.8	2.2	2.3	8.9	6.5	6.2
Recreation	7.5	4.0	3.5	2.8	1.9	1.4
Education	3.6	2.2	5.9	3.7	2.2	2.5
Health	5.0	4.4	3.8	3.6	2.6	1.6
Science	7.5	12.5	9.0	6.7	6.0	3.2
Credit and insurance	-0.1	-2.4	1.5	5.5	5.9	4.6
Government administration services	-4.5	-1.8	2.2	5.2	3.8	3.0
Military personnel	-0.8	-4.8	2.2	3.4	1.6	0.6
Other sectors	5.5	5.9	5.0	5.2	3.7	2.7

Source: <u>USSR: Measures</u>, p. 55.

Table 21. Sectoral shares (in percent of total) in investment, 1918-81.

Sector	1928-32 (First FYP) (A)	1918-81	1976-80 (B)	Percentage Point Change (B)-(A)
Industry	38.0	35.8	35.3	-2.7
Group A	31.7	31.0	31.0	-0.7
Group B	6.3	4.8	4.3	-2.0
Agriculture	15.6	18.0	20.3	+4.7
Transport and communications	17.7	11.1	12.0	-5.7
Construction	1.1	3.5	4.0	+2.9
Housing	15.4	16.3	13.6	-1.8
All other	12.2	15.3	14.8	+2.6

Source: Narodnoie khoziaistvo SSSR 1922-1982, pp. 368-69.

Table 22. Sectoral shares in industrial investment, 1959-79.[a]

	1959-65	1966-70	1971-75	1976-79
Branch of industry:				
Ferrous metals	9.3	8.3	7.6	7.1
Coal	7.2	6.1	4.9	4.5
Oil and gas	11.6	12.9	13.8	17.4
Electric power	11.7	11.4	10.1	8.7
Machinery	15.3	18.8	22.4	24.5
Chemicals	9.0	9.2	9.3	9.9
Forest products	5.6	5.8	4.6	3.9
Construction materials	6.3	5.3	5.0	4.2
Light industry	3.6	4.4	4.2	3.7
Food processing	8.7	7.8	6.9	6.1

[a]In percent of industrial investment.

Sources: Cohn 1983, p. 189.

While I cannot go into the details of the sectoral structure of Soviet growth, the abnormalities and imbalances (or, as the Soviet planners themselves would put it, the "disproportions") must be emphasized. These shortcomings--the notorious weakness of Soviet farming, underdeveloped consumer industries, housing, services, and so on--are caused by the lopsided preferences of the Kremlin, not by planning mistakes. Of the latter, there must have obviously been a great many, but that is an altogether different story. In reflecting upon Soviet industrialization, Nutter once remarked that its "pattern . . . would never be duplicated by a market economy" (Nutter 1983, p. 178). Only a system maintaining the tightest central controls and suppressing popular preferences could have continued for decades along the path characterized by Soviet macroproportions and the derivative sectoral priorities.

PROSPECTS

Much as such things are in vogue, it is impossible to second-guess Mr. Andropov's intentions. Conceivably, changes in the direction of Soviet growth may be in store. But as yet nothing indicates a drastic reorientation. There is no sign whatever of a cutback in military spending. Even if new arms control treaties should actually be concluded, the ongoing modernization of the Soviet arsenal plus assorted external commitments make major reductions of the proportion of resources going to the military (and related sectors) unlikely. Furthermore, the Eleventh Five-Year Plan, while of necessity moderate in setting overall investment targets, entails no relative improvement in the standing of consumer sectors (see Table 23).

Soviet planners are evidently hoping for a reversal of trends in the output/capital ratios. But how they can achieve it, given the demographic difficulties ahead, is not clear. Of course, there is the technology, and even more important, the possibility of a thorough reorganization. But even if Mr. Andropov should resolve to take the plunge--and probably only "more steps on the treadmill" can be expected--an acceleration of Soviet growth is not in the cards. Thus, the perennial slogan _dognat' i peregnat'_--to catch up and to overtake--is losing any vestiges of realism it may have retained.

Much is being made in the West of the Soviet economic situation, which is often described as a "crisis" (Goldman 1983). Still, in my opinion, any prognosis of an impending systemic breakdown would be far-fetched. Soviet institutions and policies are not an engine for economic

Table 23. Investment in the Eleventh Five-Year Plan.

Sector	Percentage Increase, Plan 1981-85 over 1976
Total	10
Industry	23
Ferrous metals	30
Fuels and power	52
Machinery	10
Other (inc. light and food)	8
Agriculture	7
Transport and communications	22
Housing	8

Source: Legget 1983, p. 137.

progress, but primarily a means of acquiring and exercising geopolitical power. And in the pursuit of the latter, these institutions and policies have yet to fail. In closing on this note, let me quote Walter Laqueur: "It is quite likely . . . that economic conditions in the Soviet bloc will deteriorate even further in the years to come. But there is no reason to assume . . . that this will greatly influence the conduct of Soviet foreign policy" (Laqueur 1983).

POSTSCRIPT

The new man in the Kremlin has reportedly made it "clear to a fascinated world that his country is in even worse economic shape than almost anybody had realized" (The Economist July 26, 1986, p. 7). Statistics confirm that the Soviet slowdown continued through the Eleventh Five-Year Plan, 1981-85. The annual GNP growth (see Table 7 supra) decreased to 2.4 percent during that period. Total factor productivity further declined by 0.5 percent annually, if not more.[14] Despite the exhortatory optimism of the recently approved Twelfth Five-Year Plan, it is rather unlikely that things will change for the better. The already discussed constraints persist, and there are new additional ones, most prominent among them being the drop in oil prices undercutting hard currency earnings. Neither anti-alcoholism campaigns nor the limited "reforms" which are contemplated can revive the system. Not even the Chernobyl nuclear plant disaster seems to have an effect on the Soviet inertia so deeply rooted in bureaucratic vested interests. The edifice of socialism is by now solid.

In these circumstances, rearranging _per fas et nefas_ the international political economy to Soviet advantage may seem tempting. After all, the Soviets are better at this game than they are at ordinary business. These, however, are but speculations. For the shorter run, and quite realistically, Lenin's heirs can count on capitalist assistance: yesterday, a European pipeline, today subsidized American grain.

With capitalism heading for its inevitable doom, according to official ideology, this can only be a temporary expedient. Yet, it helps to keep the socialist show on the road while the historico-dialectical details are being sorted out.

NOTES

1. In addition to earlier pathbreaking works by Jasny and Gerschenkron, among the most important works of this scholarship are Bergson 1961; Nutter 1962; and Becker 1969.

2. See Jonas and Sandy 1970 for an excellent discussion.

3. Bergson's calculations are at ruble factor cost (composite, 1937 base) from Table 51 of Bergson 1961, p. 210. The estimates in _USSR: Measures_ are in 1970 rubles; see Table A-1, pp. 52-54. The growth rates are the same as for adjusted factor cost (_USSR: Measures_, p. 51).

4. Jasny believes that "the manipulation of the statistics, whose beginning coincided with the great deterioration of consumption levels in the early thirties was largely undertaken to conceal this very fact" (of the failure to raise living standards): see Jasny 1951, p. 52.

5. U.S. indices are calculated from Appendix B in Gordon 1981 and its corrected version "Annual Data (Revised) 1930-1980." (Mimeographed).

6. This is a crude estimate using (1) the indices in Table 6, (2) the U.S. GNP figures at 1972 dollars, and (3) the assumption that Soviet per capita GNP was one-third to one-half of the corresponding U.S. figure. Accordingly, the Soviet per capita product (at 1972 prices) lagged by 1.6 thousand to 1.9 thousand dollars in 1940 and by 3.3 to 4.4 in 1980.

7. This was the subtitle of H. Schwartz's column in the issue of November 26, 1980.

8. This is an approximation on the premise that Soviet per capita GNP is one-third to one-half of the U.S. figure, and the ratios of consumption to GNP in the two countries are as shown in Table 11. (On such assumptions the Soviet consumption would be 29 to 43 percent of the U.S. level.) More elaborate estimates are on the same order, e.g., "in 1976 real per capita consumption in the USSR was 34.4 percent of that in the United States; and even that low figure was believed to be biased in favor of the USSR," according to Consumption in the USSR (1981, p. v).

9. By contrast, the Japanese have kept military expenditures to a minimum since World War II.

10. Sums of investment ($\sum_{t=1}^{10} I_t$) and output differences ($Y_{10}-Y_0$) were used.

11. Geometric means ($\prod_{t=1}^{10} \frac{\Delta Y_t}{I_t}$)$^{0.1}$ were used, with $\frac{\Delta Y_t}{I_t}$ calculated from $\frac{\Delta Y_t}{Y_t} : \frac{I_t}{Y_t}$.

12. See Feiwel 1971, vol. 2, ch. 5, for a discussion of this problem.

13. The residual can be defined as $r = y-(\alpha k+\beta \ell)$ for a Cobb-Douglas function.

14. Bush 1986, p. 4. Figures are from U.S. government research sources.

REFERENCES

Becker, A. S. 1969. Soviet national income 1958-64. National accounts of the USSR in the Seven Year Plan period. Berkeley: University of California Press.

------. 1982. The burden of Soviet defense: A political-economic essay. In World Military Expenditures.

Bergson, A. 1961. The real national income of Soviet Russia since 1928. Cambridge, Mass.: Harvard University Press.

Brzeski, Andrzej. 1971. "Intensification" of economic growth in Eastern Europe. Jahrbuch der Wirtschaft Osteuropa. G. Olzog.

Bush, K. 1986. The Twelfth Five-Year Plan: Gorbachev's blueprint for acceleration. Radio Liberty Research Bulletin, No. 28 (3389), July 9, 1986.

Cohn, S. H. 1983. Sources of low productivity in Soviet capital investment. In Soviet economy in the 1980's.

Consumption in the USSR: An international comparison. 1981. Washington, D.C.: U.S. Government Printing Office.

Eason, W. W. 1963. Labor force. In A. Bergson and S. Kuznetz, eds., Economic trends in the Soviet Union. Cambridge, Mass.: Harvard University Press.

Feiwel, R. G. 1971. Problems in Polish economic planning: Continuity, change, and prospects. New York: Praeger Publishers.

Goldman, M. J. 1983. USSR in crisis. The failure of an economic system. New York: W. W. Norton.

Gordon, R. J. 1981. Macroeconomics 2nd ed. Boston, Mass.: Little, Brown.

Jasny. 1951. Soviet economy during the plan era. Stanford, Calif.: Stanford University Press.

Jonas, P., and H. Sandy. 1970. The Gerschenkron effect: A reexamination. Review of Economics and Statistics (1970):1.

Laqueur, W. 1983. Wall Street Journal. April 17.

Legget, R. 1983. Soviet investment in the 11th Five-Year Plan. In Soviet economy in the 1980's.

Levine, H. S. 1983. Possible causes of the deterioration of Soviet productivity growth in the period 1976-80. In Soviet economy in the 1980's, part I.

Mickiewicz, E. 1973. Handbook of Soviet social science data. Free Press.

1977 World population data sheet. 1977. Washington, D.C.: Population Reference Bureau.

Nutter, G. W. 1962. The growth of industrial production in the Soviet Union. Princeton, N.J.: Princeton University Press.

------. 1965. On economic size and growth. (Mimeographed).

------. 1983. The structure and growth of Soviet industry: A comparison with the United States. In Political Economy and Freedom. Orem, Utah: Liberty Press.

Program of the Communist Party of the Soviet Union. 1961. Crosscurrents Press.

Soviet economy in the 1980's: Problems and prospects. 1983. Washington, D.C.: U.S. Government Printing Office.

Stalin, J. N.d. Political report of the central committee to the Sixteenth Congress of the CPSU. *Leninism*, vol. 2. New York: International Publishers.

Treml, V. G. 1983. Soviet dependence on foreign trade. NATO Economics Directorate. (Mimeographed).

USSR: Measures of economic growth and development, 1950-80. 1982. Prepared for the Joint Economic Committee, U.S. Congress. Washington, D.C.: Government Printing Office.

Wiles, P. J. D. 1964. *The political economy of communism*. Cambridge, Mass.: Harvard University Press.

World Bank Atlas. *Population, per capita product and growth rates*. 1972. International Bank for Reconstruction and Development.

World military expenditures and arms transfers 1970-1979. 1982. U.S. Arms Control and Disarmament Agency.

Chapter 10

THE CASE OF SELF-MANAGEMENT IN YUGOSLAVIA

By

Svetozar Pejovich*

INTRODUCTION

Most research by western scholars has traditionally emphasized the macroeconomic aspects of socialist economies. A predictable outcome of this emphasis on the system of planning and macroeconomic analysis has been a rather poor *ex ante* understanding of the economic forces at work in socialist countries. Let us look at two examples.

In the 1950s a relatively high rate of growth of the Soviet economy was taken for granted. G. Warren Nutter was among the very few economists who questioned the reported growth rate in the Soviet Union, doubted the ability of the Soviet Union to continue to grow at the same rate, and denied the importance of economic growth policies for human welfare. Nutter based his observations and predictions on the standard price theory adjusted to take into consideration the incentive effects of property rights. Nutter was castigated for defying the traditional wisdom. Yet

*S. Pejovich is professor of economics and director of the Center for Education and Research in Free Enterprise at Texas A&M University.

history has validated Nutter's predictions about the Soviet economy (Nutter 1983).

The 1965 economic reform in Yugoslavia was acclaimed as a major step in the direction of greater efficiency. The reform was supposed to transfer decision-making powers from the bureaucracy to the employees of business firms. Horvat claimed that "self-management accelerated growth of output, and technical progress beyond anything known before" (Bajt 1983). Vanek thought that self-management should be tried everywhere, and some German economists linked the idea of codetermination in Germany with the Yugoslav system of self-management. In response to these claims, a property rights micro-model was developed that suggested that the 1965 reform would generate inflation, low savings, high unemployment, and serious liquidity problems in Yugoslavia. Moreover, it suggested that those problems are generated by the labor-participatory system itself. These predictions have turned out to be correct.

The point is that price theory has one advantage over the analysis of aggregate variables: It is capable of contributing to knowledge. In the field of comparative studies, the price theory adjusted for the effects of various property rights has led to a simple general conclusion: There can be no efficient markets without private property rights (Nutter 1968), and there can be no economic development without private ownership (Pejovich 1986).

Major institutional features of the Yugoslav economic system are (1) the state ownership of capital goods, (2) the employees' ownership of the returns from capital goods held by the firm, (3) the employees' right to govern the firm, (4) the system of quasi-voluntary contracts between firms, institutions, and various agencies, and (5) the substitution of bank credit for the system of administrative distribution of investable funds. When this institutional framework is translated into the bundle of rights that defines ownership in the firm in Yugoslavia, the following picture emerges:

- The employees own the residual.
- The employees have the right to fire and hire the firm's management, including the director.

- The employees can neither sell the rights specified above nor continue to enjoy them when they leave the employ of the firm.

The right to capture the residual in Yugoslavia is contingent on the association of one's live labor with the firm's physical assets. When this association ceases to exist, one's right to capture the residual ceases as well.

PROPERTY RIGHTS IN YUGOSLAVIA AND THE ALLOCATION OF RESOURCES

Yugoslav workers are free to choose to exchange their current consumption for higher future income by leaving a part of the residual with the firm for investment in additional capital goods. Yet, they can neither sell their claims to future earnings from fixed assets acquired by the firm during the period of their employment nor continue to receive their share of those earnings once they leave the employ of that firm.

Private savings of S dinars in period one permit additional consumption of $S + i_0S$ dinars in period two. But the same number of dinars left with the firm for purchase of additional capital goods makes possible additional consumption of only rS dinars in the second period. It follows that the worker who saves one dinar out of his current wages purchases a stream of income equal to

$$y = \frac{i_0(1 + i_0)^n}{(1 + i_0)^n - 1}, \qquad (1)$$

where i_0 is the prevailing rate of interest on savings deposits and n is the common time horizon of the working collective.

The employee will then have incentive to accept a reduction in his take home pay if he can expect to receive in the form of higher wages a stream of income at least equal to (1). Given the firm's legal obligation to maintain the value of its fixed assets, the rate of return from investment which would generate the stream of income equal to (1) is

$$r_0 = \frac{i_0(1 + i_0)^n}{(1 + i_0)^n - 1} \quad . \tag{2}$$

It follows that for each given i and n there exists the rate of return r which would make the employees of the labor-managed firm indifferent between investment in nonowned assets and private savings.

The allocation of the firm's earnings between the wage fund and retained earnings then turns out to depend on the schedule of investment opportunities in additional capital goods (Pejovich 1969).

To simplify the analysis, I assume that the firm's demand for liquid assets (cash balances, new money, physical inventories) is a constant percentage (a) of its fixed assets, i.e. L= aF, and dL/dF=a. Then

$$F = \frac{X}{1+a} \tag{3}$$

$$L = X(1 - \frac{1}{1+a}) \tag{4}$$

Given the assumed proportional relationship, or for that matter any other positive relationship, between (F) and (L), a long-term loan will induce the enterprise to increase the percentage of retained earnings earmarked for investment in liquid assets. And if retained earnings happened not to be sufficient to finance the firm's need for additional liquid assets its demand for long-term loans will be accompanied by an increase in the demand for short-term credit.

The AF_b and BL_b curves in Figure 1 show the volumes of long- and short-term credits the firm would require in order to finance various levels of investment in new capital goods ΔF, given the employees' time preference and time horizon, the firm's earnings, and the schedule of investment opportunities, the rate of interest i_0 on individual savings, and the behavioral relationships discussed above. The OA investment in capital goods represents the extreme case which is associated with zero bank credit. As bank loans are made available to the firm, the level of investment in fixed assets will increase beyond A. At B the firm will be financing its entire investment in capital goods via bank credit while retained earnings will be just sufficient to satisfy its need for additional liquid assets.

FIGURE 1

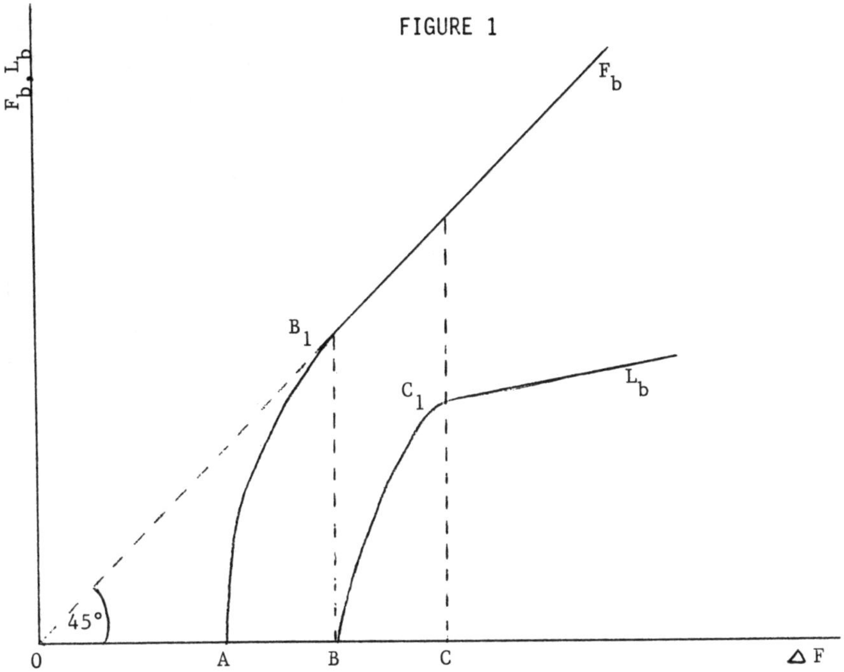

It follows that investment in fixed assets between OB and OC levels in Figure 1 will be possible only if short-term credits are made available to the firm. To put it differently, if and when the volume of investment in capital goods is in excess of OB, retained earnings of our hypothetical firm will become inadequate to finance its rising demand for liquid assets.

The slope of AF_b between A and B and the slope of BL_b between B and C conform to the analysis in Pejovich (1976) upon which this section of the chapter is based. The relationship between property rights and incentives in Yugoslavia suggests that each dinar borrowed from the bank tends to increase the firm's total investment by less than one dinar (the remainder being reverted back to the wage fund).

The set of diagrams in Figure 2 combines the firm's marginal efficiency of investment schedule with its demand for long- and short-term credit. The MM curve is the marginal efficiency of investment schedule. This schedule is traditionally taken to reflect the opportunities the given firm possesses for the use of additional fixed assets and is based on the firm's initial position, current prices and the characteristics of the existing production function. The F_bM and L_bL_b curves represent the volumes of long- and short-term borrowings which are required for each given level of investment in fixed assets. The F_bB_1 curve then represents the labor-managed firm's combined need for bank credit.

In the absence of bank credit the firm's investment in fixed assets will be OA in Figure 2. The availability of bank credit will increase its investment beyond OA. The firm's demand for bank credit will exceed the value of its investment as the level of investment in capital goods exceeds OB.

FIGURE 2

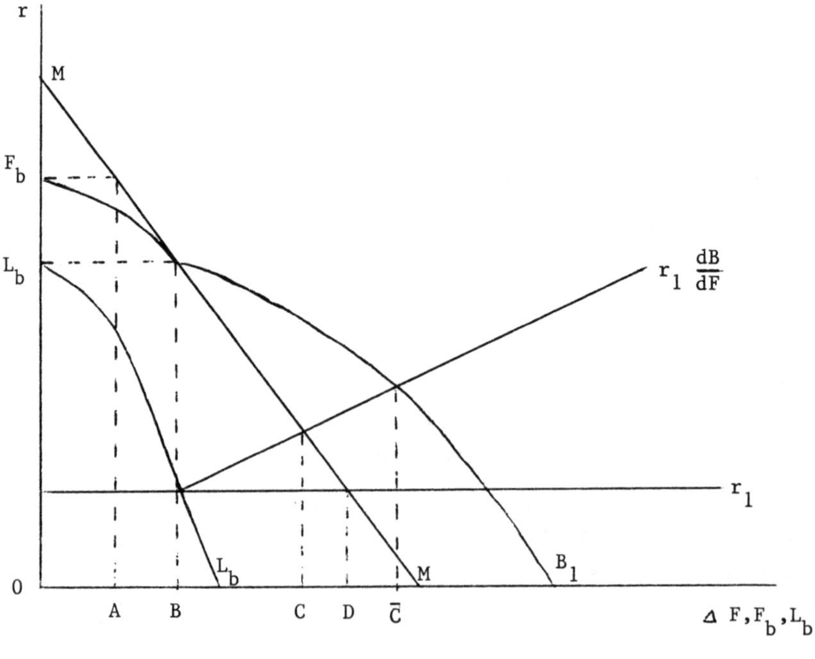

The fact that the aggregate demand schedule for investable funds and the marginal efficiency schedule of the firm do not coincide raises the problem of assigning a separate rate of return to liquid assets. In a private property free-market community those assets earn what they cost. In that case, conventional proposition that the firm's rate of investment depends on its schedule of investment opportunities and the market rate of interest is valid.

While the capitalist firm can invest its liquid assets in market securities, the Yugoslav firm has to hold them as cash balances or inventories (for financial markets do not exist in socialism). The cost of each given investment in fixed assets in Yugoslavia (or in socialism in general) is then higher than in a private property, capitalist economy. The difference in costs is a price the Yugoslav firm has to pay for not being able to capitalize the future consequences of current allocative decisions.

Property rights in Yugoslavia have a predictable effect on the rate of unemployment. New workers acquire the same rights to the firm's earnings as those already employed. That is, currently employed workers have to share with new workers the returns from past investments which they helped to finance through retained earnings. In addition, the law makes it very costly for the Yugoslav firm to lay off workers in response to changes in the economic situation. It follows that even when a worker's expected marginal product exceeds the average product of the firm's current labor force, he is not necessarily hired.

Finally, the non-transferability of the worker's right to ownership in the firm's earnings means that prevailing property relations in Yugoslavia provide no room for diversification in risk bearing among individual workers whose risk aversion is not likely to be the same. Thus, the employees of the Yugoslav firm have additional incentives to prefer those investments which promise to shift income returns forward and postpone cost. This nontransferability of the worker's right to ownership in the firm's earnings is a consequence of the constitutional requirement that the returns from capital assets belong only to those workers who work with them. Some attempts have been made by the Yugoslav government to encourage firms to invest in other firms, but the resolution of the allocation of profit and the returns from those ventures have provided no incentives for workers to explore those alternatives.

To summarize, the expected consequences of the incentive structures in Yugoslavia on the allocation of resources are quite dismal: rising unemployment, inflation, growing dependence of business firms on bank credit, seemingly insatiable demand for bank loans, high cost of liquidity and strong pressures to seek investment projects that maximize near-term cash flow and postpone costs.

PROPERTY RIGHTS IN YUGOSLAVIA AND INNOVATION

Innovation means doing something that is new. It could be the development of a new good, the opening up of a new market, a new source of supply, a new technology, or a new method of organizing activity. Innovation has two interrelated social functions: revitalizing the economy and offsetting the law of diminishing returns. It is then the engine of economic development.

The innovator translates knowledge into new choices. Innovation is a consequence of the innovator's perception about the applicability of knowledge, willingness to accept the risk and uncertainty associated with doing something new, and the ability to see the innovation through (as innovation unfolds many people have to say "yes"). The innovator must possess such traits as ingenuity, optimism, stubbornness, perseverance, and vision. Moreover, successful innovators are difficult to identify *ex ante*. The growth of knowledge being unpredictable means that specific innovations cannot be planned in advance. One cannot simply decide to have one innovation each month.

The prevailing property rights in society determine who has the right to acquire and determine uses of resources (e.g., who can innovate). Property rights also define constraints on the rights to use resources. In a private-property economy all individuals are allowed to innovate, while the freedom of contract lowers the cost of identifying the value of resources in alternative uses.

In Yugoslavia the pool of those who can innovate is restricted to the working collective. Some limitations exist even within the working collective. Individual employees cannot acquire and use resources. No individual employee is in the position to translate his perception of other people's demand for various goods into actual market outcome (supply). He has to sell his ideas to the Workers' Council. The firm's director is perhaps the only individual who can use resources to implement new ideas. However, the director must also seek the Workers' Council's approval for any major change in the firm's scale of operations. And the Workers' Council consists of people with diverse interests, different backgrounds, limited business understanding and experience, and unequal technical knowledge.

Incentives to innovate in Yugoslavia are also limited in comparison with the capitalist West. The employees' right to capture the firm's earnings links the firm's performance to the employees' wages. However, as the firm grows in size, the employees' perception of the relationship between their individual efforts and wages tends to weaken. A worker who comes up with a potentially profitable idea captures for himself only a small fraction of the total gain. Yugoslav institutions also reduce the director's incentives to innovate. A successful innovation in Yugoslavia does not reward the manager as quickly as he is rewarded in the West. A successful innovation in the West affects the price of the firm's stock and in doing so enhances the manager's opportunity cost. It is much costlier to generate this kind of information about managers' performance in the markets without private ownership rights (that is, without financial markets).

The "self-management" in Yugoslavia has constrained both the firm's efficiency as well as the innovator's freedom and ability to expand the community's set of choices. Property rights assignments associated with labor participation in the management of business firms reduce the number of potential innovators, their ability to attempt innovation and incentives to innovate. Self-management in Yugoslavia has collectivized innovations and alienated the innovator from its results.

THE PERFORMANCE OF THE YUGOSLAV ECONOMY

The property rights analysis has correctly anticipated economic problems in Yugoslavia. The rate of inflation averaged about 40 percent in the early 1980s. By 1986 inflation has approached a 100 percent rate. The rate of economic growth averaged about 37 percent in the 1980-85 period, clearly a negative real growth rate. During the same period the average real income in Yugoslavia declined at a rate of about 7 percent per year.

The rate of unemployment was 8 percent in 1973. It rose to 15 percent by 1984. Counting about 700,000 Yugoslavs working in West European countries, the unemployment rate is about 20 percent. In addition, labor input per employed worker has been falling at the rate of 1.5 percent per year (Bajt 1983). This problem of "unemployed employed" has been attributed to laxities in the organization of production, shirking and the inability of firms to lay off workers in response to changes in the level of economic activity.

One percent growth in GNP requires an investment of about 6 percent of GNP in Yugoslavia. One percent growth of GNP in Turkey, Portugal, and Spain requires investments of 3.2 percent, 2.8 percent, and 3.7 percent of their respective GNP's. A Yugoslav sociologist has calculated that between 1982 and 1984 the number of hours required to buy a pair of shoes had doubled (Beloff 1985, p. 234).

The Yugoslav external debt is about 40 percent of its GNP. Internal borrowing of the Yugoslav firms in 1984 was about equal to GNP. One of every 10 firms in Yugoslavia was in the red in June, 1986. In the first six months of 1986, loan repayments by Yugoslav firms exceeded their tax obligations by almost 30 percent (Politika 1986).

The question "What happened to the Yugoslav miracle?" has a simple answer. There has been no miracle in Yugoslavia. The Yugoslav system has, like all other variants of socialism, failed to perform. The Yugoslav experience reinforces and strengthens the lesson we have learned from other socialist experiments, which is that the fundamental institutions of capitalism (private property, contractual freedom, and limited government) are powerful and perhaps necessary conditions for economic efficiency.

REFERENCES

Bajt, A. 1983. The economic growth of Yugoslavia. Paper presented at CESES Conference in Florence.

Beloff, N. 1986. Tito's flawed legacy. London: Victor Gollancz.

Nutter, G. W. 1968. Markets without property: A grand illusion. In N. Beadles and L. A. Drewry, eds., Money, the market and the state. Athens: University of Georgia Press.

Pejovich, S. 1969. The firm, monetary policy and property rights in a planned economy. Western Economic Journal, September, pp. 193-200.

------. 1976. The labor-managed firm and bank credit. In J. Thornton, ed., Economic analysis of the soviet-type systems. Cambridge: Cambridge University Press.

------. 1986. Alternative property rights and innovation. Paper presented at the Liberty Fund Conference on Economic Freedoms, Napa Valley.

Politika. August 28, 1986.

Chapter 11

ECONOMIC AND SOCIAL CONSEQUENCES OF SOCIALIST POLICIES IN FRANCE

By

Jacques Garello*

When the Socialist party swept the elections on May 10, 1981, it was the result of three reactions of the French electorate:

1. a sanction vote, to reject President Valery Giscard d'Estaing's policy, judged too conservative by some, too "social democrat" by others.

2. an illusion vote, because many French thought that socialists had better recipes for resolving the "crisis."

3. a revolution vote, as the 110 propositions of the "communists and socialists government common program" were conceived to set up collectivism in France.

In 1986 many French found a definite similarity between the government's socialist policy and the one Raymond Barre administered before 1981. They are not all wrong in the sense that many planning elements, even elements of collectivism, could be found in French policies before 1981; the welfare state was well in place--like elsewhere. But the revolutionary aspect or, as Mises says, "destructionism" (Mises [1922] 1981, pp. 413-62) of the socialist policy has been developed to such an

---

*J. Garello is professor of economics at the University of Aix-en-Provence.

extent that French society will have a long recovery after the passage of socialists in power. The "mixed society" is one more step on the road to serfdom, and the heritage of socialism will be a heavy burden for French society.

SOCIALIST POLICY AND THE "CRISIS"

"Crisis" is an easy expression to use to point out the difficulties that most Western countries saw in the 1970s and early 1980s. But we also know that this expression is deceitful, for it was not a simple phase in an ordinary business cycle, but rather a deep implication of our organizational modes.

The electoral cleverness of the socialists in 1981 consisted in making French people believe there was not a real crisis abroad and that the economic difficulties were due only to government policies that were linked to capitalist principles. The crisis analysis was made according to the usual Marxist ideology: inflation and unemployment were the result of the worker's exploitation by the propertied class, of which the state would be the accessory.[1] So French people believed that changing their government was enough to overturn the crisis, but most of them did not understand that they were also being asked to change society. The "common program" was read by less than 5 percent of the voters, and economic ignorance did the rest.

The socialists promised to solve France's unemployment problems quickly and to abolish "social injustices" by giving large purchasing power to the "working classes." Who would disagree with those goals? However, we know that the difference between the free society and the socialist society is not so much the aims but the means.[2] How did they apply them, and which results did they achieve? The socialist policies for achieving their stated goals were not satisfactory, as we will see later. This explains why, beginning in 1983, socialists pretended to change policy to launch the idea of a "mixed society."

"French Socialism"

As do all system designers, socialists imagined it was possible to establish a new form of socialism in France that would avoid all the usual costs of socialism and keep only the "benefits." Moreover, this flattered the chauvinist feelings of the French people, who always believe they can succeed where others have failed. In fact, we can observe that French socialism was only moderately original and that its own originality was in fact an additional manifestation of its ignorance of economic problems (but was that a problem for socialism?).

Three principles summarize the "French" socialism policy: (1) full employment, (2) the extension of the public sector, and (3) the so-called "democratization of the enterprise." Full employment policy is the most ordinary aspect; it takes its inspiration from the Keynesian principles according to which unemployment is caused by low private aggregate demand and can be solved by a large program of public expenses. However, French socialists preferred to operate the reflation by consumption expenses rather than through public investment; they thought they would do two things at the same time: reflate the economy and give purchasing power to their electors. One can notice that when socialists came in power in 1936, they too had the policy of "purchasing power" with Leon Blum and Edouard Herriot.

Socialists were well aware that a revival of demand only reduces unemployment if firms could respond to this sudden market swelling. One of the dangers was that foreign firms would be the first winners of this purchasing power distribution. This is why socialists anticipated a "reconquest of the domestic market": dynamic French firms would be able to compete with foreigners and could prevent them from entering the French market. Moreover, they hoped the fast development of French purchasing power would spur French firms to "reconquer" this market, which they would have long since abandoned for external markets judged more profitable. In this reconquest of the domestic market, a decisive thing must be the extension of the public sector. As a matter of fact, socialists made a very important discovery for economic science and the French economy: during the years 1975-1980, French public firms invested more and exported more than the private firms. They did not think that these good results were achieved with the taxpayers' money at prohibitive costs. They simply persuaded the French that extending the public sector would increase the dynamism of French industrial production. The socialization of the means of production, which we will not call nationalization but only "extension of the public sector,"[3] which is the cornerstone of the collectivist process, takes an additional dimension in the French case: it must drag the rest of the economy with it!

This optimism about the goals of socialism is supported by the practice of "firm democratization." As a matter of fact, socialists think that capitalist power must be transferred, at least partly, to the wage earners. By "democratization," in the French socialist language, one means "syndicalization" (trade unionization). This syndicalization would have to take effect in all French firms, but it could be applied immediately and feel its beneficial effects on productivity in public firms. This syndicalist form of socialism is very well known (Mises [1922] 1981, pp. 239-44). It is particularly popular in France, where all self-management proponents feel drawn to the Socialist party and to one of the two Marxist trade unions, the CFDT.

This is how socialists conceived their policy in 1981: the French economy must be restarted under the double thrust of an extended market produced by the distribution of purchasing power and by firms dragged to very high productivity levels by an extended public sector and stimulated by trade unionism power.

Implementation of the Policy

The government budget was at the heart of the revival policy. For 1981, the budget deficit (which in 1980 had been set by vote at 29 billion francs) went up to 73 billion. For the 1982 budget, the increase of the public expenses would be 23 percent, and the deficit was voted to be 95 billion francs (it would come to 130 billion in reality). In 1983, the deficit would be set at 130 billion francs. Another way to give purchasing power is to increase national insurance benefits to elderly people, large families, and the unemployed. This is expressed by a very high growth of the "social security" budget[4] which, with 900 billion francs, becomes more important than the state budget. The deficit of the social security program reached 23 billion francs in 1982; it would be reduced afterward by an increase in contributions. During all this period of "revival," tax and para-tax receipts did not stop increasing (without canceling the deficits, however); the compulsory levies' share in the gross national product went from 41 to 42.5 percent within two years.

Nationalization is one of the most immediate measures of socialist policy. The September, 1981, law nationalized all banks and credit institutions not already in state hands[5] and nine large industrial groups. Following the nationalizations, the state directly controlled 95 percent of bank property, 80 percent of financial institutions, and 32 percent of the industrial sector. All in all, the "big national firms" sector represents 18 percent of the GNP.

However, we have to wait for another year (1982) to see the Auroux law complete the socialist mechanism. In public firms, this law confirms the trade unions' power on the board of directors. In private firms, the Auroux law gives to the trade union the right to contest employer authority on regulations, on redundancy and engaging procedures, on investment plans, and on staff formation. The Auroux law established also the principle of "workers' expression in the firm": meetings must be held regularly to associate the staff (always represented by trade unions) with the firm management.

The first measures hardly in place, we could already realize socialists were bound to fail. Far from diminishing, the "crisis" was worsening.

The Worsening of the Crisis

The most obvious signs of the aggravation of the crisis were the unemployment and inflation figures. Since October, 1982, the limit of two million unemployed (6.5 percent of the working population) that socialists promised never to breach was cheerfully exceeded. In one year unemployment increased 32 percent! Inflation, which had slowed in 1980, started off again all the more. Most of all, the inflation differential with

France's principal partners grew hollow: the first twelve months of socialism was marked by an inflation rate of 14.1 percent (against 12 percent the previous year), as Germany posted 6 percent, and the United Kingdom 10.4 percent (from 11 percent in 1981). The OECD countries' average rate of inflation was 11 percent (source: OECD).

France was settling into deficits. First the budgetary deficit: it was expected, but the figure was much higher than expected--80.9 billion francs for 1981 and 130 billion for 1982. The government pretense of holding the deficit under 3 percent of the GNP could not be maintained. The public firms' deficits were not expected. The newly nationalized firms, far from being the "trend setters" of the French economy, posted 13-billion-franc deficits (1982), which brought the whole bill for all nationalized firms (old and new ones) up to 54 billion. But the deficit which would most impress the French would be that for foreign trade: 93 billion francs (1982).

The deficit was not financed by resorting to the Central Bank. Two techniques were used: the borrowing of the Treasury, and outside loans. From May, 1981, to the end of 1982, the French Treasury issued 30 billion in loans on the capital market, but it mostly resorted to massive loans on the money market (150 billion; the usual volume before 1981 was around 15 billion). From May, 1981, to December, 1982, the French external debt increased nearly 20 billion dollars,[6] as the Bank of France currency reserves diminished four-fifths. At the end of 1982, French external debt was estimated to represent 9,000 francs per capita. This important use of financial resources, which must be considered unusual, prevented the swelling of the money supply.[7]

As the public sector drained a large part of the country's financial capacity, it left only a few things to the private firms. On the capital market, whose volume was around 200 billion francs, the public sector (which represents 22 percent of the GNP) took 160 billion (which is 80 percent). So the French private firms suffered a crowding-out effect. They suffered all the more because their cash flows were greatly diminished by the rapid increase of the charges (especially taxes and social contributions),[8] price controls (restored in June, 1982), and stiff international competition. All in all, the private investments decreased sharply: 10 percent in 1981 and 7 percent in 1982.[9] This is particularly the consequence of the additional charges they had to pay: state taxes increased 14.7 billion in 1982, local taxes (proportional tax) 8.6 billion, national insurance contributions 12 billion. The "Auroux laws" (to be discussed later) cost 13 billion, and the law which obliged firms to pay a fifth week of paid vacation and to reduce the work week to thirty-nine hours represented 45 billion. All in all, French firms had to pay 95 billion francs as international competition became stronger. Because price controls were set up again in June, 1982, firms could not make more profits, and a large number of them had to run into debt under expensive conditions. Bankruptcies, whose number increased from 1982 and which would put a large number of workers on the street, were up during the first two years of the socialist government.[10]

"War Socialism"

With the demand policy failing (it was practically given up in October, 1982), the socialist government's first reaction was to strengthen planning and to institute protectionism. The year of 1983 will be remembered as the "war socialism" year.[11] Price controls were strengthened. But the government also set up a wage hike, with 9 percent for private firms and 6 percent for civil servants. In November, 1982, unemployment benefits themselves were abolished for nearly 40 percent of the unemployed. After the third devaluation, which occurred soon after the local elections in March, 1983, currency outflows were limited to a minimum (1,000 francs per year). The government largely campaigned on the "buy French, produce French" theme, and the Communist party developed the most strident nationalist thesis. Some importations were stopped: hi-fi equipment (especially video cassette recorders) coming from Japan were subjected to stronger customs control. President Mitterrand tried to persuade his European partners that Europe must be organized against American and Japanese trading aggressions. Fortunately, he did not succeed.

On the fiscal and monetary field, the government suddenly passed from revival to austerity. To limit the budget deficit, the state forced taxpayers to subscribe to a loan equal to 10 percent of the tax they pay. To fill the social security deficit, a 1 percent income tax was enacted. The truth is, the state demands austerity from private individuals, which it hardly respects itself. The 1983 budget was presented as a major effort to limit public expenses. In fact, the deficit was larger than official figures showed (it increased 25 percent over 1982), and expenses increased 15 percent (official figures reported 11 percent).

At that time the socialist leaders began to systematically use the statistic lie. Not only were budget figures underestimated, but also the price index was manipulated. For example, tobacco and alcohol, whose prices went up because of the tax increase, were not taken into account; insurance premiums were left out of the index (they also had increased rapidly because of the taxes). A part of the external debt was concealed. The government reported that unemployment was decreasing when it was rising, and foreign trade was reported to balance when it was actually becoming more unbalanced.

The "Unemployment Social Treatment"

Pierre Mauroy, prime minister until July, 1984, became famous for creating a miraculous new cure for unemployment, to which would be applied a "social treatment."

The cure was to diminish unemployment figures by changing the definition of the unemployment statistic. Young people without work had now to follow formation training. If they were training, they were not unemployed. If they were not training, they were not unemployed but instead were "formation applicants." On the other end of the working life, the retired age was still sixty-five for most professions, but unemployed between sixty and sixty-five were now "anticipated retired." The unemployed between 55 and 60 were called "pre-retired." Because of this marvelous invention, around 400,000 people disappeared from the official unemployment figures in one quarter. Unfortunately, during the same period 400,000 "real" unemployed arrived on the labor market, so the government had only a very small benefit from its ingenious invention.

The Mauroy government did not limit its efforts against unemployment to this "social treatment." A certain number of old socialist ideas returned to reduce unemployment, or at least unemployment figures. The first one was the creation of civil service jobs: 200,000 in 1982, but 1983 public finances did not allow it any more. The second one was "share of labor." In 1982, the government set the legal work week at thirty-nine hours, down from forty.[12] In 1983 they wondered if they should give in to the pressure of trade unions, which asked for a thirty-five hour work week, although trade unions disagreed on the methods: CGT wanted 35 hours without wage cuts, while CFDT, the more "reasonable," would accept a wage loss amounting to half the sum that the reduction in hours would have eliminated. The government agreed to postpone this discussion. The third idea was the public works policy. It first was called "collective interest work," then from 1984, "collective service work" ("Travaux d'utilité collective"--TUC). Local administrative offices and associations could employ the young unemployed, whose wages (lower than the legal minimum wage) would be paid by the state.

French Economy Goes Deep Into Crisis

Despite the inventive genius of the socialist policy, the French economy had one of its worst years in 1984. The unemployment figure, which everyone watched closely, exceeded 2.2 million people in February, 1984, and went up to 2.4 million in December, 1984 (11 percent of the working population). This unemployment strikes the young first: one out of four unemployed was young, and 40 percent of the youth were unemployed. As the employment demand stabilized, employment supply completely collapsed: 400,000 jobs disappeared between 1981 and 1984. Business bankruptcies went from 17,375 (for 1980) to 25,018 (for 1984). Additional taxes and various "contributions" that firms had to pay continued to rise, however, from 4.7 billion francs in 1981 to 62.4 billion in 1983. The debt of French firms had increased 150 billion per year since 1981.

The only positive elements (upon which official propaganda focused) were the decrease in the inflation rate and the recovery of the balance of trade. These results are relative, though. The inflation differential with Germany was still five points (7.3 percent increase in prices in 1984 in France against 2.2 percent in Germany), and with an OECD average of two points. The external deficit was still 25 billion francs.

The most important result was the dispersion of capital, but the French population did not see it. Mises said the usual way for socialists to govern is to sacrifice the future to manage the present.[13] This is exactly what happened in France. The volume of the Treasury debt reached 700 billion in 1983. The annual service debt represented 62 billion in 1983, 80 billion in 1984. In the 1984 budget, the expense to cover this service was the item that improved the most, with an increase of 19.8 percent. The external debt was also very important, in excess of 600 billion francs. The official figure (undervalued) was 55 billion dollars in June, 1984. The load of the external debt represented 66 billion francs in 1984, 82 billion in 1985, 102 billion in 1986, and 150 billion in 1988. It will take a whole generation to absorb the deficit left by the unconsiousness of the socialist policy.

Moving on to the "Mixed Economy"

The bad conjunctive results are not sufficient to explain why socialists in 1984 denied some of their principles and turned to forms they themselves call "liberal." There was also the unpopularity of the education reform project (which led more than 2 million people to demonstrate in the streets of Paris on June 24, 1984) and a rising trend of liberal opposition.

The policy shift became apparent with the change of prime ministers: Laurent Fabius succeeded Pierre Mauroy in July, 1984, and communists left the government. The new trends would apparently be to diminish the controls, reduce taxes, and give firms the means to adjust and reorient. But we can quickly note that this changing was more apparent than real; it was directed more at electors than at entrepreneurs and families.

The lessening of controls was set for November and December, 1984, starting with "credit deregulation," which meant the decade-old credit-rationing system would be abolished. To replace it, however, was a system of reserves calculated by the credit increase banks allow. Bankers called the new system more constraining than the previous one. Obviously there is no suggestion of reversing the nationalization of the banks or the "selective" policy that gives advantages to some sectors over others depending on the goodwill of the government. Then came the "exchange liberalization." This meant that the French would have the right to remove abroad 1,500 francs per month instead of 1,500 francs per quarter, and French firms could invest on the EEC (European Economic Community) territories in France for 50 percent of their investments (instead of 25 percent), and they could borrow in European ecus. The situation was far from being a free-exchange market; this did not stop newspapers from saying "Beregovoy (minister of finances) is playing one more time the 'liberal card' by 'releasing the prices.'" In fact, this measure involved only about twenty industrial goods, which represented 6 percent of the industrial turnover. More than a third of industrial goods were still framed; the increase must be negotiated with the government and would not exceed 3 percent in 1985. As for services, prices had to increase in 1985 between 3 and 5 percent after negotiation.

The illusion for the "tax cut" was also effective. It is true socialists now do say "too much tax kills tax," as Mitterrand says, a real Arthur Laffer follower. The income taxes anticipated by the 1985 budget decreased 5 percent, but after being increased 8 percent in 1984. High incomes will not have the advantage of this favor and still pay a surtax of 3 percent if they exceed 30,000 francs. The highest income bracket was taxed at 73 percent. The "exceptional" 1 percent income contribution to fill the social security deficit was likely to be abolished in 1985. But the deficit appeared again (forecast at 20 billion in 1985), and social contributions were raised. At the same time, local taxes also were raised. All in all the French saw compulsory taxes increasing instead of decreasing, as the government was saying.

However, the "industrial policy" field is the one where socialists surprised their followers and shocked the communists. They developed the idea that employment stability is not an absolute right and that firms could make staff redundant if absolutely necessary. This contrasted with the fact that the state still subsidized a certain number of insolvent public and private firms (this subsidy can be as high as 100,000 francs per year and per job).[14] A new ministry was also created: the minister of industrial changes, which proves that socialists have a limited trust in the market to restructure the French economy and that they count on the administration initiatives to guide investments and create jobs. However, socialists are finally conscious that it might be better to allow certain liberties in wages and working conditions to create jobs. The government encouraged negotiations between employers and trade unions to admit the "flexibility of contracts of employment": to allow definite time jobs, temporary jobs, part-time jobs, to set the wage level by firm (and not by branch or national negotiations), and to introduce elements of "personalization" into wages (premiums). All those things were forbidden by French labor legislation. Trade unions refused to accept those changes, and the government did not do anything to modify this legislation.

In these conditions, we can seriously doubt the sudden conversion of the socialists to liberal ideas. The mixed economy invented by Mitterrand was designed to hide the failures of the policy followed since 1981 in order to calm dissatisfactions and to regain the growing sympathy that liberal theses got in the French electorate.

The mixed economy has only one item of interest left for economic analysis: it is testimony to a socialist policy's failure to overcome a crisis. But it does not really touch the socialist principles. It is only a stopping point; during a certain period socialists compromise with the private sector and the market, which coexist with the public sector and the socialization of the means of production. Francois Mitterrand declares it, so there is no doubt: "The coexistence of two kinds of societies will be long. It squares with a stage of evolution which western economy knows when progress forces are in power . . . From this mixed economy I am not making a theory. I describe the present practice the way it develops in the actual present forces, although it is breaking with capitalism to nationalize credit and the large industrial poles."[15]

Here is the most important point: the socialists never stop pursuing the march to collectivism, and despite the misfortunes of their conjunctive policy, they put in place (or worsened) measures that inevitably turned French society away from capitalism. Crisis might have overcome socialism, but socialism wants to kill capitalism.

SOCIALISM AND THE REVOLUTION

When they came to power, the socialists socialized. Without doubt the work is not finished as we are still in the "mixed economy" ("société d'économie mixte"). But there were enough changes in France between 1981 and 1985 to compromise deeply the future of the market economy.

Breaches in Property Rights

The nationalizations were enacted in September, 1981, and they constitute one of the most revolutionary measures that new governments can take while they are in a "state of grace"[16] that immediately follows their election. They concerned nine industrial groups, some of which were in a bad situation (as Usinor and Bollac-Sacilor, two iron and steel groups).[17] But most affected were banks, except for the very small ones (less than 5 billion in deposits), foreign bank branches, and mutual banks (which were already dependents of the state). These bank nationalizations did not inspire any desire to control the credit policy. Through the central bank, which controls the monetary market; through the old nationalized banks, which represented 60 percent of the deposits; through public bodies of saving and financing, the French state already had total control over the financial flows. The survival of the private banking sector, even in the minority, gave a positive spirit to productivity and to competition. It was not enough for the state to control; it wanted to orient. To socialists, banks are the symbol of capitalism, and abolishing the private property of the banks seemed to them to be a decisive step in the establishment of socialism. The old dream of the Saint-Simonian socialist was realized: public banks giving credit at low cost, or even free, to ensure general prosperity. Alas, socialists had to find out then that credit was not free, that capital still flew abroad, that interest rates were still determined by the market. Francois Mitterrand vented his anger against the American interest rates and made a long speech at the 1982 Versailles meeting to persuade President Reagan to do something to reduce the rates.

The fiscal system is the second form that breaches in property rights took. It is an old and familiar tactic throughout the world. But in

France in 1981 it had a deliberate revolutionary face: the rich have to pay because they are rich, not because the state needs money. French socialists being indifferent to Laffer's reasoning--they do not believe it matters much whether fiscal yields diminish--wanted to penalize economic success. In July, 1981, a "high-income surtax" was established. It was 25 percent for that part of the superior tax over 100,800 francs. It concerned only 108,000 taxpayers. In September, 1981, tax cuts for large families (7,500 francs per child) were abolished: this concerned 130,000 families. At the same time, an "unemployment tax" of 10 percent was levied on taxpayers who paid more than 25,000 francs in taxes (2 million taxpayers). Finally, the most revealing: a tax on "large wealths." Those whose wealth was estimated at over 3 billion francs (estimation measures are completely arbitrary) would pay between 0.5 and 1.5 percent of their wealth every year in taxes. This tax has negative yield; it puts only 4 billion in the treasury, which had to spend 5 billion to put the necessary control system in place. It is obvious that during all those years the progressiveness of the income tax was increased, with the creation of the 65-percent bracket in September, 1982, surtaxes of 8 and 5 percent for superior brackets, and these "brink effects" are more and more pronounced. This contributed much to discourage the most enterprising French and to encourage all kinds of tax evasion, but it was not socialist business who wanted overall to repress capitalists with socialist fiscal policy.

This hatred of capital and prosperity inspired the Quillot law. This law was to end the exploitation of tenants by landlords. It not only enforced rent control but practically forbade the termination of leases: a renter who was settled could not be expelled. More "renter associations" had control of leases, of rental charges; only a few associations were considered "representative" by the law (these have communist and socialist tendencies). The consequence of this law would be the immediate collapse of the building market, and the worst housing crisis since 1945. Capitalists wanted out of the real-estate market to turn to others (especially in bond investment on the stock exchange, favored by the fiscal law).

The Auroux law meant to enterprise what the Quillot law meant to housing. Its aim was to contest "the absolute power of employers in firms." The hierarchical and disciplinary power were placed under control of trade union representatives: loft rules, sanctions against an accused employer must go to the joint production committee, and so on. Besides, workers now had "right of expression" in the firm: discussion sessions could be organized at which the employers must listen to the staff's complaints and suggestions. Of course the staff is not talking directly but through the compulsory intermediary of the trade unions. In firms without any trade union division, trade unionists coming from other firms can take part in the discussion sessions. These measures would have an immediate effect as negative as that of the Quillot law: the total confusion of production, mainly in the public firms. As a matter of fact, in the private firms employers often succeeded in neutralizing the Auroux laws by organizing direct discussion sessions with the staff (as part of the "quality circles"), which turned the sessions with trade unions into inefficient and ridiculous exercises. On the other hand, small firms could escape by decreasing the number of their employees (the Auroux laws did not apply when the number of employees is less than ten and are easier when there are fewer than fifty employees). This wasted time, for those useless exercises represented a total cost of more than 50 billion francs per year for the French firms, a quarter of their investments.[18]

The real-estate law is another breach in property rights. Under the pretext of defense of the natural environment, and of town-planning harmonization, the government increased ways of eviction by the local administrations. Real-estate administrations were created and could impose land sales and seize inheritances.

The common point between Auroux, Quillot, and real-estate laws is the will to contest any kind of power built on property and to deny the reality of contracts: the rental contract or the labor contract are meaningless as responsibility is held by only one party (Mises [1922] 1981, pp. 32ff.) The free conventions between private people must give way to collective bargaining with the parties whom the law designates. These are the trade unions or renter associations, formed and supported not by workers' or renters' support but by political parties. The only doubt is to know whether the trade unions or the state will conclude the discussion. Sometimes the state imposes the solution (especially in insolvent firms for which the government allowed redundancy); sometimes the trade unions do (for example, they refused to allow flexibility of the labor contract). Anyway, the private property of capital has been damaged, and the liberty to form enterprises and make contracts has been diminished by all these measures.

Breaches in Private and Public Liberties

Breaches in private property and in economic liberties go with an aggression against other liberties, and most of the French who voted for Francois Mitterrand did not expect that.

The two most "heated" areas are education and information. But we should not forget the socialist revolution in the field of culture, of family, and so on.

The "common program of the government" planned the establishment of a "large unified and laicized public service of the national education." Consequently the Savary law project, which was taken to the parliament in 1984, planned the abolishment of private schools. Those schools had at the time a third of all pupils, and, since the Guermeur law, had had state subsidies in order to guarantee near exemption from fees to families or to diminish the school fees sharply (public education is free). In a counterpart to this aid, the state controlled programs and the pedagogy of the private schools, and these schools needed the state's permission to open new classes. This system was considered too "liberal," and socialists campaigned on the theme "to public money, public school." So the Savary project planned the fusion of the two kinds of schools: teachers would be appointed at random to one or the other school, subsidies would go only to schools that had administrators appointed by the state or by the local administrations, the schools' distribution could be modified, and some schools could be closed. This project caused such a violent outcry (a demonstration in Paris on June 24, 1984) that the government had to retract. However, there is still a succession of measures that tend to abolish private schools but in a more circumspect way: diminution of subsidies, denial of class openings, and so on.

In the higher education field, the socialist government wanted to overturn university traditions. Another Savary law, enacted in December, 1983, abolished the old universities and transformed the studies system in the "democratization" mode, which means a total absence of selection and competition. Also, as in Eastern countries, the law separates research from education. The recruitment of professors has been greatly modified: it is less selective and some positions of titular professors were abolished. Pride in the French university system disappears. The whole new system is now under the power of the minister of national education and a puzzle of elected assemblies (with trade union participation).

Information is another battle front for liberties. In December, 1983, the government passed the Fillioud law which was meant to "organize competition in the written press." This law forbids integration of newspapers beyond a certain number. This number was set specifically to affect the Hersant group (Figaro group) and to protect all press groups owned by the followers. Hersant succeeded, for the time being, in canceling this law, but the largest press group of the opposition is still threatened. Apart from the written press, there was a large battle around the radio and television groups. The socialist power allowed free radio (which the previous "liberal" government refused). But it imposed such administrative conditions that they could only establish with the permission of the High Authority (appointed by the state), and only if they do not wrong the state-run radio group. The broadcasting power of the free radios has been limited in that sense. Free radio was in a very delicate situation. For instance, when the government decided to close "Radio-energy," the most powerful private radio station in Paris, it set off such a reaction of the press and entertainment industry that the measure was postponed. State controls have long governed the three channels of national television. In 1984 a fourth channel, a commercial one (with subscriptions) was allowed, but under the state's direct control! Government uses state television a great deal. During 1982, there were ninety-seven hours, forty minutes of the majority party's presence on television and twenty-three hours, twenty-five minutes for opposition politicians.

All government measures and all positive economic indexes go immediately into state television and radio propaganda. The disinformation is established (Hayek 1972, pp. 153-66).

But socialists want to go further: it seems that the French should not learn how to think, so a major policy aims to establish a state culture. It belongs to the minister of culture, Jack Lang, who is particularly sectarian. Fidel Castro's and guerrilleros' friend, Lang is strongly against American culture. He gave instructions to decrease the number of American films on television and to obstruct American production in France. Lang also subsidizes shows that do not interest French viewers but which give work to artists (who will give their support to the government). On another front Lang invented "democratization of culture" by forcing the sale of a book at a set price all over the country. Lang estimates that reading cannot be left to the market process (<u>Le prix unique du livre</u> 1983).

The socialist culture goes naturally with the socialist morality. For example, the French government imposed on the French its preference for cohabitation, abortion, and feminism. The fiscal system is more favorable for unmarried couples with children than for a traditional family. Abortion, legalized under the administration of Valery Giscard d'Estaing, is now backed by social security. By paying their "social contributions," some French are unwilling parties to what they consider a crime. "Women's rights" were conceived as the obligation not only to open all jobs to women but also to impose a required minimum of women in job areas. A "minister of the women's condition" in France is headed by Minister Roudy, who is very determined: "If [the] left wing [had not] come in France, women would have been pulverized!" Official culture broadcast through all medias controlled by the state is a permanent fright of moral and religious values to which many French cling. The family is not only dishonored but also culturally depreciated and fiscally penalized. A family with three children and a high income pays more taxes and gets no family allowances beyond a certain amount; it is better to be poor and without a child. The demographer A. Girard, although he is close to government, had to admit that "socialists are innermost malthusians" (<u>Le</u>

Monde, January 30, 1983). This is shown in the decrease in marriages and the birthrate and the increase in the number of divorces and abortions.

Taking stock of socialist actions in culture, information, and education, we have to think of E. Carr's statement, quoted by Hayek: "It is significant that the nationalization of thought has proceeded everywhere *pari passu* with the nationalization of industry" (Hayek 1972, p. 153).

The French are so much under socialist control that the private sector, which could back the opposition to totalitarian projects, has been progressively denied existence in favor of the public sector. This is what Mitterrand calls the "mixed society," but it would be better to call it a dualistic society.

The Dualistic Society

The dualism phenomenon noticed in the poorest countries is devastating French society. What we mean by dualism is the juxtaposition of a developed modern sector ruled by the market and a traditional sector with low productivity ruled by administration and hierarchy. The long-term question is whether the modern sector will manage to communicate progress to the traditional sector, or whether it is killed by it. This is what is happening now in France.

The public sector, the tribal sector, is now taking nearly a third of the French national product. There are 6.5 million civil servants and public firm wage earners, which is 30 percent of the working population. This public sector is a millstone around the private sector's neck. It is the cause of the nonstop increases in taxes and contributions to fill deficits and create new civil service jobs. It consumes the large part of savings resources to the detriment of private investments; it keeps interest rates high and causes the rationing of credit. It is competing with the private sector in an unfair way. Peugeot pays taxes in an amount equal to the subsidies its competitor, Renault, gets from the state. Local administrations establish centers of health, of architecture, or legal advice, which ruin professions. Overall, this public sector is against any change. The staff has a quasi-guarantee of work for life. It does not feel concerned by the difficulties in the country, and it always complains about its condition. It shows its protest through nonstop strikes and poor quality work. In 1982 the number of wasted worker-days in the industry because of the strikes went up to 2,256,900 (compared with 1,495,600 in 1981, which is an increase of 51 percent in one year). These strikes concerned mainly the nationalized sector: iron and steel, coal mining, and Renault, which in 1983-84 had the strongest and the longest strike of all French social history. Trade unions used strikes to weaken private groups such as Peugeot, which had not been nationalized. Strikes are increasing in the "public services" such as the railways, postal services, electricity. The service is sabotaged, and some sorting offices refuse to deliver newspapers and even letters that do not appeal them.

Trade unions in the public sector are sure of impunity and of the backing of the socialists, who have guilty indulgences for everything public. This situation makes a large number of workers and employers of the private sector angry because they are conscious of their enterprise problems, they have no guarantee, and they realize the public wasting is ruining the economy. In a speech French bishops themselves noticed what was immoral in such a situation.[19] Public opinion, which favored nationalizations in 1981, is now against them, and some polls show that the French would agree with the privatization of a certain number of administrations or public firms.[20] The conscientious and sincere people working in the public sector are very surprised about the sudden worsening of the working and management they observe. So the rift is getting deeper between the French who realize state socialism's damages and those who do not want to change anything in the present situation because it gives them more income without any effort and with an absolute guarantee of work. This is what Mitterrand is calling socialism's victory over capitalism.

Mental Confusion

If a majority of the French are now desperate about the mixed economy, it must be explained why this same majority voted socialist in 1981 and why there is still more than a third of the French population which is either undecided or even satisfied. This explanation is in the confusion socialists maintained in the people's minds, using ambiguous language and exploiting feelings or resentments dear to the French heart. These techniques have already been described by Mises and Hayek: end of truth, destructionism.[21]

Concerning language, all the usual cleverness has been used. "State control" has never been used, but always "nationalization," or even better, "extension of the public sector." Never did we hear "trade unionization" but always "democratization." The misuse of the term "democracy" allowed the justification of the Auroux and Quillot laws that abolished private property. It is in the name of "competition" that the state monopoly over the press and information has been justified and that the official price of a book has been established. The compulsory laicization has been called "school liberty." It is in the name of "public service quality" that trade unions are allowed to disrupt transports, energy, and postal services. It is in the name of the ill that professional medicine and private hospitals are pushed into a corner. At the time taxes increase, the government says they diminish, and when unemployment increases quickly, the government says it slows down.

Socialists are very clever to subvert many aspirations of the French. They seduce ecology interests by promising to stop nuclear power and to slowing the sale of armaments. In fact, the nuclear program slowed for only one year and then started off again. Concerning armaments, gone are the days when Mitterrand was taking armaments off the French planes exposed at the Bourget; the government no longer hides the equipping of armies and territories all over the world. Socialists also abused the clergy and all people who saw in the new regime a hope for better "social justice." Those who did not see that socialists were tyrants and sectarians also did not see that they created the "new poverty."[22]

However, the worst deceit was the justification of all the revolutionary measures by the vote of May 10, 1981. Entrusted with the "popular will" and having the majority in the parliament, socialists thought they had the right to change the laws, the whole society. The best way to explain this attitude is the one used by the socialist deputy André Laignel when he spoke to the opposition deputies: "You are juridically wrong because you are politically in minority." The socialists did not stop breaking the law, but did stop abiding by legislation! Everything was done in a mystic way of the "10 May." "The 10 May French exceeded the limit which separates the day from the night," said Jack Lang, and echoing, Prime Minister Pierre Mauroy: "A new day is rising, with us the truth is raising." However, it is certain as we move away from the May 10, 1981, socialists have more and more difficulty behaving as absolute masters of the law and of the country, first because they are not politically in the majority, as the ballots have shown since 1983,[23] and second because the truth (not the socialist one) raises the French. Without doubt, at the present time the socialist dismissal phenomenon becomes irreversible. But the socialist dismissal, in our strange country, does not mean the dismissal of socialism.

The Liberal Counterrevolution

At this writing, it is practically certain that despite the manipulations of the electorate law, socialists will be expelled from the government in 1986, but nothing will oblige President Francois Mitterrand to resign his office.

But are we sure that new leaders will turn away from socialism and start the liberal counterrevolution? We should not forget that the seven-year term of Valery Giscard d'Estaing was a very social democrat one. The socialists did not create the socialization; they speeded it up. On another point, even if electors (in polls) say they feel attracted by the "liberal solution," politicians are frightened by the entirely new orientation that will take place in the country of Colbert, Napoleon, and De Gaulle. So the proposed programs of the opposition parties are very careful and often closer to the good old social democracy.

Without doubt the new parliament will abolish quickly a certain number of "wicked" laws affecting education, the press, and bank nationalizations. But will they go as far as abolishing what the left wing already calls (with cleverness) the "social attainments"? The social attainments are the charges firms must pay and which reduce the liberty of action of the entrepreneurs, the trade union privileges, and the recognition of the public monopolies. Finally, there are primarily an enormous amount of social transfers, with a social security budget of 1 trillion francs, and taxes now exceed 50 percent of the GNP. About all these items the opposition is cautious. And if everyone promises a reduction of taxes and the limitation of public expenses, nobody explains precisely how to do it and nobody will commit to a real program of privatization. In France, status quo tyranny is already in place before a political change occurs!

It is true that the task of the new government will not be easy, and its officials are right to be frightened. Indeed, the mixed economy will leave a double heritage: on the one hand a disastrous conjuncture, high debt, enormous deficits, enterprises ruined by taxes and trade unions, but on the other, half of France will be, tomorrow as today, against any adjustment, attached to its privileges, and troubled by communists and socialists. So government officials will have to be particularly decisive and well backed by public opinion to establish right away the needed reforms to help the liberal counterrevolution.

There are, however, reasons to hope that it will be so. The first reason is that France would not long stay isolated from the international context based on competition and free enterprise. The second one is that the French more and more want a real change and that more than one-third say they are against a simple restoration of the social democracy.[24] The third reason is that the trend for liberal ideas is getting stronger in the intellectual class in the last five years; we discover again that France is the country of Montesquieu, Jean-Baptiste Say, Bastiat, and Tocqueville. We can share Mises' opinion, which is "we can only fight ideas with ideas. Only ideas of capitalism and liberalism can triumph from socialism" (Mises [1922] 1981, p. 460).

NOTES

1. According to L. Jaspin, prime secretary of the Socialist party, "Inflation is the economical form for class struggle." June 16, 1982.

2. Mises (1922)/1981, p. 47: "The systems, in fact, differ not in their aims but in the means by which they wish to pursue them."

3. "Rather than 'nationalization,' a word full of ideological connotation . . . I prefer the expression 'extension of the public sector,'" said Pierre Joxe, domestic affairs minister.

4. In France, "social security" covers not only retirement pensions but also medical bills and support to families.

5. In 1945, the "big four" deposit banks (which had 60 percent of all deposits) were nationalized.

6. The external debt (in billions of dollars) evolved as follows: 26.9 at the end of 1980, 38.2 in 1981, 44.2 in 1982, 53.7 in 1983, and 54.4 in 1984. These figures were underestimated.

7. "There was a crowding-out effect, to the detriment of the productive sector." Renaud de la Genière, director, Banque de France, in the May, 1983, annual report.

8. From 1979 to 1982: gross cash flows from 22.5 to 12.4 percent, profitability rate from 10.3 to 5.6 percent, wage costs 75 percent (production) to 79 percent, and financial costs from 33.8 to 60.6 percent.

9. Self-financing for French firms was 76.1 percent of the total formation of capital in 1979 and less than 51 percent in 1982. The ratio of indebtedness increased from 52 to 63 percent.

10. The number of bankruptcies increased 10 percent in 1983. See under the section French Economy Goes Deep into Crisis.

11. "War socialism," in the sense used by Mises, quoting Wissel, "an adherent of the most unpopular concepts of duty and coercion" (Mises [1922] 1981, p. 227).

12. The idea behind share of labor is that if workers work fewer hours, the unemployed will have more hours of job opportunity available to them.

13. "'Après nous le déluge' is an old maxim of government" (Mises [1922] 1981, p. 162).

14. A notable case of costs of a "saved" job per year and per job: Manufrance 91,465 francs; Chappelle d'Arbley 71,000 francs; Charbonnages de France, 112,931 francs; Usinor 85,204 francs; Chantiers Navals de l'Atlantique 54,166 francs.

15. Francois Mitterrand, interview with Les Echoes, November, 1984.

16. Jean Francois Revel's 1982 book is L'Etat de grâce. This idea is also developed by M. Friedman in Status quo tyranny.

17. The other industrial groups were Dassault (aeronautics), Pechiney Ugine Khulmann (aluminum, chemicals), Rhône Poulenc (chemicals),

C.G.E. (electrical industry), Thomson Brandt (electrical industry), St. Gobain Pont à Mousson (glass making, chemicals), and Honeywell Bull (computers).

18. "The generations which grew up in the last decades have been taught from childhood that membership in trade unions was workers' most important social duty. A strike came to mean a sort of holy action, a social ordinance. On this ideology rests the power of the workers' associations. It would break down if the theory of its social utility were superseded by other views on the effect of trade unionism" (Mises [1922] 1981, p. 439).

19. "Attention: nouvelles pauvretés." Speech of the social commission of the French bishops, December 15, 1984.

20. Poll, October, 1980: 50 percent of the French agree with the nationalization policy. Poll SOFRES, January, 1983: 61 percent of the French think nationalizations have been useless; 45 percent would agree to privatization of nationalized firms.

21. "Perhaps the most alarming fact is that contempt for intellectual liberty is not a thing which arises only once the totalitarian system is established, but one which can be found everywhere among intellectuals who have embraced a collectivist faith and who are acclaimed as intellectual leaders even in countries still under a liberal regime" (Hayek 1972, p. 163). "If the work of socialization had to be carried on, it was not possible to do so by the old methods. The voice of reason which warned men not to venture any further on this path must be silenced, criticism must be obliterated by the intoxication of enthusiasm and fanaticism, opponents must be killed, as there was no other way of refuting them" (Mises [1922] 1981, p. 444).

22. Speech of the social commission of French bishops.

23. Local elections (March, 1983): Left 46 percent, Opponents 54 percent; European elections (June, 1984): Left 38 percent, Opponents 62 percent; District elections (March, 1985): Left 43 percent, Opponents 57 percent.

24. Poll SOFRES Expansion, February, 1985, 41 percent of the French are for liberal policy, only 18 percent for socialist or social democrat policy.

REFERENCES

Friedman, Milton. 1981. Status quo tyranny. New York.

Hayek, Friedrich von. 1972. The road to serfdom. 2nd ed. Chicago: University of Chicago Press.

Le prix unique du livre. 1983. Ch. Fauvelet. Paris: Institut Economique de Paris.

Mises, Ludwig von. (1922) 1981. _Socialism_. 2nd ed. Liberty Classics.

Revel, Jean Francois. 1982. _L'Etat de grâce_. Paris: Fayard.

Chapter 12

THE CASE OF CODETERMINATION IN WEST GERMANY

By

Christian Watrin*

In the task of analyzing the influence of socialist ideas and programs on the West Germany economy and economic policy, three problems must be overcome.

1. What is actually to be understood as "socialist policy" in the German case?

2. Even if it proves possible to describe the contents of socialist policy in a more or less satisfactory way, can single measures taken in the democratic process actually be identified accurately as the consequences of the socialist way of thinking? Expressed differently, could it not equally be the case that the particular measures taken could be ascribed to other political or ideological schools of thought (e.g., the program of the social market economy, economic planning concepts, the social teachings of Christian churches, or any of the diffused interventionist doctrines, which partly dominate the public debate)?

---

*C. Watrin is professor of economics at the University of Cologne.

3. Only if both of the above questions are answered satisfactorily can one approach the question of identifying the influence that socialist concepts have had in the German experience.

DEMOCRATIC VERSUS TOTALITARIAN SOCIALISM IN THE GERMAN DEBATE

Post-war Socialist Currents

According to its own self-conception, socialism is a doctrine that makes proposals about how people should live together. Indeed, its supporters have presented very different plans. The list begins with those socialists who under Marx's influence later became known as the utopian socialists (R. Owens, Saint-Simon, Fourier, Weitling); it continues with the scientific socialism of Marx and Engels and its offspring, Leninism-Stalinism; it then includes the different variations of religious and ethical socialism, as well as the ideas of self-management socialism of the Yugoslavian model. It proceeds with the countless forms of socialism in developing countries and finally ends with the different shades of the newly developed ecology-socialism. In comparison with these variations of socialism, most of which belong to the totalitarian camp, democratic socialism developed in the free part of Germany after the end of World War II attempts to develop a free version of the socialist credo and to use it as the basis of practical policy, in particular of economic policy.[1] Indeed, for a variety of reasons it is not easy to describe the basic concepts of this approach. In the first place, for an understanding of it the experiences with the Stalinist socialism of the 1930s and 1940s are of importance. What must be kept in mind is the policy of sovietization, practiced after World War II by the occupying force and its viceroys in that part of Germany which later was to become the German Democratic Republic (GDR), where an unbroken line of repression of human rights and freedoms has occurred. Another, not unimportant, role is played by the intellectual discussion of the social and economic order of the German Federal Republic. The parties and schools of thought in competition with the democratic socialists--partially after the initial hesitation--devoted themselves to the Western ideas of a free society. Therefore, the advocates of socialist ideas in post-war Germany soon found themselves under pressure from competing intellectual currents, despite all the prophecies in intellectual circles, that, to paraphrase Schumpeter (1950, p. 350), the "march towards socialism" was inevitable. Besides this and because of the influence of Ludwig-Erhard, an abrupt departure from economic planning, which had survived the demise of national socialism, was completed in 1948, and the shift toward a market-oriented economic system was finalized.[2] Erhard's economic policy speedily enabled the rules of the market economy to prevail, among other things by deregulating countless markets and establishing free economic relations with the Western world. Against this political background the first important step taken for the development of democratic socialism was the final departure from the Leninist doctrine of the dictatorship of the proletariat. According to this doctrine the communist party has the right of absolute power because, it is said, it alone is in the position to fulfill the law of history established by Marx and Engels; that is, it alone can lead human society after the anticapitalist revolution through the interim stage of socialism and ultimately to communism. However, democratic socialists oppose this claim to unlimited sovereignty with their faith in the rules of the democratic party competition (see Schwan 1984). To what extent this simultaneously implies a deviation from Marx's central message--that the human race would collectively turn from the capitalistic mode of production, renounce the competitive capitalist spirit, and come to experience the perfection of its creative possibilities in a Kingdom of Freedom (Harrington 1970, p. 367)--is a problem that will be addressed below.

Besides the question of which procedural rules are to be applied to the field of political decisions, the second important socialist theme is the organization of society's production. Marx was decidedly of the opinion that in the Kingdom of Freedom the means of production would be communal and that the coordination of economic activity would be achieved according to the rules of collective planning and not according to those of the market. In this regard the deviation of the protagonists of democratic socialism from the older examples is in no way as unambiguous as with the question of political competition. Here the conviction that equal freedom for all citizens can be guaranteed only if each can partake in all decisions that affect him, is basic to socialist conceptions (see

Deist, in Schmid et al., p. 202). This should be understood as the principle that each should be able to place his vote, as it were, on the scale in the case of important common decisions. As a result the extension of political democracy to economic democracy and the wish for co-determination at both the company and economy-wide levels are central concerns of the democratic socialists.

Simultaneously, the conviction expressed in Marxist philosophy, that man should be master of his own fate,[3] is closely connected with the expectation that the economic process should be controlled in a multiplicity of ways and be aligned to economic policy goals that have been determined in the democratic process. What Hayek (1970, p. 7f.) has termed "constructivism" accordingly plays a decisive role. This constructivism should serve the management possibilities of the modern state and its bureaucracies so as to achieve the desired aims by means of influencing the forces that activate and motivate human beings. Consequently, confidence is expressed in neither the evolutionary forces of a free society, nor the self-guidance of the market, nor the dynamics of the competitive economy. Contrary to what Adam Smith described in his invisible-hand theory, it is not believed that these coordination mechanisms can lead to the desired results.

Constitutional State, Social State, and Democratic Socialism

In some respects the socialist view encounters conceptions that are also represented by its political competitors. For instance, criticism of the social conditions of the nineteenth century, which the older socialism took as its point of departure, is widely encountered in other political schools of thought. A conviction that is also widely found in many political positions is that the economic liberalism of the nineteenth century failed largely because it was not able to overcome the social questions of the newly formed industrial society in accordance with its own rules.

In this context the double strategy followed by Bismarck (Rustow 1971, p. 20) between 1878 and 1890 marks a turning point for German development. At that time Bismarck wanted politically to outmaneuver the followers of German social democracy and separate them from their voters with the help of his infamous Socialist Laws (Sozialistengesetz) on the one hand and his social legislation on the other. With respect to social policy he assumed a conservative-patriarchal stance, according to which it was the duty of the state "to further the well-being of the worker."

Historically, Bismarck's position describes the renunciation of the liberal state of the nineteenth century and a move toward the social and welfare state convictions, which were already present in the eighteenth century. In the German debate, however, in contrast to that in other European countries, the relationship between the liberal constitutional state on the one hand and the social and welfare state on the other became a dominant theme at an early stage.

In its present version Bismarck's conception maintains that the state is no longer a formal constitutional state and the sole guarantor of law, but that it should also ensure full employment, social security, equality of opportunity, and aid to the disadvantaged. These convictions are expressed in the German Basic Law in the form of the entrenched social state principle (Sozialstaatprinzip).[4] Nevertheless, this entrenchment is made without the boundaries of social state activity simultaneously having been determined. Because disparate interpretations can be made of what "social" implies, a never-ending debate exists on the scope of the tasks that the state should perform in compliance with the social state commandment and on how these tasks are to be accomplished.

In the opinion of many lawyers, the social state principle implies an "executive, redistributive and apportioning" state that "comes to the aid of its citizens by dispensing concessions to the individual" (Wiedmann 1980, p. 1218). This wide interpretation of the state's tasks does not, in the opinion of many, exclude measures for economic planning; it is further compatible with countless forms of intervention in the market process. Besides this, it provides numerous points of departure for the public organization of fields that in other countries are primarily organized through markets.

It is a moot point in this context whether the principles of a constitutional state and those of a social state are compatible. From the abundance of answers to this question, only that of the federal constitutional court (Bundesverfassungsgericht) is quoted briefly. This court is of the opinion that no contradiction exists between the constitutional state on the one hand and the social state on the other, even when the latter is adorned with many interventionist capacities. The court gives expression to this by referring to "the ideal of a Social Democracy in the form of the Constitutional State" (Wiedmann 1980, p. 1218). It continues by maintaining that this "ideal exists in the tension between the protection of the individual and the requirements of a Social State system." This can be interpreted in an economic sense to mean that a trade-off exists between the principles of the constitutional state and those of the social state, without, however, any specifics as to how this trade-off is to be achieved.

If one agrees with this view of the federal constitutional court, then one arrives at the conclusion that social state conceptions and the doctrine of democratic socialism are not necessarily in opposition to one another. The socialist view does indeed have a completely different basis than does the idea of the social state. The former is rooted in criticism of the liberal notions of the nineteenth century (the so-called critique of capitalism) and the social conditions of the time. The latter has its origins in the countless social reform movements of the nineteenth century. Nevertheless, in particular cases both can lead to exactly the same conclusions with regard to measures of social and economic policy. What may appear to be socialist policy to the one could be demanded by the social state principle for the other. What is socialist policy often becomes blurred against the background of the social state idea and vice versa.

THE RELATIONSHIP BETWEEN STATE AND SOCIETY IN DEMOCRATIC SOCIALISM

One of the principal themes of continental liberal philosophy is the relationship between state and society.[5] One of the main concerns of liberalism is the curtailment of the state's power (i.e., limited government) on the one hand and the accentuation of individual rights of freedom on the other hand. Wilhelm von Humboldt describes this view in his "Limits to the Effectiveness of the State," as did J. S. Mill in his often misunderstood laissez-faire principle (Mill 1869, p. 691). According to this, noninterference of the state in the affairs of its citizens should be the rule, from which deviations are to be allowed only in limited, clearly defined cases.

In the German legal tradition expression is given to these liberal convictions in the form of the doctrine of the separation of state and society (Böckenförde 1976, p. 395f.). In its present form this says that in the terrain of the state, that is, with respect to public affairs, the legitimized use of coercion is allowable through democratic processes, and that in the field of society, that is, with respect to civil affairs, the individual is free to pursue his own interests. Expressed in the language of property-rights theory, the terrain of society is every sector in which rights of ownership are acknowledged and are exchangeable.

In comparison to this, the question arises as to how democratic socialism interprets the relationship between state and society, that is, between the public and private spheres. Of paramount importance for the subtleties of the debate is the influence that Marxist philosophy has had on the one hand and that the revisionist schools of thought (Lassalle, Bernstein) have had on the other.

As is well known, Marx and Engels saw the state as the instrument of repression of the dominant classes and predicted its demise in the ultimate stage of human development (Avineri 1969, p. 202). Consequently, as the separation of state and society is extinguished society is no longer the sector in which the individual is free to make decisions within the framework of the law. As a result, in the Marx-Engels conception the position formerly held by the state and its agents, which were equipped with the power of authority, is assumed by the "organs of society," which should be composed in such a way that everyone takes part in the communal decision-making process. With everyone participating, the freedom of each should simultaneously be ensured. Therefore, the democratic decision-making process is itself made subject to no boundaries.

In the history of ideas this radically democratic concept can be traced back to Rousseau's doctrine of volonté générale, according to which the interests of the individual and those of the community become one in the ideal society (Rousseau 1959, p. 91f.). In this context one is tempted to recall Voltaire's famous contrapuntal remark, which reads: "I do not deliver myself up to my fellow citizens without reservation. I do not give them the power to kill and to rob me on the basis of a majority decision" (Rousseau 1959, p. 137).

Lassalle, one of the founders of German social democracy and a political rival of Marx, takes a less radical stance on the question of the relationship of state and society. This does not, however, imply that he can be described as a supporter of liberal political philosophy. As do Marx and Engels, he expects that in socialism there will be a concurrence of interests between the individual and society. The conflict of interests between people because of "mine" and "thine," which is the basis of Hobbes's philosophy, should belong to the past in the universal community. Simultaneously, however, Lassalle supports universal suffrage and pleads for "the representation of the working class in the legislative bodies of Germany" (Schwan 1984, p. 6). This demand would be sensible only if the existing legislative assemblies were granted the right to make binding decisions for all citizens, including the working class. Approval of participation in the democratic bodies, nevertheless, does not include support for the institutions of the liberal constitutional state, by which the individual would be shielded from the power of the democratic state.

In the history of the Social Democratic Party it was the revisionist wing (Eduard Bernstein) that first fostered understanding of the liberal principles of shielding the individual from state arbitrariness. Bernstein introduced into the socialist debate the ideas of the constitutional state, the separation of the executive form, the legislative and judiciary functions, and the protection of minorities (Schwan 1984, p. 9). However, the revisionist-socialist position is characterized by the fact that, besides the protection of individual freedoms, the establishment of equality is considered equally important. Nevertheless, the equality principle is not interpreted by Bernstein and his many followers in the liberal sense that all citizens are equal before the law; rather, it is understood to mean that equality should be achieved in a material sense through the use of coercive public measures.

Under the influence of Kurt Schumacher, who was the most prominent party leader of the Sozialdemokratischen Partei Deutschlands (SPD) immediately after the collapse of national socialism, the accentuation of human rights and freedoms along the revisionist road taken by Bernstein, was increased. The crowning finale of this line of thought in democratic socialism is generally considered to be the SPD's Godesberg program, which was passed in 1959 (Grundsatzprogramm 1959). The essence of this program was announced with the statement: "We are fighting for democracy. It must become the general basis of our public and civil existence, because it alone expresses appreciation of man's dignity and his personal responsibility. We resist every dictatorship, every form of totalitarian and authoritarian rule, because these deny man's dignity, destroy his freedom, and obliterate the rule of law" (Grundsatzprogramm 1959).

This passage is a clear renunciation of the totalitarian democracy of Marxist form, for which the subjection of the individual to the decisions of the collectivity is the fundamental idea. At the same time a move toward the liberal individualistic principles can be detected in the accentuation of personal responsibility and human dignity. Further, as already mentioned above in a different context, the fact that the state system determined in the program was that of parliamentary democracy was also unequivocal, just as was the willingness to submit to democratic competition for votes.

Despite all this the Godesberg program does not amount to the taking over of the liberal ideas of the constitutional state from the left because the basic question of the limits of the state, which liberal political teaching accentuates so repeatedly, was not answered at all unambiguously. This is especially the case because, since the passing of the Godesberg program, a shift in socialist theoretical discussions toward the Marxist position was observable.[6] As noted at the beginning, "democratization" can be understood to be the desire that political democracy should be completed on the social and economic side. This can be interpreted in the sense that a process, which one believes will of necessity take place, can be accelerated with supporting measures. It could, however, also be meant in the radical sense, that a "change of systems" is the aim.

With respect to German development, the second interpretation must be attributed the greater weight. In that respect, however, at least the supporters of the radical line of democratic socialism returned to the position taken earlier by the older Marxist socialism, with its demand for the suspension of the separation of state and society and its metaphor of the withering away of the state.

This becomes exceptionally clear if one keeps the demands of Marx and Engels for the socialization of the means of production in mind. The need for such a socialization is to be deduced from the diagnosis that private ownership of the means of production is the basic evil of the so-called capitalist economy, because it allows the workers to be exploited by the capitalists. It is consequently required that all means of production should be withdrawn from private ownership and transferred to "society." The socialization of the means of production in the Marxist utopia should not, however, be understood to mean simply the transfer of property rights to other holders. Rather, the demand should be considered as more attuned to the idea of "socialized man," who will only develop to his full potential within the collective system (Harrington 1970, p. 77).

Therefore, "socialization" does not imply, as often erroneously thought, that the means of production should be nationalized (or placed in the hands of the commune or municipality). The holder of property rights to the means of production should instead be "society." The demand for the democratization of the economy--or, alternatively phrased, for the democratization of society--takes up this idea again. At this juncture, however, socialism is confronted by a fundamental problem. As long as "society" is not a politically structured entity, the possibility of becoming the holder of rights to the means of production is lacking. The Soviet solution to this problem is that the Communist party assumes this task, which, however, leads to the well-known problem of a totalitarian domination by the party.

Socialist parties in other parts of the world have in the past often adopted the method of rather subtly and insidiously changing the Marxist socialization postulate into demands for the nationalization of industry. This mostly implies, as was the case recently in France, that the small and medium-sized firms are spared and only the large concerns are converted to state property. At best a new "state socialism" or, as often falsely said, a "state capitalism" can result from such a policy.

Nevertheless, this is as far removed from Marx's concept as the communisme de caserne of the previous example.[7]

If these two solutions are not considered suitable, then those who stand up for liberal socialist ideals face the problem of either renouncing the socialization idea, which amounts to destroying the foundations of the whole concept, or of developing an institutional alternative without the shortcomings already mentioned.

"Democratization of the economy and society" is the catchphrase that refutes the nationalization of the means of production (in the sense of its being transferred to the state) just as it causes the rejection of single-party rule and economic control. The question is whether the suggestions for the practical application of the phrase "democratization of the economy and society" are really capable of leading to the desired liberal solution of the problem under modern circumstances.

ATTEMPTS AT APPLYING THE DEMAND FOR DEMOCRATIZATION

Particularly toward the end of the 1960s and in the 1970s, countless initiatives were launched in the German Federal Republic to translate the demands for the democratization of the economy and society into reality. In so doing the ideas were to a certain extent coupled with those of the syndicalist system of economic organization of the 1920s, in which industries are owned and managed by workers.[8] In the discussion two aspects can be distinguished: (1) the demand for economy-wide democratization, and (2) democratization at the firm or company level. In the second case well-developed codetermination legislation exists. In the first case one could possibly say that limited first attempts within the framework of the economie concerté (concerted action) have been made. In any case, the theoretical discussion is sufficient to fill whole libraries.

Industrial Codetermination: The Way to the Corporate State

In their attempts to develop an alternative to the so-called capitalist economic system, the supporters of socialism are continually faced with the question of developing suitable institutions to replace the market's coordination of economic plans. Insofar as central planning of the Soviet type proves to be unacceptable because of the limitation it places on freedom and because of its serious inefficiencies, new proposals must be developed. These initially began with the syndicalist movement and finally found expression in the idea of social self-administration, which was developed particularly lucidly by some of the supporters of the Yugoslavian model of socialism (Watrin, forthcoming). According to this, the separate producer-labor collectives should not coordinate their economic plans by means of markets, in the orthodox sense, which would entail a relapse into a group-egoistic economic form, burdened with all the shortcomings that socialism particularly strives to overcome. Therefore, instead of market coordination, a community process of voting, constructed in a stepwise fashion, should be deployed. This starts at the level of the commune (or municipality), proceeds with the method of sending delegates from the lower units to the separate provinces or states, and terminates in an institution at the level of the national state.

This is the basic model of collective decision-making that is represented in the German discussion by, for example, the supporters of the social control of investment or social structural planning, but also by the advocates of the introduction of economic and social councils at the different levels of a federal state (Hennis 1977; Scherping and Wallner 1973; Roth 1976).

It is apparent that in a world of limited resources, in which information is costly, voting systems that require the participation of all citizens, as in the classical Grecian polity in which the assembled citizenry makes decisions, are no longer practicable because of the sheer numbers involved. The decision-time costs of applying such a procedure in a mass democracy would be enormous, and it is doubtful if consistent plans could ever be achieved in this way, not to mention optimal national economic plans. This would also be the case if, in an exuberant delight of experimentation, a new Computopia (computer and utopia) were to be imagined, by which every evening the nation could make the political decisions for the next day through the manipulation of a few buttons on a telephone (Schimmelbuch 1971, pp. 28ff.)

Compared with the high rhetoric of socialist theory, the measures that have actually been taken in a world that was not previously subjected to a tabula rasa process of revolution seem modest. In this regard German history provides enough for consideration. After the collapse of the Kaiserreich, attempts at socialization were made in the newly formed Weimar republic, in which social democracy came to power rather abruptly, without, however, possessing any precise proposals for establishing a socialist system. Socialization plans therefore did not get further than the discussion stage (Röpke 1926, VII, p. 576). In the later years of the Weimar republic, which unfortunately the leading socialists of that period dismissed as mere "formal" democracy, the German General Trade Union Congress (Allgemeiner Deutscher Gewerkschaftsbund) succeeded in having revised plans for democratization accepted in the form of a Preliminary Reich's Economic Council (Reichswirtschaftsrat) (Naphtali et al. 1969, p. 9; Beck 1962, p. 24). It was to be a kind of third chamber, with the function of advising on governmental economic policy. Its members were not chosen in general elections, however, as would have been appropriate for the democratization idea. Neither was this body composed of delegates from subordinate levels, as the model sketched above would imply, as this level had simply not been created. Rather, the Reich's Economic Council comprised representatives of established associations, who were chosen according to a proportionally based formula.

The practical importance of the Reich's Economic Council was small, and it was eventually dissolved in 1934. It should nevertheless not be overlooked that as an institutional solution such a form of democratization of economic policy is far removed from the conceptions that connect Marxist socialism to the socialization of the means of production. The same applies to the democratization idea if, thereby, the social self-administration sketched above is implied. In reality the solution eventually found is of the nature of the corporate state--a system of collusion between big unions, big business, and the state. That implies that it may be sure of meeting with approval from the representatives of completely different political convictions, for example, those who believe in the corporate stratification of society, a view that was popular in the 1930s, and not only in Germany. Of course the same applies also to all representatives of group interests who are primarily interested in increasing their own influence.

The second important attempt to introduce socialist economic planning concepts, which also ended in failure, was undertaken in the 1970s. On the one hand, the ideas of economic democracy that led to the Preliminary National Economic Council (Vorläufiger Reichswirtschaftsrat) were taken as a starting point; on the other, the ideas of French "planification," which in the history of economic thought can be traced back to Saint-Simon, also played an initiating role. It should nevertheless be noted that the drawn-out theoretical discussion concerning the relevant questions was out of proportion to the meager results that were finally attained.

The key concept to understanding the debate reads: concerted action. Its meaning is, however, easily misunderstood, not only in English but also in German. Initially, "concerted action" was understood to mean any market strategy taken by firms that was described by the American anti-trust act as a conspiracy against the public interest (Hoppmann 1971, p. v). However, in the German discussion, "concerted action" is to be understood in terms of the French _action concertée_, a concept which was derived from the planification debate. It denoted the cooperation of the state with the large economic interest groups, in particular the trade unions and the employers' associations, with respect to economic policy. In the well-known writings of Naphtali (1969, p. 26), in which the strongly socialist-influenced trade union viewpoint of the 1920s is formulated, the history of the labor movement is described from a Marxist perspective in the chapter entitled "Democratization of Economic Policy." Included were considerations of which position the trade unions should taken from then on in the Weimar republic. It was not only required that they, as every other interest group, should contribute their wants and ideas to the public discussion, but it was also demanded that they should have direct participation in public economic policy. The decisive sentence reads: "The democratization of the economy . . . requires that direct participation of the workers organized as producers, i.e. the trade unions, be continually extended in all agencies of economic policy" (Naphtali 1969, p. 137).

How was this socialist idea to be put into practice? The situation in the 1960s was in no way the equivalent of that in the 1920s, when this idea was first formulated. In the Federal Republic of Germany the rules of a market economy becames a much stronger reality than in the interventionist Weimar republic, with its benevolent attitude toward cartels. Ideas of socialization were as politically unpopular as demands for nationalization. Accordingly, socialist economic policy could not launch any changes in property rights. In fact, its starting point lay in a completely different field, namely that of incomes policy. Consequently, the developments led to results that were far removed from the concepts of economic democracy's supporters.

In its second annual report, the Council of Economic Advisers (Sachverstandigenrat), founded in 1963, called for the introduction of a "concerted stabilization action" and described this measure expressly as a "new social contract."[9] It was suggested that representatives of the trade unions, employers, and the government come together so as to come to an agreement about determining wage increases, in such a way that the increases would not destabilize the economy; in particular, it was argued that inflationary developments, which would endanger full employment and economic growth in the long run, should be avoided.

This proposal becomes clear when one briefly considers the German system for determining wages. This system is such that negotiations are undertaken at an industry-wide level between trade unions and employers' associations, as, for example, between all metal workers and all companies of the metal industry. In these wage negotiations, contrary to, for example, the British system, a company only belongs to one employers' association, that is, it negotiates with only one trade union. In the labor market the employers' cartel is confronted with only the workers' cartel. In the German one says that "autonomous groups" negotiate with one another, the technical expression used in reference to the entire system being "collective bargaining autonomy."

Wherever two monopolies (in this case, cartels) oppose each other in the market, it is known that the solution is indeterminate. It follows, therefore, that wage increases far in excess of the rise in labor productivity could result. When that occurs, the government is faced with a dilemma. It can either follow an inflationary policy so as to ensure job security, or it can maintain the value of money by risking unemployment. The supporters of concerted action believe that one could best avoid this dilemma by persuading the employers' associations and unions to agree on wage settlements that do not cause the problem mentioned above. However, to achieve the permission of the unions and employers' associations to use such a procedure, it was considered expedient to grant them a measure of influence upon the formulation of governmental economic policy within the framework of a concerted action program.

Undoubtedly, other possibilities would also be available to solve the problem sketched here, for example, compulsory mediation or the renunciation of the government's responsibility for ensuring full employment. Compulsory mediation was often practiced to settle wage differences in the Weimar republic, but it did not prove to be satisfactory, as the government became embroiled in countless wage disputes. The government's attempts at mediation usually led to its being attacked by both trade unions and employers, which in the long run damaged its public reputation. Nevertheless, the other alternative, that of renouncing governmental responsibility for full employment, found very little public support in the 1960s, as the Keynesian full employment doctrine was then widely accepted in all political quarters. A reconsideration only occurred toward the end of the 1970s, when it was generally realized that full employment programs of the Keynesian type could give rise to "stagflation." This led, albeit only in the last few years, to the conviction that the promise made by the social liberal government coalition at the beginning of the 1970s--that the government could guarantee full employment--was incorrect. Increasing reference is nowadays made to the view that the level of employment depends strictly upon the wage level, that is, the trade unions and their partners, the employers' associations, are primarily responsible for whether full employment is maintained or not.

The practical implementation of the concept of concerted action took place in § 3 of the Stability and Growth Act of 1967 (Stabilitäts- und Wachstumsgesetz). According to section 3 the government was required to place wage guidelines for a "simultaneous, coordinated procedure (concerted action) at the disposal of the trade unions and employers' associations," whenever a macroeconomic disequilibrium threatened to arise (Stern, Munch, Hansmeyer 1972, p. 16). These guidelines were not formally binding upon the participants. In practice, however, the trade unions and employers' associations were expected to abide by them because these parties had been involved in considering and compiling the wage guidelines. Consequently, the right to take part in the discussions about the guidelines was seen as the price for achieving voluntary·compliance with the agreement. Without a doubt, the consideration was continually in the background that if the equilibrium between the conduct of the two parties (i.e., the concerted action) were to fail, the government could be induced to limit the collective bargaining autonomy of these cartel-like associations.

Several times a year "meetings for concerted action," to use the terminology of the official announcements, took place under the chairmanship of the federal minister for economic affairs (for further details see Watrin, Konzertierte Aktionen). During the initial stages agents of the most important associations of employers, industry, the trades, and retail trade, as well as representatives of the trade unions, participated. At the first talks 9 organizations were represented, with 34 persons being present. Later, however, the numbers of participating institutions and persons increased rapidly and included the Council of Economic Advisors and the German Federal Bank. By the beginning of 1977 the number of participants had increased to 79 persons representing a total of 24 organizations. In this way the concerted action followed a course that in many ways is similar to that taken by the Preliminary National Economic Council. Initially, it was intended that this committee be kept small (80 to 100 persons). Nevertheless, the political pressure of private interest groups quickly led to the numbers being inflated until, finally, the number of seats amounted to 326.

The sessions of the concerted action were not public. They were also preceded by preparatory talks with representatives of companies and unions, who formed a steering committee that was well shielded from outside scrutiny. The meetings were, as a rule, concluded by, first of all, the minister of economic affairs commenting on the business cycle, to which then were added the opinions of the remaining participants. The communiqués published on the meetings initially brought to the fore what the represented opinions had in common, but in later years differing points of view were also stated. After the thirtieth session general announcements were no longer published.

During the period in which concerted action existed, various attempts were made to extend the list of topics to be handled. However, these endeavors achieved little.

In the public debate suggestions were often made to develop the concerted action procedure toward a federal economic and social council with increased responsibility for economic planning, or toward a committee capable of making binding decisions with respect to wages or investments. In the first case the supporters based their arguments on the ideas of the democratization of the economy and economy-wide codetermination, which had already been advanced by Naphtali, Baade, and others in the 1920s. In the second case, the binding force of the decisions which were to be taken was emphasized by the consideration of suitable sanctions. Neither proposal, however, was of any practical significance.

In the course of the judicial altercations surrounding the Codetermination Act of 1976, the trade unions refused to participate further in the sessions of the concerted action program. Attempts to revive the meetings after the decision of the federal constitutional court were not successful. At present (1985) meetings between the federal minister of economic affairs and private interest groups have taken the place of the former multilateral talks.

Whether or not concerted action ever really achieved the desired procedural balance has been questioned by those participants who have since publicly spoken out on the question. It is often maintained that "despite its description, concerted action was from the start less an instrument of concrete action than an information forum." It is said that it "ultimately never rose above having the character of a non-binding discussion committee" (Tietmeyer 1969, p. 179).

Despite this conclusion one should nevertheless not obscure the questions of principle that arise from having interest groups participate in governmental decisions. If interest groups are included in the public sphere in an official capacity, the danger arises that either they could manipulate the governmental apparatus to further their own special interests or they could become part of the governmental power machinery. In the first case the result would be a "socialization of the state," that is, one would move in the direction of a corporate state. In the second case a "takeover of society by the government" would ensue, that is, one would move in the direction of those social democracy ideas that attempt to obscure the distinction between state and society.

Even if in the German case no decisive results were obtained in either direction, it cannot be denied that concerted action touched upon a question of great importance to the liberal economic system, namely, that of the boundary between public affairs and private self-determination. This it achieved through its attempts to create a procedural balance between public agencies and private interest organizations. Even if no concerted action was achieved with respect to particular matters, there was exposed the basic question of what legitimization the unions and employers' associations have for participating in governmental decisions. In the case of these associations, unambiguous legitimization through general, equal, and secret ballots, which are normally required in a liberal democracy, are lacking. Neither can they maintain that they represent large sections of the population, for without a doubt, the role of consumer or taxpayer is more important to most citizens than that of being a member of an employers' association or trade union. However, neither consumers nor taxpayers had positions in the concerted action committees or in comparable institutions. The opinion that one has to do with a kind of functional representation stands on thin ice, if one believes that in an economic order the interests that either have not been or are not easily organized into collective groups (according to Olson [1968, p. 163], taxpayers, consumers, savers, and others) also require consideration.

Nevertheless, developments that point toward concerted action are fostered by democratic socialism and its political philosophy. This is particularly the case because lately, on the basis of the same model, democratic socialism has pleaded for the social steering of investments.

This does not imply that new obligations will be transferred to the government; rather, according to the ideas of the advocates of investment control, institutions would allow unions, representatives of employers and perhaps also those of the public interest, whatever is to be understood by that, to have a say. They should either allocate investments directly into definite branches of the economy or in some or other way sanction and authorize investment plans. However, all this is just as irreconcilable with a market economy and the orientation of economic subjects to price signals as are the principles of a liberal democracy. The socialist ideas of economic democracy therefore ultimately favor a condominial, combined form of government by associations which have not been legitimized democratically, or they lead to the inclusion of freely formed societies (which is more probably in the long run) representing interest groups in the public power apparatus, thereby weakening the freedom of the individual.

Codetermination in Firms: A Step toward Workers' Self-management Socialism?

Economy-wide codetermination versus codetermination in firms

In socialist thinking, workers' self-management plays an important rule, so much so that to many socialists it seems to be the primary aim of the socialist movement. Despite this, there are others who are strongly opposed to any form of syndicalism. According to the arguments of the latter group, self-management by workers would only further the self-interests of those working in a particular company rather than the general welfare of society and therefore would be steering society off the road to socialism. In the past both these views have surfaced in German debate. After World War I when the German social democrats came to power for the first time, following the dissolution of the Second Reich, they opposed the system of workers' soviets, which had sprung up in Bavaria and elsewhere during the revolution of 1918. They changed this system by enacting a law on "works councils," which gave the employees of a firm rights to express their views collectively to the management, but which did not give them self-management rights according to the syndicalist or socialist views held in many quarters at that time.

In addition, the introduction to the above mentioned Preliminary National Economic Council must be seen in this context. It is also interesting to note the attitude that the German Trade Union Federation adopted at that time toward codetermination in firms. It was argued by high-ranking union officials that (entrepreneurial) co-management would tend to increase the extent to which firms promote only the interests of their own workers, to the detriment of society as a whole. Unions should therefore support codetermination in the economy as a whole, but not within firms. (Critics suspected that the true reasons why the Trade Union Federation abstained from pushing codetermination in firms was their fear that they might lose their grip on their members, if co-management was allowed to become too widespread in industry.)

After World War II the priorities were reversed. The unions and their many intellectual supporters attached prime importance to codetermination in firms, while the introduction of codetermination at an economy-wide level in the form of economic and social councils became a secondary matter. Nevertheless, the concept is still on the agenda, and the idea of setting up such councils as an instrument for macroeconomic planning or the steering of investments has to be borne in mind for an understanding of the whole problem.

The point of departure for the development of codetermination after World War II was the granting of co-management rights to workers in the coal and steel industry in 1951.[10] The 1951 law on codetermination in mining enterprises and the coal and steel sector laid down equal representation for labor and shareholders in the "supervisory boards" and the appointment of a worker director on the "board of managers." Despite opposition from the labor unions, a labor/management act (sometimes known as the Works Constitution Act) followed in 1952. This stipulated that one-third of the membership of the supervisory boards of joint stock companies was to go to the employees. In 1972 the Labor Management Relations Act was amended. A few years later, in 1976, the Federal Parliament adopted the Codetermination Law, providing for the extension of codetermination in the coal and steel sector to <u>all</u> large commercial corporations, though in modified form. In total, 470 companies, including all the well-known names in German industry, are now working under this law. The main point is that the supervisory boards comprise between twelve and twenty members (depending on the number of employees). Half of the seats are held by the shareholders' representatives and the other half by the employees', but in a very peculiar manner. Among the six to ten seats on the employees' side, two or three are reserved for labor union representatives from outside the company. The other seats go to the representatives of the workers, the white-collar employees and to those senior executives who do not belong to the board of managers. All representatives must be elected by separate group elections. For instance, the senior executives choose their representatives, and so on.

The central question is whether or not codetermination, as it was introduced in Germany company law, is a step toward the socialist ideal. Of course, socialists backed the 1976 legislation, which is the most important of the laws mentioned above; it also cannot be denied that the socialist vision of a fully democratized society has had a major impact on the debate. However, even among nonsocialists the introduction of codetermination rights in many fields of public life was not questioned during the last round of the debate. The Codetermination Act was passed by the German parliament nearly unanimously, and today no major party or any interest group challenges workers' participation, apart from calls for minor alterations of the existing legislation. Even the private or public owners of codetermined enterprises do not raise their voices against the measures taken.

This development is not easy to explain. It can be argued that the prevailing consensus signals that the "Germans are all socialists now." This is not very convincing in view of the 1983 election, which was won by the conservative parties in a fierce ideological attack against the socialist views put forward in the election campaign. Another explanation may be that the German codetermination legislation does not have severe effects on German companies and their efficiency. Therefore, the debate can be left, as many think, to the ideologists, which means that it is practically of minor importance.

In the following paragraph it will be shown that the German codetermination legislation did not have the dramatic effects that were expected by many of its critics. But this does not mean that it is an unimportant change in the legal structure of the country. It causes a situation which is notable in many respects and may become the starting point of some measures which are steps not to the socialist goal, but to a more corporativist economy.

Economic effects of codetermination

The question of equal powers. The German Codetermination Act, which has been in force for nearly nine years, has only recently come under investigation by economists (Benelli 1979, 1983; Wickenkamp 1983; Monissen 1978, pp. 58-84; Jensen and Meckling 1976; Prosi 1976; Pejovich 1978b, pp. 3-21). One major question which had already been discussed before the legislation was passed by the German parliament is the issue of whether equal representation of shareholders and employees on the supervisory board, that is, the introduction of the "parity" principle, would imply that both groups would have equal rights. In a case that went to the German Constitutional Court in 1977 a group of managers in codetermined companies complained that they were no longer free to make decisions on wage settlements since the workers had achieved parity in the supervisory boards and could influence the board of managers not to be too tough when wage agreements were to be settled. The case was, however, dismissed. The court decided that the rule allowing shareholders and workers to send equal numbers of representatives to the supervisory board does not mean that true parity has been introduced. The court's decision was based on two arguments. First, the chairman of the supervisory board is normally nominated by the shareholders' representatives. Therefore, he belongs to that group. According to the law, the chairman has a casting vote if there is a deadlock. Second, it was emphasized that as a rule, wage contracts are not settled between an individual company and its local union, but between the employers' association to which the firm belongs and their trade union counterparts at a region- and industry-wide level.

These arguments do not take into account the dynamics of codetermination and the strong political elements on which it rests. It is the principal object of the legislation that in the companies' decision-making process the interests of the employees, as well as those of the shareholders, should be taken into account. Therefore, a strategy of the shareholders, which was to be based solely on the second vote of the chairman, would not just give rise to further political demands to install "true" parity via legislation. It could also be a real source of industrial disputes and offer a strategy for employees' representatives to lay all the blame for unfavorable business operations on the shareholders. In many cases it would therefore be a better strategy for the shareholders' representatives not to override the employees' side but, instead, to seek compromise and to follow the strategies known in politics as implicit logrolling. Thus, the seemingly paradoxical outcome that most decisions made in codetermined supervisory boards are reported to be taken unanimously can be explained as the consequence of package deals. What information is available suggests that they are normally agreed upon outside the board in deals between the Works Council and the Board of Managers.

The argument that de facto parity has been achieved (Wickenkamp 1983, p. 125), and that employees' representatives have a decisive influence on matters, can be strengthened when looking at the appointment of the members of the board of managers, undoubtedly the most important decision to be made by the supervisory board. The contracts are normally for five years, and as a rule board members are reelected two or three times before retirement. The election procedure that they must undergo is very complicated. In the first ballot the law prescribes a two-thirds majority of the supervisory board members, which means that a managing executive needs at least some votes from the workers' side. If this fails, then a committee must be established and within a month must place one or more candidates on a new list, which could, if desired, include the candidate who lost the first round. The next ballot will be decided by simple majority, and only if it results in a stalemate does the member who chairs the supervisory board have a vote.

An election procedure like this attracts the attention of the general public. Therefore, it is in the interests of management to find candidates for the board of managers who will be elected on the first ballot. Therefore, above all, the candidates who have the best chance are those who can bridge possible conflicts of interest between shareholders' representatives on one side and the employees' representatives on the other.

The result of the above-mentioned voting rules is clearly an attenuation of the shareholders' property rights. They no longer have full control over the members of the board of managers who, as their economic agents, act in their interests. On the other hand, a rational number of the board--or someone who plans a career as a board member--will adjust early to the change of institutional environment brought about by the codetermination legislation and will try, in time, to be approved by the workers' representatives as well.

It is obvious that this will influence the policy pursued by the members of the managing board, especially their investment decisions, their labor relations strategy, and their dividend policy. Seen from the employees' point of view, the impact of a company's investment policies on job security and wages--not on profits--is important. Their representatives will prefer less risky investment alternatives and more capital-intensive projects to risky, growth-oriented policies. Empirical findings (Benelli 1979, 1983) prove that management under codetermination is included to ask its supervisory boards for approval only for those investment projects that fulfill these criteria.

Further, it is obvious that employees' representatives have a special interest in working conditions and in payments, which are not part of the wage contract but benefit workers one way or another. These payments range from extra retirement benefits out of a company fund to the sponsoring of local sports clubs. It is held that bargaining in all these fields plays an important role when agreement in supervisory boards is sought on more controversial matters.

Profit policy is another domain within the scope of interest of labor representatives. It is in their interest to plow profits back into the business as much as possible. This attitude is frequently shared by the management, which prefers self-financing to outside financing under many circumstances. It could be argued that policies of plowing back are also in the interests of the shareholders because they will influence share prices in a positive way. However, spending the earnings on non-wage benefits for workers and fringe benefits for managers is also an alternative.

During the downswing of the business cycle in the early 1980s even codetermined companies had to dismiss large numbers of workers and close plants. It is interesting to see how codetermination worked under these circumstances. Present legislation permits companies to terminate operations anywhere at any time. The employees must be informed in advance, but they cannot prevent the dismissal. Yet those laid off have a right to a compensation payment. An agreement on the amount paid must be reached with the Works' Council, not with the supervisory boards or its labor representatives. In practice this does not matter much, for, as a rule, the employees' representatives on the board are also members of the Works' Council. There are no statistics available as to the amounts paid in the final agreements, but it is known that the sums are large and that it is extremely costly to come to an agreement. In addition, the board of management must justify any shutdown to a supervisory board with employees' representatives who cast a vote for the board's reelection.

"Evasive action" and "exit" of shareholders. Shareholders facing a law that attenuates their property rights have two strategies at their disposal. The first strategy, "evasive action," can be launched via changing the legal form of a company, changing the company's bylaws, qualifying for exemption by cutting down the numbers of employees to fewer than two thousand, or via relocation of productive capacity out of the country.

At least 150 companies out of 620, which prior to the legislation would have been candidates for enrollment in codetermination, are said to have evaded the law by changing their legal form or reducing their number of employees to fewer than two thousand (Wickenkamp 1983, p. 156). And there are reports that several companies, which are for the time being subject to the law, are pursuing policies which will bring them out of the domain of mandatory codetermination.

"Exit" is the strategy of selling shares of codetermined enterprises and looking for other investment opportunities. Whereas some striking examples for the first strategy can be cited, evidence of the second cannot be produced easily. It must be remembered that the financial markets in Germany anticipated the reduction in shareholders' wealth. The public debate about the pros and cons of workers' participation went on for many years, and the main legal provisions were known at least a year before the law was enacted (Benelli 1983, p. 156).

However, it would be shortsighted to argue that, apart from a decrease in the price of shares of codetermined companies when the law became effective, there is no lasting impact from the changes in the legal order. Most of the large companies in Germany have been confronted with a problem of long-term financing, which cannot be attributed primarily to the stagnation period of the early 1980s. For many years a public debate has been going on as to how companies could attract more share capital. However, a 1976 change in corporate tax law to bring this about did not prove successful. Of course, the financing problems cannot simply be attributed to codetermination mandated by law as there are many factors that influence competitive financial markets. But it can nevertheless be said that codetermination is costly, that decision-making costs go up, and that risk-aversion policies instead of growth policies are universally preferred. These are all factors that have to be paid for and that, even in the long run, cannot be easily overcome.

Furthermore, for the time being large shifts of investment funds from codetermined companies to non-codetermined firms--or into foreign investment--have not been reported. The reallocation of capital itself is not without cost, but on the other hand, the attractiveness of codetermined firms to those investors who have access to the world capital market may be too small to raise the funds required. If this is correct, there must be at least some evidence that codetermined companies have in the past been less efficient than their national and international competitors, including those enterprises where the workers' side had only a minority representation on the supervisory boards.

A pathbreaking study by G. Benelli (1983) indeed demonstrates that in national and international cross-sectional studies the variations in returns on shares in industries that have been under codetermination legislation since 1951 (coal mining, iron and steel production) have been the lowest compared with other industries within and outside Germany.

It could be argued that coal mining and steel producing are so-called "sunset" industries, which have to struggle with falling demand. But the proper question is whether or not the restructuring process and the efforts to get into new markets have been hampered by codetermination. It cannot be proved that codetermination has been the main obstacle to the adjustment process to which both industries have been submitted. But coal mining, with a state-regulated monopoly introduced in the 1960s, has been one of the most heavily subsidized industries in Germany for decades. Equally, the iron and steel industry has been under the special regulations of the European Coal and Steel Community for many years. Today, the relevant market is heavily protected against competition. In addition, considerable subsidies are paid, and yet, this highly concentrated industry seems to be unable to solve its adjustment problems.

Beneficial to workers as well as to the owners of capital? One major argument suggests that mandatory codetermination does not pass the test of Pareto-superiority because it did not result from voluntary agreements between the owner-shareholders of the respective companies and their workers and that the introduction of codetermination by act of legislation is in itself proof that there are winners as well as losers (Pejovich 1978b). There is, indeed, some evidence in favor of this argument.

The German unions, which own a number of very large companies and have some hundreds of thousands of employees,[11] have not been "progressive" as far as the introduction of co-management rights in their own enterprises is concerned, despite the fact that they are fighting politically for even more codetermination. According to their line of argument in favor of codetermination, which states that competitive advantages are to be gained through its introduction because of its humanizing effects in the workplace, the trade unions as employers should, through the voluntary introduction of codetermination in their own firms, be able to secure this decisive competitive advantage for their undertakings. In fact, they did not put their own line of reasoning into practice. The reason the unions gave for publicly "renouncing" voluntary codetermination in their own firms was the following: it would allegedly be disadvantageous for their companies if they should have to compete with non-codetermined "capitalistic" firms. Interestingly enough, this blatant contradiction, which seems to prove that codetermination is obviously not advantageous to capital owners as well as employees, was not used as an argument by their opponents.

The argument that codetermination would originate from voluntary contracting, if it were beneficial to owners of capital and to workers, could also be questioned from the viewpoint that it rests on the implicit assumption that the initial distribution of property rights was fair. Indeed, this seems to be one of the implicit arguments in the whole debate. Contrary to the view of many economists that an enterprise consists of a nexus of contracts among owners of productive resources and that "the firm . . . has no power of fiat, no authority, no disciplinary action any different . . . from ordinary market contracting between any two people" (Alchian and Demsetz 1972), it was generally held in the German debate that an enterprise is a hierarchical organization with unequal partners. For instance, the Mitbestimmungs Commission,[12] established by the government to report on codetermination, stated that when a wage earner signs a wage contract, he "submits himself to the authority and prerogatives of his employers," and, the commission continues, that this is compatible with human dignity only if "the subordinate or his representatives can directly influence the formation and the content of the decision-making process in an enterprise." Therefore, the inequality between the contracting parties was seen as the central argument for the introduction of codetermination via state intervention. But the real question is whether this is an argument to call the allocation of property rights, before the law was enacted, "unfair." Further, it must be asked whether a transfer of property rights via mandatory codetermination in the supervisory board is an efficient measure to strengthen the bargaining power of workers. Finally, it is interesting to see how workers value codetermination rights. Most opinion polls come to the conclusion that they are not highly ranked and that job security, high salaries, and safety provisions are valued more highly.[13] Of course, in opinion polls the one who is questioned may not necessarily reveal actually held opinions. The revelation of true preferences would only occur if codetermination were to command a price and were to be traded in a market. But when codetermination is compulsory, such market transactions are prohibited. Therefore, the question of whether codetermination in the supervisory boards is of any value for the workers who are supposed to gain from its introduction cannot be answered.

Do codetermined enterprises gain more political influence? The introduction of codetermination laws constitutes a long-term change of the company law and the legal structure of an economy. A much-debated question in this context is whether codetermined companies gain more political influence than their non-codetermined competitors. It is said that under the rules of the modern welfare state big companies are "unsinkable" because they will be bailed out by the democratic government whenever they suffer severe losses. Especially in the Germany case it has been argued that the "producers" in a codetermined enterprise, that is, labor and management, have a good chance of placing political pressure on a democratic government when asking for subsidies, tariff protection, and interventionist measures.

There is some evidence in favor of this argument, but it is difficult to decide whether it is valid or not. As already mentioned, codetermination was introduced in the coal-mining and steel-producing industries as early as 1951 via the Montan Act. Both industries are so-called "sunset" industries. Coal mining has been highly subsidized since the 1960s, and hard-coal mining is now a large monopoly as a result of government intervention. The steel industry is also subsidized and protected against competition from the world market via minimum prices, import licenses, and quantitative restrictions. The question is how far this has been caused by the rigidities codetermination has imposed on the companies in those industries, how far the industry could have delayed adaptation to new economic conditions by successful lobbying, and, especially, how successful unions and work councils have influenced political decisions in favor of both industries.

It can be argued that constraints upon competition in steel and coal mining have also occurred in countries that abstained from codetermination legislation, for example, France and Belgium. But this is no answer to the problem of lobbying activities in codetermined firms--a field of empirical research that still has to be covered in Germany.

EPILOGUE: CONTRADICTIONS AND UTOPIAN AND ANTILIBERAL ELEMENTS IN THE ECONOMIC DEMOCRACY MODEL

In the long series of socialist models developed in the last hundred years, that of democratic socialism is a serious attempt to overcome the utopianism of Marxist thought. As many have been fortunate enough to experience, the Marxist vision of a New Society and a Kingdom of Freedom has not been proven to be a foundation for establishing efficient and humane economic relationships in a society or for ensuring the freedom of the individual. On account of these circumstances, the question to be answered is whether the shortcomings and faults of Marxist thought will ultimately be overcome by democratic socialism.

The answer is negative. Economic democracy, the model developed by democratic socialism as a counterconcept to the so-called capitalist economy, is itself contradictory; as is shown by the German example, it contains utopian elements and does not develop a clear conception of how individual freedom can be ensured on the economic terrain.

The contradiction is to be found in the incompatibility of economy-wide codetermination and codetermination in the firm. It is thus no historical accident that the supporters of socialist ideas in the Weimar republic accentuated their realization of economy-wide codetermination, whereas their successors in the German Federal Republic have shifted the emphasis to codetermination at the company level. Contrary to the claims that democratization at the firm and economy levels are compatible, a trade-off can be seen to exist between the two concepts. A system of economy-wide codetermination--however it may be organized in detail--means in essence that central planning of economic processes is desired. The property rights to the allocation of resources must be vested in a central body that gives directions to individual firms as to what they are to do.

In this way the freedom to make decisions at the company level is attenuated. Inversely, a high measure of freedom in decision-making at the company level implies that higher-level authorities must delegate property rights to lower levels. However, the simultaneous centralization and decentralization of decision-making with respect to resource use is not possible.

The economic democracy model suggested by the democratic socialists, however, contains not only a fundamental conceptual contradiction but also a strong utopian element. The political attractiveness of economic democracy lies in the promise that at the company level the so-called hierarchy and domination of capital will be removed. Those who work in a company should themselves decide what they should do; they should be emancipated; accordingly, the catchphrase is "Control by the controlled."

As can be seen from the German example, the implementation of such an uncontrolled, anarchistic order is not possible under modern circumstances. If "lack of control" is to be taken seriously, the unanimity rule must be made compulsory for all collective decision-making in large group; the unanimity rule, however, in all probability quickly leads to increasing decision costs, so that the balancing of "democracy" against "efficiency" becomes inevitable. As a result a trade-off occurs between the aim of having individuals partake in decisions and the costs this participation incurs. Accordingly, a price must be placed on what codetermination is allowed to cost.

This discussion is, however, evaded by the democratic socialists. They create the impression that economic codetermination is "costless." This utopian approach to concrete questions makes the practical implementation of their ideas far removed from the original concept. Again, this can be clearly seen in the German case. The codetermination legislation applicable to large companies that was broadly sketched above makes it clear that a highly complicated system of rules must be created, over which the individual has only minimal influence.

All the problems that focus criticism on present-day political democracy are once again to be found in those firms that have introduced codetermination and which are enthusiastically referred to as "industrial democracies." Because the rules of indirect democracy must be applied in large companies, new classes of officialdom develop, as was to be expected. What Michels (1925) describes as the oligarchy problem arises. Further, the known phenomena of political control come to the fore, and the well-known problem exists that it does not pay the individual worker or employee to offer resistance. If special interests are politically organized, the probability of their being able to override the general interest is greatly enhanced.

Finally, democratization at the company level has many shortcomings compared with the constitutional state in its modern form. Whereas in the constitutional state system the individual is guaranteed certain rights of freedom that can be maintained, if need be, against the will of the majority, equivalent rights are not in principle secured in democratized companies. In this case the freedom of the individual is at best limited to participating in decision-making by voting. As a rule in the larger concerns this is done by the election of representatives, who then have considerable discretionary power; in smaller firms the decision can still be made by personal participation in the voting process. Nevertheless, in both cases the rights of the individual are restricted to codetermination (in the literal sense of the word). As far as the results of the voting process are concerned, the individual is subjected to the opinions of the majority. In the history of philosophy on securing the individual's freedom, this is, however, a retrogressive step toward a situation in which the individual's property rights are not clearly defined.

NOTES

1. See Schmid et al., Grundlagen, esp. the contribution of Gert von Eynern, Heinrich Deist, and Karl Schiller.

2. For details see Willgeroldt 1976, p. 61f.

3. See the interpretation of Marxian theory given in Lowenstein 1970, p. 89 and in Avineri 1969, ch. 8.

4. See Articles 20.2 and 28.1 of the German Basic Law (Grundgesetz).

5. See, e.g., Wilson and Skinner 1976, esp. the contributions of Alexander Caircross, James M. Buchanan, and Richard A. Musgrove.

6. Cf. Sozialdemokratische Partei. Ökonomisch-politscher Orientierungsrahmen für die Jahre 1975-1985 in der vom Mannheimer Parteitag der SPD am November 14, 1985 beschlossenen Fassung, Bonn, 1975.

7. This is an allusion to the phrase Marx coined when criticizing Bakunin's communism. See Avineri 1969, p. 239.

8. A description and critique of the syndicalist movement was delivered by Ludwig von Mises (1981, p. 239).

9. Sachverständigenrat zur Begutachtung der gesamtwirtschaftlichen Entwicklung. Jahresgutachten 65, no. 186. For details, see Watrin, Die Demokratisierung, p. 125f.

10. An overview of institutional aspects of German codetermination was published in the Bullock Report (1977, p. 72). The texts of several acts can be found in "Mitbestimmungsgesetze in den Unternehmen" (1977, pp. 21, 232, 264).

11. These would include the Neue Heimat, the Bank for Gemeinwirtschaft, the Co-op consumer cooperative, and many medium-sized companies, which employ several hundred thousand blue-collar and white-collar workers. For details see Friedl 1964.

12. (Mitbestimmungskommission). "Mitbestimmung im Unternehmen," Deutscher Bundestag, 6 Wahlperiode, Drucksache VI/334, February 4, 1970.

13. See, e.g., the empirical investigation by Ralph Darendorf (1963, p. 115). See also Blume 1962, pp. 55-304; Brinkmann-Herz 1972; Darendorf 1965; Voigt 1962; Clegg 1960, pp. 52-55.

REFERENCES

Alchian, Armen A., and Harold Demsetz. 1972. Production, information costs and economic organization. American Economic Review 62:777.

Avineri, Shlomo. 1969. The social and political thought of Karl Marx. Cambridge: Cambridge University Press.

Beck, Markus. 1962. Wirtschaftsdemokratie. Zürich and St. Gallen: Polygraphischer Verlag AG.

Benelli, Giuseppe. 1979. The codetermination movement in the west. Paper presented at the Forty-ninth Annual Conference of the Souther Economic Association, November 7-9, 1979, Atlanta, Georgia.

------. 1983. Mitbestimmung und Selbstverwaltung. Eine ökonomische Analyse der Arbeitnehmerpartizipation. Cologne.

Blume, Otto. 1962. Zehn Jahre Mitbestimmung-Versuch einer Bestandsaufnahme. In *Zwischenbilanz der Mitbestimmung von Erich Patthoff*. Hans-Böckler Gesellschaft.

Böckenförde, Ernst-Wolfgang. 1976. Die Bedeutung der Unterscheidung von Staat und Gesellschaft im demokratischen Sozialstaat der Gegenwart. In Ernst-Wolfgang Böckenförde, ed., *Staat und Gesellschaft*. Darmstadt: Wissenschaftliche Buchgesellschaft.

Brinkmann-Herz, Dorothea. 1972. Entscheidungsprozesse in den Aufsichtsräten der Montanindustrie: Eine empirische Untersuchung über die Eignung des Aufsichtsrates als Instrument der Arbeitnehmermitbestimmung. No. 15, *Beiträge zur Verhaltenforschung*, ed. G. Smölders. Berlin.

(Bullock Report). 1977. Report of the Committee of Inquiry on Industrial Democracy, Lord Bullock, Chairman. Presented to Parliament by the Secretary of State for Trade by Command of Her Majesty. January. Cmnd. 6706.

Clegg, H. A. 1960. *A new approach to industrial democracy*. Oxford: Basil Blackwell.

Darendorf, Ralph. 1963. *Das Mitbestimmungsproblem in der deutschen Sozialforschung: Eine Kritik*. Tübingen.

------. 1965. *Das Mitbestimmungsproblem in der deutschen Sozialforschung. Eine Kritik*. 2nd ed. Munich.

Deist, Heinrich. Wirkschaftsdemokratie. In Schmid et al.

Friedl, Gerhard A. 1964. *Die Gewerkschaften als Unternehmer*. Stuttgart.

Grundsatzprogramm der Sozialdemokratischen Partei Deutschlands. November 13-15, 1959, Bad Godesberg.

Harrington, Michael. 1970. *Socialism*. New York: Saturday Review Press.

Hayek, Friedrich A. 1970. *Die Irrtümer des Konstruktivismus und die Grundlagen legitimer Kritik gesellschaftlicher Gebilde*. Munich and Salzburg: Wilhelm Finke Verlag.

Hennis, Wilhelm. 1977. *Organisierter Sozialismus. Zum "strategischen" Staats- und Politikverstandnis der Sozialdemokratie*. Stuttgart.

Hoppmann, Erich, ed. 1971. *Konzertierte Aktion. Kritische Beiträge zu einen Experiment*. Frankfurt: Athenäum Verlag.

Jensen, Michael C., and William H. Meckling. 1976. Theory of the firm: Managerial behavior, agency costs and ownership structure. Journal of Financial Economics 3:305-60. Reprinted in Karl Brunner, ed., Economics and social institutions. Boston, Mass: Kluwer, 1979, pp. 163-231.

Lowenstein, Julius I. 1970. Vision und Wirklichkeit. Marx contra Marxismus. Basel.

Michels, Robert. 1925. Zur Soziologie des Parteiwesens in der modernen Demokratie. Leipzig.

Mill, John S. 1869. Grundsatze der Politischen Ökonomie, trans. Adolf Soetbeer. Leipzig.

Mises, Ludwig von. 1981. Socialism. An economic and sociological analysis, trans. J. Karhane. Indianapolis: Liberty Classics.

Mitbestimmungsgesetz in den Unternehmen. 1977. Introduction by Peter Hanau. Deutscher Taschenbuchverlag.

Monissen, Hans G. 1978. The current status of labor participation in the management of business firms in Germany. In Pejovich 1978.

Naphtali, Fritz, et al. 1969. Wirtschaftsdemokratie--Ihr Wesen, Weg und Ziel. Introduction by Ludwig Rosenberg. Reprinted by Europaische Verlagsanstalt.

Olson, Mancur. 1968. The logic of collective action. German ed., Die Logik des kollektiven Handelns. Tubingen.

Pejovich, Svetozar, ed. 1978a. The codetermination movement in the West: Labor participation in the management of business firms. Lexington, Mass. and Toronto.

------. 1978b. Codetermination: A new perspective for the West. In Pejovich 1978a.

Prosi, Gerhard. 1976. Vokswirtschaftliche Auswirkungen des Mitbestimmungsgesetzes. In Grundlagen: Eigentum und Politik, ed. Otto A. Friedrich-Kuratorium, Vol. 4. Cologne, 1978.

Ropke, Wilhelm. 1926. Sozialisierung. In Handworterbuch der Staatswissenschaften. 7th ed.

Roth, Wolfgang, ed. 1976. Investitionslenkung. Ergebnisse einer Diskussion zwischen jungen Unternehmern und Sozialdemokraten zum Problem von Markt und Lenkung. Hamburg: Rowohlt Verlag.

Rousseau, Jean Jacques. 1959. Staat und Gesselschaft, trans. and ed. Kurt Weigand. Munich: Goldmann Verlag.

Rustow, Alexander. 1971. Sozialpolitik diesseits und jenseits des Klassenkampfes. In Bernhard Külp and Wilfried Schreiber, eds., Soziale Sicherheit. Cologne and Berlin: Kiepenheuer and Witsch.

Scherping, Rudolf, and Friedhelm Wallner, eds. 1973. Demokratischer Sozialismus und Langzeitprogramm. Diskussionsbeiträge zum Orientierungsrahmen '85 der SPD. Hamburg: Rowohlt Verlag.

Schimmelbuch, Heinz. 1971. Kritik an Commutopia. Tübingen.

Schmid, Carlo, Karl Schiller, and Erich Potthoff, eds. Grundlagen moderner Wirtschaftspolitik. Frankfurt: Europäische Verlagsanstalt.

Schumpeter, Joseph A. (1942) 1950. Kapitalismus, Sozialismus und Demokratie. Bern.

Schwan, Gesine. 1984. Die ideologische Entwicklung der SPD am Beispiel ihres Verhältnisses zum Staat. (Mimeographed).

Stern, Münch, Hansmeyer. 1972. Gesetz zur Förderung der Stabilität und des Wachstums der Wirtschaft. 2nd ed. Stuttgart: Verlag W. Kohlhammer.

Tietmeyer, Hans. 1969. "Konzertierte Aktion." Konzept, Praxis und Erfahrungen. In Kredit und Kapital. Berlin.

Voigt, Fritz. 1962. Die Mitbestimmung der Arbeitnehmer in den Unternehmungen. Eine Analyse der Einwirkungen der Mitbestimmung in der Bundesrepublik Deutschland auf die Unternehmensführung. In Zur Theorie und Praxis der Mitbestimmung, ed. Walter Weddigen. Schriften des Vereins für Sozialpolitik n.s. 24/I:87-536.

Watrin, Christian. Die Demokratisierung der Wirtschaftspolitik in der Bundesrepublik Deutschland. In Arthur F. Utz and Heinrich B. Streithofen, eds., Demokratie und Mitbestimmung. Stuttgart: Seewald-Verlag.

------. Collective ownership and workers' control--A way towards the humanisation of society? forthcoming.

------. Konzertierte Aktionen. Handwörterbuch der Wirtschaftswissenschaften 36/37:782.

Wickenkamp, Rolf. 1983. Unternehmensmitbestimmung und Verfügungsrechte. Cologne.

Wiedemann, Lothar. 1980. Sozialstaat. In Theodar Schober, Martin Honecker, Horst Dahlhaus, eds., Evangelisches Soziallexikon. Stuttgart: Kraus Verlag.

Willgerodt, Hans. 1976. Planning in West Germany: The social market economy. In *The politics of planning: A review and critique of centralized economic planning*. San Francisco, Calif.: Institute for Contemporary Studies.

Wilson, Thomas, and Andrew Skinner, eds. 1976. *The market and the state. Essays in honour of Adam Smith*. Oxford: Clarendon Press.

INDEX OF NAMES

Underlined page numbers indicate that the author's name appears in a reference list. Names marked with an asterisk indicate authors of chapters in this volume.

Acham, Karl, 84

*Albert, Hans, 84

Alchian, Armen, 63, 79n15, 84, 310

Allen, William R., 79n15, 84

Arrow, Kenneth, 30n6

Avineri, Shlomo, 310

Bajt, A., 249

Barone, Enrico, 68, 151, 152, 172

Barro, R., 206

Barry, N. P., 141n65, 142

Bartley, W. W., III, 85

Baumgarth, W. P., 142

Beck, Markus, 310

Becker, A. S., 235

Beloff, N., 249

Benassy, J. P., 206

Benelli, Giuseppe, 303, 310

Bentham, Jeremy, 14, 16, 26, 31, 90

Bergson, A., 210, 211, 215, 235

Berlin, Isaiah, 83n40, 85, 136n24, 142

Bernholz, Peter, 80n16, 85, 172

Blume, Otto, 311

Böckenförde, Ernst-Wolfgang, 311

Böhm, Stephan, 81n25, 85

Boulding, Kenneth E., 85

Brandt, Arno, 172
Brenner, Reuven, 85
Breyer, Friedrich, 80n16, 85
Brinkmann-Herz, Dorothea, 311
*Brunner, Karl, 26-27, 31, 52
*Brzeski, Andrzej, 235
*Buchanan, James M., 74, 85, 97, 98, 110n5, 112n16, 112
Burton, John, 30n1
Bush, K., 235

Carter, M., 207
Caspary, Adolf, 85
Cheung, N. S., 31
Chow, Gregory C., 34, 52
Clegg, H. A., 311
Coase, Ronald, 12, 19, 20, 21, 22, 29, 30n3, 31, 139n43
Cohn, S. H., 235
Cunningham, R. L., 142

Darendorf, Ralph, 311
Deist, Heinrich, 311
Demsetz, H., 23
Dickinson, H. D., 161, 164, 172
Duesenberry, James, 85
Dumont, Etienne, 16
Dworkin, R., 31, 31

Eason, W. W., 236
Efron, Edith, 52
Engels, Friedrich, 13, 31, 278, 283
Eucken, Walter, 79n10, 83n34, 85

Fehlbaum, R. P., 85
Feiwel, R. G., 236
Fellner, W., 181, 206

Festinger, Leon, 85
Friedl, Gerhard A., 311
Friedman, David, 63, 85
Friedman, Milton, 177-78, 206, 275
Furubotn, Eirik, 23, 30n1, 143, 144, 172

*Garello, Jacques
Goldman, M. J., 236
Gordon, R. J., 236
Gray, John, 112
Grossman, H., 206

Hamel, Hannelore, 174
Hamoway, R., 136n23, 143
Harberger, Arnold C., 27-28, 31
Harrington, Michael, 311
Harsanyi, J. C., 31, 31
Hayek, Friedrich A. von, 9, 55, 59, 63, 75, 79n9, 79n12, 85-86, 112, 115-42, 143, 150, 151, 152, 172, 275, 280, 311
Hazlitt, Henry, 134n1
Hegel, G. W. F., 13, 31, 90
Hennis, Wilhelm, 311
Hirsch, Fred, 30n6, 31
Hobbes, Thomas, 3, 7
Hoppmann, Erich, 311
Horvat, Branco, 172
Humboldt, Wilhelm von, 282
Hume, David, 12, 14, 30n2, 30n3, 31, 99-100, 112
Hurwicz, Leonid, 163, 172, 173
Hutcheson, Francis, 12

Jasny, 234n4, 236
Jensen, Michael C., 173, 312
Jonas, P., 236
de Jouvenel, Bertram, 83n41, 86

Kelley, D., 143
Kelsen, Hans, 86
Kempski, J. v., 137n29, 143
Keynes, J. M., 133-34n1, 143
Knight, Frank H., 31, 99, 112
Kornai, Janos, 160, 162, 173, 175, 181, 185, 207
*Kowalski, J., 207
Krueger, Anne O., 27, 31

Lange, Oskar, 148, 151, 161, 164, 165, 166, 173
Laqueur, W., 236
Lassalle, Ferdinand, 283, 284
Legget, R., 236
Leipold, Helmut, 173, 174
Lepsius, Karl, 86
Lerner, A. P., 148, 164, 173
Levine, H. S., 236
Liptak, T., 162, 173
Locke, John, 140n47
Lowenstein, Julius, 312
Löwith, Karl, 86
Lucas, J. R., 131, 143
Lucas, R. E., Jr., 207

Machlup, F., 117, 134n7, 143
Maddock, R., 207
McCloskey, H. J., 144
Manne, Henry G., 30n1, 31
Marshall, Alfred, 15
Marx, Karl, 13, 56, 57, 58, 59, 65, 90, 105, 112, 278, 279, 283
Meckling, William H., 173, 312
Medawar, Peter B., 86
Merton, Robert K., 86
Michels, Robert, 309, 312
Mickiewicz, E., 236

Mill, James, 14, 90
Mill, John Stuart, 14-15, 16-17, 32, 312
Millar, John, 12
Miller, F. D., 143
Mises, Ludwig von, 59, 60, 61, 62, 63, 64, 66, 67, 68, 69, 74, 75, 78n5-8, 79n11, 81n23, 86, 97, 112, 135n12, 135n16, 144, 148, 150, 151, 152, 153, 173, 251, 274n11, 275n18, 275n21, 276, 312
Monissen, Hans G., 312
Montesquieu, Charles Louis, 12
Murrel, Peter, 173
Muth, John, 176, 207
Myerson, R. B., 173
Myrdal, Gunnar, 67, 80n20, 80n21, 86

Naphtali, Fritz, 294, 312
North, Douglass C., 29, 32
Nove, Alec, 80n17, 87, 105, 112
Nozick, Robert, 5, 9, 63, 77, 79n14, 87
Nutter, G. Warren, 209, 210, 222, 236, 239, 249
Nutzinger, Hans G., 173

O'Driscoll, G., 142n69, 144
Okun, Arthur M., 111n7, 112, 207
Olson, Mancur, 312

Paqué, Karl-Heinz, 113
Pareto, Wilfredo, 23, 148, 151
Paul, E. Frankel, 143
Paul, J., 143
*Pejovich, S., 23, 30n1, 113, 143, 249, 312
Pigou, A. C., 15
Polthoff, Erich, 313
Popper, Karl, 56, 57, 59, 77n1, 77-78n4, 79n9, 87, 138n38, 144
Posner, Richard, 12, 22-23, 24, 25, 26, 27, 32, 144
Prosi, Gerhard, 312

Rawls, John, 97, 98, 99, 113
Raz, J., 144
Revel, Jean Francais, 276
Richter, R., 144
Rizzo, M., 142n65
Robbins, Lionel, 17, 32, 67, 70-71, 82n30, 87, 130, 144, 151
Roberts, Paul Craig, 87
Robertson, William, 12
Röpke, W., 132, 144, 312
Ross, Alf, 87
Rossi, Alice, 86
Roth, Wolfgang, 312
Rothbard, Murray N., 63, 87, 144
Rousseau, Jean Jacques, 90, 283, 312
Rubin, Paul H., 30n1, 32
Runciman, W. G., 87
Rustow, Alexander, 313

Sahlins, Marshall, 87
Samuelson, Paul A., 148, 174
Sargent, T., 207
Schäffle, Albert, 147, 174
Scheffrin, S., 207
Schelsky, Helmut, 84n43, 87
Scherping, Rudolf, 313
Schiller, Karl, 313
Schimmelbuch, Heinz, 313
Schlict, Ekkehart, 174
Schmid, Carlo, 313
Schmidt-Häuer, Christian, 87
*Schmidtchen, Dieter, 144
Schüller, Alfred, 173
Schumpeter, Joseph A., 56, 57-58, 59, 64, 68, 77n2, 81n24, 87-88, 108, 113, 313
Schwan, Gesine, 313

*Schwarz, Pedro
Seidl, Christian, _174_
Sen, Amartya, 30n6
Sidgwick, Henry, 15
Skinner, Andrew, _314_
Smith, Adam, 9, 12, 13, 14, 110n3, _113_, 280
Spencer, Herbert, 4
Stalin, J., _237_
Steiner, Hillel, 122, 123, 137n30, 137n33, _144_
Stephenson, Matthew A., _87_
Stigler, G., 139-40n46, _144_

Taylor, Fred, 148, 161, _174_
Thomas, R. P., 29
Thompson, Earl A., _174_
Tideman, T. Nicolaus, _174_
Tietmeyer, Hans, _313_
Tinbergen, Jan, 34, 48, 52
Tocqueville, Alexis de, 134n5
Topitsch, Ernst, 88
Treml, V. G., _237_
Tullock, Gordon, _113_
Turgot, Anne Robert Jacques, 13

Usher, Dan, _88_

*Vaubel, Roland
Vaughn, Karen I., _174_
Vining, Rutledge, 80n22, _88_
Voigt, Fritz, _313_

Wagener, H.-J., _174_
Wallace, N., _207_
Wallner, Friedhelm, _313_
Ward, Benjamin, _174_

Watkins, J. W. N., 141n62, 144

*Watrin, C., 313

Weber, Max, 65, 82n31, 88

Weitzmann, Martin L., 174

Weizsacker, Carl von, 174

Wickenkamp, Rolf, 313

Wiedemann, Lothar, 313

Wieser, Friedrich von, 80n21, 88

Wiles, P., 207, 237

Willgerodt, Hans, 314

Williamson, Oliver S., 174

Wilson, Thomas, 314

Wolf, Charles, Jr., 30n5, 32